2020

New Rules for the New Age

Other books by Garth Turner

2015: After the Boom
The Strategy: A Homeowner's Guide to Wealth Creation
The Defence: Guarding Your Money in Uncertain Times
Garth Turner's RRSP Guide (annual)

2020

New Rules for the New Age

Garth Turner

KEY PORTER  BOOKS

Canadian Cataloguing in Publication Data

Turner, Garth
        2020 : new rules for the new age

ISBN   1-55263-057-9

1. Finance, Personal.   2. Investments.   I. Title.
II. Title: Two thousand and twenty.

HG179.T877 1999   332.024   C99-931501-3

The Canada Council | Le Conseil des Arts
FOR THE ARTS | DU CANADA
SINCE 1957 | DEPUIS 1957

The publisher gratefully acknowledges the support of the Canada Council for the Arts and the Ontario Arts Council for its publishing program.

Canadä

We acknowledge the financial support of the Government of Canada through the Book Publishing Industry Development Program (BPIDP) for our publishing activities.

Key Porter Books Limited
70 The Esplanade
Toronto, Ontario
Canada M5E 1R2
www.keyporter.com

Design: Peter Maher
Electronic formatting: Heidy Lawrance Associates
Printed and bound in Canada

99 00 01 02 03   6 5 4 3 2 1

This book is dedicated to Dorothy

Contents

The Argument

Times are good today—Very good. And they are about to get even better, throughout the first decade of the new millennium and beyond. This is due to a heady technology, demographics, globalization, deflation, cheap money and smaller government.

Canada is in the early stages of a dramatic economic and financial boom that will prove to be an astonishing time to build wealth. However, it will not last forever. As in the 1920s, imbalances are building that will lead to a serious reversal. Unless more Canadians change their spending and investing habits, casting off those that were successful for their parents, financial regret lies ahead.

This book looks back at the 1930s to discover what people should have known and could have seen coming, and to the future for the same insights. There are key actions and attitudes to adopt now —while there is still time.

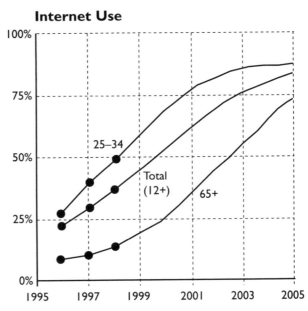

Internet Use

The Premises

Generations

The generation now in retirement will be the last one to retire in comfort.

Most people in the generation now middle-aged will face a retirement crisis.

The generation now entering the workforce will have to cope with a depression in mid-life.

Rules

The rules that used to guarantee financial success now hasten financial failure.

To prosper in a society that has no loyalty or workplace justice, you must follow new rules.

The Future

The immediate future is incredibly promising — a time of prosperity.

The experience of the 1930s could be repeated by the 2030s.

You have a dozen good years to prepare for what is coming.

Archie

Maybe your father was like mine.

Archie Turner believed in the system. No, he loved the system. In fact, he helped create it. His unshakeable faith in progress, his belief that newer was always better and his defiance of adversity, from the weather (he braved winter in a trenchcoat, and snow squalls in toe rubbers) to the disease that felled him (he hid his Alzheimer Disease for years)—these things defined him.

He came from a rural background when stagecoaches still stormed through southwestern Ontario. Just 90 years ago there was no electricity there, or running water. My father's father would eventually become president of the first little telephone company that strung up a few wires in the hamlet of Fingal, Ontario, eventually joining 503 families to the outside world, and he ran the hardware store. Eventually he got cataracts, went blind, and sat on the verandah a lot, in a sweater.

My father always refused to wear a sweater, saying they were for old men. He got cataracts, too, but had them removed. And he got as far away from the simplicity and uncertainty of rural life as he could.

Maybe your father was like mine. He craved financial security, and found it by immersing himself in a large corporate culture where you forged a lifelong career, advanced according to your talents, loyalty, seniority and desire, achieved success and retired with a good pension. Then came golf, Florida, cigars.

Archie and my mother had four kids and one salary, and got by—not always great, but okay. You could do that in the fifties, and still have a house. There was a female boarder for some time and I never had new hockey equipment, just used stuff. But my father reminded me that when he

Archie Turner

had played, they had used rolled-up magazines for pads and a frozen horse dropping for the puck.

He lived by the rules

Archie lived by the rules. He trusted his country. He believed in his job. He supported the social system. He was loyal to his wife. He saved and shunned risk. And it worked.

The money my parents made apart from the salary, especially in the sixties, seventies and eighties, was made from real estate. They would buy a house, my mother would spend the next couple of years wallpapering it to within an inch of its life, and then they'd sell it. You could make good money doing that, and get a better house. Prices were always going up. In fact, during their whole marriage, from 1939 to his death in 1995, it was pretty much the same environment—growth, progress, advancement, achievement and improvement. How could a guy not be optimistic? Despite that, they would never invest in stocks or anything else that was so risky. Paying off the mortgage was the key to security. So they did.

In his career, Archie was linear, and he was a rocket. He jumped from one position of responsibility to another and was an architect of Ontario's modern school system, from principal of a backwater two-room school in Mount Elgin to CEO of the country's largest educational mega-system, surrounding Toronto, a founder of the province's community college program, an op-ed contributor to the *Globe and Mail*, a trusted adviser to the government and a man with buildings and scholarships named after him.

He did not achieve these things by intellect, but rather by the kind of dogged determination that just wears down opposition and runs roughshod over doubts and negative thoughts. He was a man of faith. Faith in government. Faith in the future. Faith that he would do right and so would everyone else. When I saw him on his knees at night at the side of the bed, his hands clasped tight and his forehead upon them, I wondered why a successful man would need to do that.

The Premier would come to visit our house. As a child at the dinner table, I remember him asking my father for direction about things that were beyond my understanding, while the limousine driver and OPP bodyguard waited outside. Amid clouds of smoke from his Brigham pipe, purchased with ritual every year at the Sportsman's Show, Archie would dispense it.

I was in public school when I heard my father say he was making more than $10,000 a year, and he said it with pride. We were solidly middle-class with a two-storey house in the suburbs, a cottage and a new car in the driveway, and yet my mother would save tinfoil, re-engineer leftovers into phoenix food and spend hours turning one child's worn jacket into the next one's trousers. At the same time, Archie would spend huge amounts of money on hand-tailored suits and shoes, and I thought he was vain. If you look like a success, he told me during my phase of shoulder-length hair and leather jackets, you will be a success.

When he died, my mother buried him in his best clothes, a splendid blue wool suit and gold cufflinks. He looked magnificent. Archie had been an obvious success story and his death attracted media attention for days. His public legacy was substantial, while in private, he left behind a small amount of cash, a terminating pension, a nicely wallpapered four-bedroom home and a new Buick.

His rules left, too. They passed with him.

The Last Generation

THE ARGUMENT
The Canada you have lived in is ending. The generation now in retirement is the last one that will be rewarded for employee loyalty and family values. Corporations have no loyalty and the pillars most people anchored their lives to are crumbling. In the future, after a dozen good years, those who are not self-reliant stand a large chance of being caught in a retirement crisis.

My father lived for 85 years. For nine of those years, between 1930 and the start of World War II, the economy went down. It was hell, but Archie was lucky to find a job building what would become Highway 401 across Ontario. He earned a dollar a day, supplementing his salary as an Ontario public school teacher, for which he was paid $600 a year.

For the other 76 years of his life, the economy mostly went up. It was wonderful. During that time there were constants—rising prices, rising wages, rising quality, rising opportunity, better cars, bigger cities, bigger government (of which he was a part), an improving standard of living and growing personal security.

For Archie's generation, which endured the Depression and World War II, the last few decades have been payback time. Today, Canada's seniors reap far more in social benefits than they ever paid in, and they will die the best cared-for people in history. Those currently retired will enjoy about seven dollars back in social programs for every dollar they ever contributed—it will be the first, and the last, generation to have that experience.

Some will say, this is the death of opportunity. It is not. It is, however, likely the end of a time when young men, like my father in 1932, could expect nothing but unbridled expansion to lie ahead for his entire life. Today's young people must brace for almost exactly the opposite.

But in the short term, there will be growth, and progress, and advancement that will rival anything Archie witnessed. It will be great, while it lasts.

The summer of your life is at hand

We're becoming so cheerful!
WARREN JESTIN

CHIEF ECONOMIST

SCOTIABANK

JUNE 1999

The next decade or more will be the summer of most people's financial lives. The economy will flourish in the absence of inflation, with low interest rates, surplus government budgets and globalization. Incomes will rise while technology will amaze us and make our days entertaining. Threats and risks will fade. Stock markets will soar and yet consumer prices will fall. Many people will feel richer than at any other time in their lives. Certainly, wealth will be more possible than in the past, so long as you know the strategies to pursue.

Inevitably the summer will turn into autumn, and eventually a harsh winter for those people abiding by the wrong set of rules, the ones that worked for the last generation. But those who have made the right preparations, and spent the warm days getting ready, will be isolated from the blast that will chill so many. This book is a guide to prepare by. It will lay out for you the new rules.

For the children of the last generation, it is clearly turning into a contradictory time. Born, like me, into optimism and prosperity, the baby boomers who do not

Archie in 1932: Things could only get better

heed the changes could finish their lives in conditions that rival those of the 1930s all over again. The signs of what is to come are already visible, but too few are seeing them. A majority of these Canadians instead are doing the wrong things, putting their money in the wrong places, fearing the wrong risks and making the wrong assumptions.

Perhaps they learned too well from their parents, believing now that government will care for them, universal health care will cure them, social programs will support them and their children will tend to them. But, for most, it won't happen. Life is changing fast, and not all for the better. In fact, some of the most stunning advances—like vastly increased life expectancy—could hasten our biggest problems—such as an epidemic of impoverished seniors.

If you are a 65-year-old Canadian woman today, you will live, on average, another 20.7 years. If you are a 15-year-old girl, you will live to be 89. If you look after yourself, you will live to well over 100, whether you want to or not.

A time of contradictions

• In recent years inflation has turned into disinflation, and now deflation. The cost of cars, computers and houses is falling, along with interest rates. Technology is making everyone more productive, with the result being falling prices. Deflation will rob most people of wealth as it decreases the value of residential real estate, since that is where most of us mistakenly keep the bulk of our net worth.

• Interest rates have collapsed around the world, and this will continue despite short-term adjustments made by nervous central bankers. The impact on savings, and savers, will be dramatic. The time is clearly over when they could grow their money without risk.

• Global corporate restructuring, mergers and acquisitions have destroyed the linear career that Archie sought and rode. In this economy whole careers are ending while others emerge. The receptionist is gone; the webmaster has arrived.

• Without inflation, and as technology improves, commodity prices have stumbled, crippling whole sectors of the economy. Coal mines have closed in Cape Breton. Gold shafts in Ontario have been shuttered. Pulp and paper mills have shut down in British Columbia. The miners and mill workers of today are the blacksmiths and milkmen of my father's youth.

• Even the very existence of the money we denominate our lives in is in question. The Canadian dollar will probably not survive as long as I do, because of an inevitable Euro-style union with the U.S. dollar or because Canada as an independent nation will simply disappear before the baby boomers retire.

In 1977, Canadians saved almost 13% of what they earned. Two decades later, they saved less than 2%. In 1999, the savings rate hit zero. Family incomes peaked in 1989, the same year that residential real estate did. Taxes have doubled in the last 25 years. People get married later, delay having children and there are twice as many dual-income families as a generation ago. Despite that, most people think they have no job security.

Now Statistics Canada is plotting the rise of intergenerational households. The federal agency found the number of three-generational homes rose a stunning 39% in a decade, from 150,000 in 1986 to 208,000 in 1996. That rate of growth was more than twice than for all family households. Why would children, with their own children, move in with parents? According to University of Toronto professor Bob Schlesinger, because "the younger generation goes to school longer and entry-level jobs don't pay enough; and on the other end, you have seniors who may be living on a pension." A changing economy is reinventing the family along lines not seen for more than a generation.

Many people are beginning to fear the future. As the old century ended, that was reflected in declining mutual fund sales and the clamour to get guaranteed investments, despite their lower rates of return. In the near term, we should not be fearful. The best days of your life are at hand. But they won't last.

In the long term, the country as we know it could well be doomed. This is because too many people are still playing by my father's rules—

trusting the government, avoiding undue risk, giving employers unquestioning loyalty and craving security.

But the government is treading water as it floats towards the Niagara Falls of fiscal problems, $600 billion in debt. It will not be there to help you decades from now. Risk is all around us yet most people are blind to it. The larger that employers get, the less loyalty they exhibit. And the only lasting security you will have in the next two decades, before things really unravel, will be what you create for yourself.

A retirement crisis is certain

Does all of this sound dark and frightening? Well, look at the facts: there are over eight million Canadian baby boomers who will each need, in the 1999 estimation of a Bank of Montreal economist, $660,000 to $950,400 in savings by the time they reach 65 to live reasonable lives. And that optimistically assumes that the Canada Pension Plan will be there for everyone. But it won't.

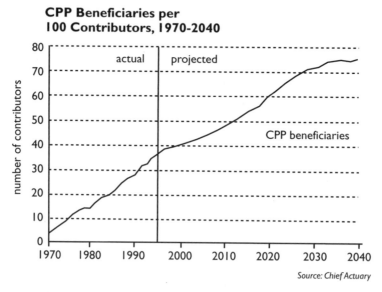

Recipe for trouble: The number of people who will be claiming a public pension over the next 40 years will soar, relative to the people who are actually funding the system.

At the outset of the millennium, with only 15 years left before retirement for most boomers, the average RRSP contains a paltry amount. In fact, RRSP contributions have actually started to decline for the first time in years as incomes stagnate and people divert money into other areas of their lives. That means today's middle-aged are short hundreds of thousands of dollars in savings and will have to find tens of thousands a year for the next 15 years to make it. But with a savings rate now at zero, that will not happen.

What does this mean? Eventually, disaster. And every day that we cling to the old rules that worked for our fathers and mothers, but today are bringing us down, that disaster will seep into our lives.

It happens in insidious ways.

• We do what we were always told was the right and best thing, and spend 15 years paying off the mortgage—just in time for the value of our property to start a 15-year erosion.

• We eschew risk, and follow the safe course to long-term stability, putting our savings into investment certificates, savings bonds and term deposits, but interest rates collapse so that after even modest inflation and raging taxes, we earn absolutely nothing.

• We listen to the voices in the daily media warning us away from the volatility and uncertainty of stock markets and products based upon them. But as we followed a "safer" course, the market more than doubled from 1995 to the turn of the century, and is set to do so again within the next decade, or far less, for the reasons set out in this book. Afraid it will go down, we watch opportunity pass us by.

• We shun the danger and unpredictability of self-employment for the security of the large corporation. Then, in our fifties, our jobs are taken away. We are unemployable in a world voracious for cheap, over-educated twenty-somethings who are resentful of the whole baby-boomer culture they grew up in the shadow of.

• We sacrifice for our children, forgo our own security for theirs in the future. A university education will soon cost a huge sum and yet a university graduate after 2020 could have the worst job prospects in nine decades because of the decline that's coming. We wonder, could our family have used that money better, for everyone's benefit?

• We subscribe to a value system that is the foundation of society, respecting others, surrendering to the common good, deferring to authority, accepting leadership. Then we discover that the International Olympic Committee is corrupt, the blood supply is untrustworthy, the U.S. President is morally bankrupt, and the guy in charge of our company engineered a big layoff that swelled his stock options.

We must ask ourselves: Are they right or are we naive? Can you really still succeed today playing by the old rules, working hard, paying your taxes and raising your kids? In a world where morality appears to be dead, is Archie's steady-Eddy approach to life now a one-way ticket to failure? How could this have happened in just one generation?

Today many of us have reason to be disillusioned, bitter and angry. Without something big happening—a major tax reduction, an economic union with the United States, a return of inflation and runaway real estate values—many people, millions, are facing personal financial ruin.

In 2020

There will be three times as many senior citizens as there are today. Baby boomers will be moving into their seventies, and starting to withdraw investment funds because they have little else to live on. The pressures on the economy and financial markets will be intense. The existing generation of taxpayers, already staggering under the burden, will be unable to pay more in taxes to save health care or pension benefits for the boomers who did not prepare.

The financial markets could head into a decline that could last 20 years. Depression-era deflation could easily bring the value of homes below the amount they are mortgaged for. The federal government's budget surplus could turn into a protracted deficit as the cost of social programs rises and tax revenues fall. The accumulated billions in debt, largely ignored during the fat years that are on the immediate horizon, will be an anchor thrown to a drowning nation.

Born into prosperity, many of my generation will die in poverty, between 2020 and 2050, wondering how it happened. After all, they followed the values their parents instilled in them. They knew the rules.

But they did not know, until it was too late, that those rules were for the parents, not the children.

The old Canada is gone

In fact, all of western society is morphing into something very different. When prices go down instead of up; when the cost of money is falling and the value of a dollar is rising; when there are more old people than there are children; when nobody has a secure job anymore; and when it's obvious the government will not meet its future obligations, then you cannot act as your father did. In this environment, your father would fail. You will too, unless you change your ways.

But most people are not changing, and will not. A wonderful economy and rising financial markets for the next 10 or 12 years will mask what lies ahead. They will lull people into thinking things are okay—the way they have always been. That will be a mistake.

There is no remedy for an aging population

We know now that the pension system will be defeated by demographics and that trying to maintain a universal health care system will bankrupt the country. For most people, there will be no pension and, unless you are willing and able to pay for it, no instant access to a doctor, either.

That means people today who do what their parents did—avoid risk, buy a house, save and hope for the best—are at real peril. Unless they put their money in the right places, aggressively reduce their tax burden, do the sane thing with real estate and exploit the decade-long, dramatic rise of the stock market, they will almost certainly fail.

Sadly, it will happen to millions. We can easily see today that most middle-aged Canadians are in no shape to take care of themselves, let alone to weather the coming financial hurricane.

• In a good year Canadians make only 15% of the RRSP contributions allowed them. Only one in 11 contributes the full amount, while two-thirds contribute nothing.

• We have hundreds of billions of dollars in the wrong assets—savings bonds, GICs, term deposits and like instruments—earning shards of interest and attracting too much tax.

• We seriously overpay our taxes, missing deductions and credits and taking income in the wrong forms.

• We cling to outmoded and dangerous ideas about the security of our homes.

• We underestimate how long we are going to live, or what it will cost to spend 30 or 40 years without a paycheque and, for many, without a cheque of any kind.

Even if the economy we have today were to be maintained, most middle-class Canadians would enter retirement in a state of financial crisis. Government pensions account for a maximum of a few hundred dollars a month. Only one in three people has a corporate pension. And with life expectancy shooting higher, the modest amount that most people have saved would be used up in a few years, if not a few months.

But the economy will not stand pat. There is a good argument for believing that after boom conditions in the first decade or dozen years of the new millennium, it will go down the tubes, starting around 2015.

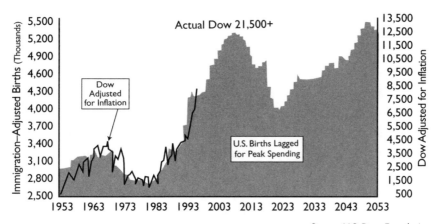

Source: H.S. Dent Foundation

American demographer Harry Dent's famous chart, showing the Dow Jones index superimposed over births, on a 46-year lag. So far, it is an accurate match, and if it continues, more boom times, followed by a major decline.

The four pillars are falling

Is the situation hopeless? Far from it. Even if you are 45 or 50 years old and have saved little and made the wrong investments, you can still change things. You can have a chance at living the rest of your life in relative comfort, but only if you act now, because the money-making years will not last forever. If you are younger, you must be an aggressive investor. If you are retired with a pension, thank your lucky stars.

That is what this book is about—avoiding the fate that will engulf so many, so deeply, so tragically in the future, as it did once in the past.

But reading it will not be enough. This must be a guide to action. And as you follow these suggestions, at times you will feel very alone, a minnow swimming against an overwhelming current. Many will mock you, saying the old rules still work and there is no need to change your thinking so radically. I certainly know the sting of such criticism, but it comes from people who fear the future and long for the past.

Some critics, I am sure, will be among the majority of Canadians who wander into personal crisis, still believing that the four pillars of support are intact:

1. That owning a home is the cornerstone of financial success.
2. That spending your money raising a family rather than saving and investing is enough, as the kids will be your future providers.
3. That it's enough to pay your taxes so you can collect public pension plan payments.
4. And that it's best to work for big corporations and institutions because that is where financial security lies.

The social commentators who tell us this are wrong. The things they hold out as intergenerational truths are, in reality, dangerous myths. Here is why:

1. Home is no safe haven

My father spent his salary on his family. He spent his pension on my mother and himself. The extra money he made came from buying and selling residential real estate. The house my parents bought outside Toronto in the early 1950s cost $18,000. They sold it in the seventies for more than $200,000.

Most boomers have had similar experiences over the last 20 years. In fact, during most of the eighties, your house probably made more money than you did. But that was then. This is now, and as the new millennium dawns, residential real estate in just about every major market in Canada is either static or declining in value because inflation has disappeared and demand is sliding as the population ages. Of course, there are exceptions —brief flare-ups, because real estate is an intensely local commodity whose value is affected by a number of factors, chiefly supply and demand.

In 1999, for example, there was an outbreak of buying fever in some of Toronto's toniest neighbourhoods. Buyers were bidding against each other, offering tens of thousands of dollars over asking prices while at the same time the average house price across the region languished.

"It's madness out there," the *National Post* reported a potential buyer saying, after he'd lost a house despite offering a $50,000 premium to the asking price. "It's frustrating. We'd rather stay in our house than go up against that. The only drawback is we want to sell our house in this market."

The vice-president of one of the mortgage corporations run by a big-five bank told me in early 1999 that he'd been caught in a bidding war for his new home in midtown Toronto, and was forced to pay $36,000 above the asking price as six parties competed for the property. Three months later, with the deal still not closed, he confided in me that he could resell the property on closing day for $100,000 more than he paid. My advice: sell. This was temporary inflationary gain in a market destined to deflate.

Archie would never have entered any kind of bidding war. He bought cheap, added value and sold higher.

But today the media are enamoured with this kind of story, because it reflects Canadian society's distorted love affair with real estate. Because this has represented the cornerstone of personal financial planning for the past 40 years, we are reluctant to give it up and face reality. Too many people today cling to the notion that buying a home and paying it off will just about guarantee security down the road. After all, it worked for their parents. Won't it work again? I don't think so.

If you have the bulk of your net worth in a home, you are probably at risk. You certainly will not see your wealth grow over the next 20 years. In fact, you may see a large chunk of it evaporate.

And young people also need to be warned. Because real estate is no longer an inflating asset, buying a home and spending the next 15 years paying down the mortgage could be disastrous. Not only will the house likely be worth less at the end of that period, but the buyers could well have missed the best decade and a half in their lives to grow money in financial assets like stocks and mutual funds. Far better that extra money be put into high-growth assets like equity mutual funds than fed to a mortgage with a low interest rate.

Why is the trend of the last 40 years—steadily rising real estate values—about to be reversed? Actually, it's already turned. Commodity prices are in a steady decline, and real estate is no exception, despite the inability of most people to see it. There are two inescapable negatives for home prices.

- Mild deflation is the enemy of real estate equity, and it is eroding the value of homes now. This is a long-term trend that will hold steady despite temporary spikes of inflation and seasonal buyer madness.

- Demographics across North America are not supportive of higher home prices. In fact, our aging population just about guarantees a continuing decline. What made real estate go up in the 1970s and 1980s will make it plunge in the 2020s and 2030s.

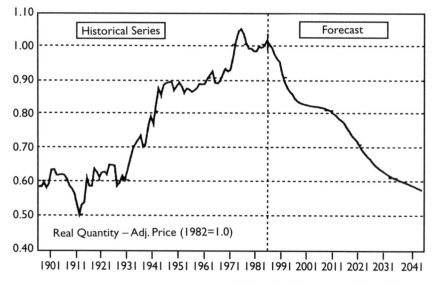

Source: Daniel McFadden, National Bureau of Economic Research

A major U.S. study of housing prices has concluded that they probably peaked in the early 1980s and will decline to levels not seen since the 1930s as the baby-boom generation falls into retirement and old age. With our proportionately largest boomer population, Canadians could see an even steeper slide.

DEFLATION. A misunderstood force that, like inflation, can work both for you and against you. Like inflation, if you harness it, you can profit from it. If you have your money in the wrong assets at the wrong time, however, it can destroy you.

That's just what happened in the 1930s, when deflation went completely out of control, for a variety of reasons. Between 1930 and 1933—

the darkest of the dark time—consumer prices in Canada fell by a third as the jobless rate jumped to the same level. People stopped buying things because, with prices falling so fast, it made sense to wait and buy cheaper.

House prices plunged as wages declined. But mortgage debt, of course, held steady. Many people actually found their equity falling below the mortgage amount—a situation briefly repeated in Alberta in the 1980s.

Today, deflation is mild. It's unlikely that the 1930s experience will be repeated—until, perhaps, the 2030s. But today's environment is still deadly for most real estate ownership. Why? Because most people have not had a salary increase for years, so demand for houses has been soft. That led to real estate values in many urban centres being lower at the end of the 1990s than they were at the end of the 1980s. And, meanwhile, the price of money (which is interest) has collapsed. That decline in mortgage rates has masked for many people the fact that the value of their homes has also declined.

This situation is the polar opposite to that of the eighties, when real estate flourished and was an outstanding investment. Then inflation, which raised wages and housing values, actually facilitated affording a home, since the mortgage in constant dollars would become easier to pay. Now, were it not for declining mortgage rates, those home loans would be harder to service as real family income is on the decline. As the economy deflates, real assets become less valuable and money becomes worth more.

For the first time in 25 years—most of the working lives of the entire baby-boom generation—the value of a dollar is climbing. It buys more car, more computer, more financing and more house. It also means financial assets that represent liquid wealth—stocks, bonds and mutual funds, for example—are rising as well. It's obvious where the bulk of your net worth should be if you want your money to grow and insulate you against what is coming.

In other words, the Dow Jones Industrial Index could rise from 10,000 to 20,000 in the same period of time as the value of your home falls by about 20%.

This does not mean you should sell your house and live in a tent. Far from it. With lower home values and cheap mortgage rates, it actually makes sense for many people to buy, rather than rent, because that will increase their monthly cash flow.

But it does mean that sitting on a paid-off home whose equity is eroding is insane. Better that you should remove some of that equity and use it to buy financial assets that have a better future, and create a tax-deductible mortgage at the same time, as scary as that seems. And, no, my father would never have done it.

DEMOGRAPHICS. It's the science of studying the composition of the population, and nothing is as startling as the impact of the baby boomers.

People my age form the single-largest age group in the entire population and our tastes, desires, habits and hormones have shaped Canadian society for the last 50 years. From a big jump in the baby-food market in the fifties to Top 40 radio and the Beatles in the sixties, yuppie egotism in the seventies and then the inflation-driven real estate boom of the eighties—this "big generation" has been omnipresent and is about to have its biggest impact ever. The infatuation with monster houses is gone, to be replaced with a radical downsizing and a corresponding rush into financial assets that has only just begun, as more and more people wake up to the fate that awaits them.

Changing demographics means changing real estate needs and goals. The developments that we know will take place are nothing short of breathtaking. According to government statistics, the average family size will shrink; the number of people living alone will jump by 70%; and the number of two-person households will double by 2016. More than half of all "families" will have just two people in them. In fact, households with singles or doubles will constitute an amazing 80% of all the family units in the country.

And that raises a fundamental question: Who will want to buy all those four-bedroom suburban homes that the boomers are now rattling around in? The answer: very few buyers, indeed. And as sellers compete for those scarce buyers in 10 or 20 years, the value of such properties will likely fall sharply, robbing wealth from those who did not foresee the inevitable.

Other real estate trends that appear certain to emerge include a resurgence in interest in bungalows, condominiums, "age-proofed" homes, prime recreational properties and houses that can serve easily as places of work in the new Internet economy.

Commodities are in a long-term downtrend

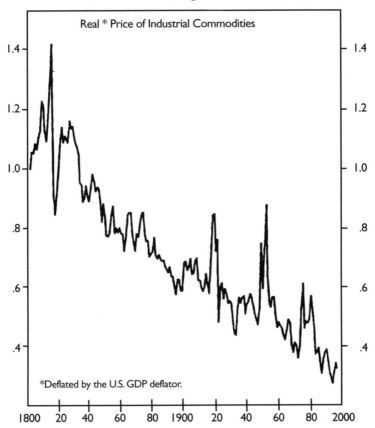

Real * Price of Industrial Commodities

*Deflated by the U.S. GDP deflator.

Commodity prices have been in a steady decline for the past 200 years. Why? Because as we develop better technology, our reliance on many natural resources decreases. Notice when there have been inflationary spikes in the last 100 years—during the Industrial Revolution, after the First and Second World Wars, and in the 1980s, thanks to demographics.

If you have the right kind of real estate, the money you have put there will be protected. If you have the wrong kind of real estate—and most middle-aged people unfortunately do—your equity could be lost. If you wait too long to sell it, you may be unable to find a buyer at any price.

Just imagine how it will be in 2015, when there will be more than eight million 60-year-old boomers with $8 trillion worth of real estate equity trickling away daily. They will be desperate to sell—to get their net worth into assets that have a future, like equities and investment funds based upon them. It could be chaos.

Demographics do not lie. There is no cure for an aging population. Not even immigration, unless it were massive. There is simply nothing to be done to reverse the inevitable changes that lie before us.

But demographics also make a large part of the future completely predictable. If you know that, then logic will tell you that much of the real estate that people want to own today could turn into a wealth trap.

Sadly, real estate is still a big part of the Canadian culture. Too many of us have clung to our parents' outmoded beliefs. The price to be paid for that mistake is incalculable. Home is no safe haven. You are on your own.

2. No Leave it to Beaver any longer

And what of the traditional argument that raising a family is the best investment you can make? That your children will support you? That sacrificing their future for your own, by saving and investing, is somehow greedy and wrong?

The reality is that in the future your children will probably have a hard time looking after themselves, let alone you. The economy of North America could be in the soup in two decades, dragged lower by the demands of an aged population. American demographer Harry S. Dent, Jr. forecasts a depression there, starting somewhere around 2009 and troughing around 2023, with the Dow Jones falling from a high of more than 21,000 to a low of 6,500. If it happens, that would severely impact children now in high school or university, right in the middle of their peak career years.

Already, it is getting harder and harder for young adults to make the transition from years of education to a rapidly changing workforce. It is putting them vastly behind in terms of income growth and wealth accumulation. A 1999 Statistics Canada survey found that more young people are delaying their move out of the family home than at any time in the previous 15 years, thanks to a poor economy, higher tuition fees and a tendency to later marriages.

In 1996, more than half of all unmarried men between the ages of 20 and 34 lived with their parents, while 47% of unmarried women did the same. To most baby boomers, who could not wait to fly the coop, this is a major social departure, and it suggests that their children, getting a late start, will be ill equipped to care for them later.

Meanwhile, the urgency of saving and investing to deal with the coming financial and economic crisis has been challenged by a dangerous media misinterpretation of the words of one man—Malcolm Hamilton, a

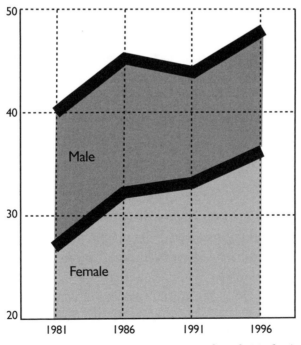

Home to Roost
Percentage of unmarried young adults,
aged 25 to 29, living with parents

Source: Statistics Canada
The Globe and Mail

pension expert with William Mercer Ltd., and a frequent media commentator. Hamilton is as controversial as he is smart. He knows how to get attention. In late 1998 he got lots of it by suggesting that Canadians would be just as well off spending their money raising their kids and paying off their houses as scrimping and saving for retirement.

The media loved that, as it reinforced the popular myth that amassing retirement wealth is simply impossible for the average person. Within months, the message was being repeated as a justification for people not making RRSP contributions.

But what Hamilton said was wildly different from the interpretation given his words. He spoke of Canadians with lower incomes—under $30,000 (which, sadly, includes over half of all adult Canadians)—who, if they did not invest in RRSPs, would get about the same income in government retirement benefits. The *Financial Post Magazine* reported and interpreted it this way, "As Hamilton observes, a couple earning an annual income of $20,000 can live quite comfortably, especially if they've paid for their home and raised their children."

Quite comfortably?

I don't know about you, but my goal is not to live, with my wife, on $20,000 a year in retirement. In fact, that would represent a loss of more than half the average family income of $54,000 reported in 1999, and a serious drop in living standards. With Canadians now routinely spending 20 or 30 years in retirement, that is hardly something to look forward to.

3. Expect no government support

And what of the universal pension system? My father collected Canada Pension Plan (CPP) benefits until the day he died, despite the fact that he had a large, secure and indexed pension (as none of his children did later). Is it conceivable that the government would break faith, and have no payments for you when you reach retirement age in a decade or two?

It is. In fact, I think you should count on it.

First, do not believe for a minute that you can live a middle-class lifestyle on the money you receive from CPP. As I write this, the maximum monthly pension at age 65 is less than $750. The maximum pension for a person with a disability is less than $900 a month. The public pension plan was never set up to be an income-replacement vehicle in retirement —only a supplement. You have always been expected to augment this stream of income with your own RRSPs and with the corporate pension you receive after a career of working.

But things are coming unglued.

Only five million Canadians will have any corporate pension income coming in. We are vastly behind on our RRSP contributions, with two-thirds of eligible Canadians making no annual contributions whatsoever.

Too much of what we have is put in entirely the wrong places, like guaranteed investment certificates (GICs), money market funds, savings bonds and treasury bills, especially among Canadians over the age of 50.

Projected depletion of CPP fund

billions of dollars

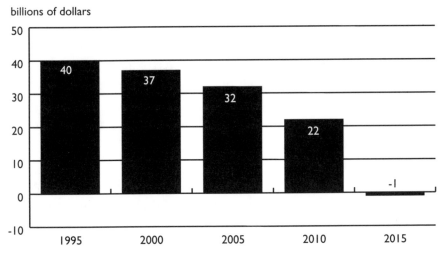

Source: Canada Pension Plan

The Canada Pension Plan is no longer self-sustaining. More is paid out to today's seniors than is collected from today's workers. That means the CPP Reserve Fund is being depleted, and is scheduled to be gone by 2015—as Baby Boomers begin to retire—without some kind of radical change.

Meanwhile, well-meaning but unhelpful politicians have reassured Canadians that the pension plan will always be there, despite the obvious. As a public document from the CPP Consultations Secretariat pointed out in the dying days of the 1990s, "For the past 30 years, we have paid much less than the benefits we are receiving, or will receive, from the CPP are worth. Future generations will be asked to pay considerably more than the benefits are worth. Will they be willing and able to do so?"

Of course not. In a country with some of the highest tax rates in the world, and an expensive and aging population, that is an absurd question. Today's 20-year-olds will not pay more to support today's baby boomers. Already the CPP is in sad shape. The amount that employees and employers pay into the plan is rising sharply, from 5.5% of earnings to a projected 10.1% in 2016, and up to 14% after that unless some kind of reform takes place. But even with that sharp jump in contribution levels, the money in the CPP could be all gone by about the time the first boomers are expecting a cheque.

Already today the plan is clearly in reverse. In 1996, for example, 10 million working Canadians contributed $12.5 billion to the CPP. But the 3.5 million seniors who collected benefits were paid $17.5 billion. The shortfall of $5 billion was partially offset by interest earned by the $36 billion CPP reserve fund, which is mostly invested in low-rate provincial bonds. But even with that income, the CPP had to use $700 million of its savings just to break even.

If this continues, the CPP will be dry in 2016.

Ottawa has moved to try and ease the CPP crisis by establishing the Canada Pension Plan Investment Board (CPPIB), with its first president and CEO being former Nesbitt Burns head John MacNaughton. Starting in the autumn of 1999, the board invested public pension money in financial assets like Canadian and foreign index funds. Using the additional amount of money that higher CPP premiums will bring in, the CPPIB could have as much as $88 billion under management by 2008.

Is this the solution we have been waiting for? Will the public pension system always be there for us?

Far from it. Today's seniors chew through more than $17 billion a year in retirement benefits. By the time the baby boomers retire, the number of seniors will have tripled, which means (unless benefits are drastically reduced) by 2015 the CPP will face an annual cash requirement of more than $50 billion. Even with an astounding investment track record under John MacNaughton and his successors, pension fund reserves will, at best, hold out for three years, perhaps four.

Clearly, the plan is fundamentally flawed. Too many people are taking out too much money, or too few are contributing too little. So, do we tell retirees and future retirees that they will have to live on a lot less, or do we burden workers today and in the decades to come with a massive new tax?

The answer is evident: There is no room for more taxes. The next generation will not pay them. And in a world of globalized free trade where tax rates have a direct impact on a country's competitiveness and productivity, taxes must fall, not rise. Already Canada is hugely uncompetitive with the United States, thanks largely to our substantially higher tax load. What Ontario and Alberta have done in the battle against these high taxes will surely spread to every level of government, if the country is to remain productive.

So, the CPP is cooked. It will not exist in a decade as it exists today. It will not be universal but instead be an income supplement for the destitute. How could those who framed the CPP in the 1960s have been so terribly wrong? Well, they made some major miscalculations:

• They underestimated how long we would live. On average, Canadians now live more than three years longer than anticipated and that will increase to almost five years by 2030. This increased longevity makes a huge difference to the CPP payout.

• Birth rates have collapsed. In fact, if it were not for immigration, the population of Canada would eventually reach zero. This means the number of workers supporting each senior is falling, from five over the next decade to just three by 2030.

• The economy has slowed substantially. This is not the inflationary, rapid-growth 1960s any longer. In fact, today we have deflation, static wages, falling commodity prices and stagnant real estate values. We blew the chance to build up a big reserve fund for the CPP when the economy was booming. Today, when the inflationary boom is behind us, when the population is aging, the pay-as-you-go CPP system just doesn't work anymore.

CPP contribution rates

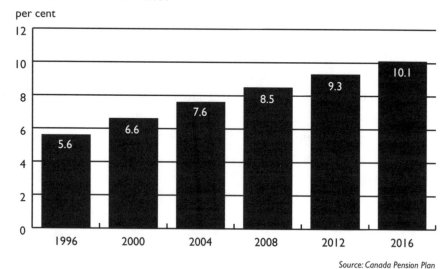

per cent

Source: Canada Pension Plan

Depletion of the Canada Pension Plan's Reserve Fund will come about despite a dramatic rise in the contribution rates for employers and employees and the establishment of the Canada Pension Plan Investment Board. There has been a lot of controversy as to whether, at almost double the 1996 rate, the new level will be high enough.

• The benefits paid to seniors are probably too rich. Political leaders made big mistakes, like indexing benefits to inflation, letting people take early retirement at age 60, loosening the definitions of "disability" so many people qualified, and allowing people to keep survivor benefits even after they remarried.

The bottom line for Canadians, especially baby boomers now in their forties and fifties, is that the CPP as our parents came to know it in their senior years will not exist in ours.

Many people will not receive any money from Ottawa, and most will pocket far less than they expected. This will deepen a retirement crisis already clearly forming on the horizon. And it will happen just as the economy of Canada, and possibly all of North America, takes a huge stumble into darkness, sometime around or after 2020. You must know this now. You are on your own.

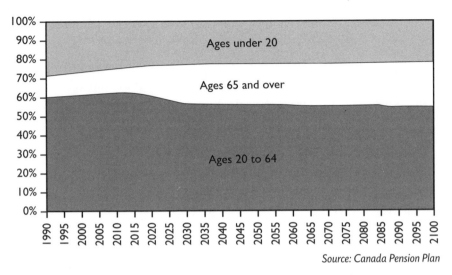

Source: Canada Pension Plan

Living too long: At least for the public pension plan. As life expectancy rises, the number of people over 65 will, for the first time, outnumber those under age 20.

4. There is no workplace justice

Today's world is one in which corporate mergers can sweep away tens of thousands of jobs without warning. For example, in one recent month:

• Volvo said it would shut four production facilities, including one in Halifax, costing 5,300 jobs. This preceded the company's marriage a few months later to Ford Motor Company, of Detroit.

• Aerospace giant Boeing revealed it would be cutting 48,000 workers from its payroll as part of a two-year plan to cut production costs, wiping out 20% of all its positions in Canada and the United States. Five months later, the company laid off 7,000 more employees.

• ITT Industries announced a $400 million restructuring and the elimination of 1,200 jobs.

• Citigroup said it would be laying off 10,400 people, or 6.5% of its workforce in a $900 million restructuring.

• The newly combined Mobil and Exxon shed 9,000 jobs.

Commenting to CNN, First Union Corp. economist Joel Naroff said, "Job security is not something you even talk about anymore." And he's right. So workers who leave their posts and join a picket line for a secure job—as CBC technicians, Toronto school janitors, Air Canada pilots and Bell Canada technicians did as the 1990s ended and as U.S. air traffic controllers did when Ronald Reagan was U.S. president—are misguided and tragic figures.

In this world without corporate loyalty, the only security is that which you can create for yourself. Small companies are invariably better than large ones because they often have stronger balance sheets, typically less debt, entrepreneurial leaderships, more flexibility and the ability to adapt to rapidly changing marketplace conditions. Self-employment is better than working for someone else because you can better control your own destiny, choose better how you will be taxed and better chase opportunities when they arise. Holding equity in your employer is better than holding a title and a salary than can evaporate on a Friday afternoon when a "superior" walks into your office with a letter.

Like it or not—and many Canadians with employee mentalities recoil at this reality—we are returning to an era of rugged individualism, when to protect yourself and your family, you must be doing business on your own. It might be as an entrepreneur, creating, selling, doing deals with others and adding mutual value to your efforts. Or it might be as an intrapreneur, using your job to leverage up other opportunities within the corporation, thinking laterally, not vertically.

Always remember: The president has no more security than you do. But she might have equity. And having equity beats having a job, ten times out of ten.

Is this a hopeless situation for the average person?

Absolutely not. But it is dramatically different from the past. The employees of one large Canadian media corporation learned that lesson. Company management took it private after the major corporate shareholder pulled out, but that involved a "one-time" round of layoffs to make it attractive to the holders of company debt.

Soon management decided to take the company public again, with an initial public offering. But to make the company attractive to investors, and raise the share value, it "trimmed costs" again—with more layoffs. The IPO was a success and senior managers made millions. Soon after, a competitor announced a hostile takeover, which was ultimately defeated as the company found a "white knight" investor who paid a huge premium to buy control.

Employees cheered before television cameras in the company's head office lobby. Senior managers made millions more on their bloated stock options. Within six months the new controlling shareholder was forced to lay off hundreds of people, to keep the bond rating agencies happy. Several months later it sold off enough shares in the company to retire its own corporate debt, while leaving its subsidiary mired in indebtedness—paving the way for more troubles and adjustments to come.

Who won? Those holding equity. The losers? Loyal, long-term employees who thought doing a good job counted for something. Today, it counts for nothing, and the sooner you learn that lesson, the better.

When loyalty dies, there is no workplace justice. You are on your own.

By 2020

The four pillars will be a memory for most. They simply will not be there to support society as we knew it in the 50 years leading up to the millennium.

A job with one employer spanning decades and leading to the kind of secure corporate pension that Archie enjoyed until his 85th year will be, for all but a handful of people, a memory. A lifetime government pension cheque every month for every citizen, as he received, will also be an unaffordable luxury when there are more 65-year-old women than 10-year-old girls, as there will be in a couple of decades. The working generation at that point will be unable, not just unwilling, to shoulder that burden.

The financial support of your grown children is also a great uncertainty as the economy takes an inevitable hit and the number of seniors mushrooms by 300%. In 2020 being 100 years old will not be noteworthy—it will be commonplace. Health care costs will explode as will the taxes to support them. It will not be a happy time to be mid-career, trying to raise a small family in a Depression-era economy and still worrying about your struggling parents.

And the house? Far from being a refuge and a source of financial security, it could be a symbol of all that is going wrong with your life—a depreciating asset that is taking down the bulk of your net worth with it, unsaleable and expensive to maintain.

Is hope lost?

No, far from it. Not if you understand the nature of the changes rapidly taking place in our society. Nothing in a few years will be as it was a few years ago. The rules my father successfully and expansively lived by are now being struck down. You cannot trust the system today, because it is crumbling before your eyes. There are few jobs for life. No guarantees of a guaranteed income. No secure support systems. You will be on your own, as Archie and everyone else was during the last Depression.

But the good news is that opportunity abounds now and during the next decade before the most fundamental change rolls over us.

You have a distant warning of what is to come, and a huge chance in the meantime to prepare. You can survive and prosper, build your wealth and therefore your insulation from change. If you know where the economy, interest rates, financial markets and commodities are headed, you can do the right thing. Put your money in the right places. Know the true risks. Take the proper action and avoid the fate that awaits so many.

Are you ready?

The Last Depression

THE ARGUMENT
Let us look back. Following an era of unprecedented prosperity and technological advance, the Great Depression of the 1930s was a shock to most people. Had they seen it coming, they would have doubtlessly prepared.

There are ominous parallels today, far in advance of the next depression.

Stock prices will stay at high level for years to come, says Ohio economist.

NEW YORK TIMES

SUNDAY, OCTOBER 13, 1929

Prices of stocks crash in heavy liquidation, total drop of billions. Many accounts wiped out.

NEW YORK TIMES

THURSDAY, OCTOBER 24, 1929

Fundamentally, business conditions are sound and there is no reason for pessimism. It is well that in times like these we should not overlook the general soundness of the Canadian situation.

MORRIS W. WILSON

GENERAL MANAGER, ROYAL BANK OF CANADA

OCTOBER 1930

An enduring image of loss—desperation sale of a luxury automobile on Wall Street, 1929

For just about every Canadian or American who has lived for more than 70 years, there are two defining events: the Second World War and the Depression. If you lost family in the war, that was the worst. If you did not, the Depression was a bigger reality, because it touched just about everyone. It was shocking, unforeseen and right off the economic radar screen. For those who lived through the event, it was incomprehensible. But, in retrospect, it could have been one of history's most predictable events. Today, it could be our largest lesson.

The lost decade

The Great Depression took middle-class people and made them poor. In 1929, there were 13,447 Canadians with taxable income of more than $10,000. By 1934, that number had plunged by more than 50%. By 1932, the unemployment rate in Windsor, Ontario—the heart of the Canadian auto manufacturing industry—was a crushing 38%. In 1933, a full 15% of the Canadian population, some 1.5 million people, were on government relief. By 1938, just a year before World War Two started, there were still almost 900,000 in desperate straits. This would be the lost decade, after one that had seemed to promise nothing but growth, rising markets and rampant technological advance.

This Depression took hard-working people and made them unemployed and, ultimately, hopeless. It took away farms and destroyed the fabric of rural Canada where, in the 1930s, 80% of the population lived. Countless western communities defaulted on their financial obligations. The local tax base melted away as farm incomes ran down to almost zero. It evaporated life savings. It swept away governments, with the defeat in 1930 of Conservative, pro-business Prime Minister R.B. Bennett by Liberal Mackenzie King. In the United States, hapless President Herbert Hoover went down before the interventionist policies of Franklin Delano Roosevelt in the spring of 1933. Economic collapse on an unparalleled scale was about to transform the very way people viewed society. This was the death of rugged individualism, and the birth of the social safety net, the New Deal and state-run enterprise. Capitalism turned the other cheek, in embarrassment.

This Depression forever changed the way North America would work. It tested economics, and economics failed. It turned into a global event that would help spawn the next world war. It made houses worth less than the mortgages placed on them. It took mothers and thrust them into bread lines. It forever discredited those who preached that life would only get better; who said history was no guide.

BY THE BEST ACCOUNT, it was in mid-1931 that Clayton and Georgina Bacon realized the family was going down fast. The Ontario farm economy was collapsing as commodity prices deflated. There was just no cash to buy seed, feed or food. There were no government income support programs, no baby bonuses, no unemployment insurance, no well-off friends. Just five kids, a broken-down truck, an unpayable mortgage and desperation.

One day Clayton said to Georgie, let's go West. It had to be better, because anything was more than nothing.

The truck made it, piled high with everything they owned after a *Grapes of Wrath*–like odyssey across a country vaster than any of them had imagined. Every day there had been another breakdown, another heartache and the humiliating need to live off the generosity of strangers. As it turned out, that horrible, dehumanizing journey was a dream compared to what was coming.

In Saskatchewan, the drought came. Crops turned into brittle sticks. Wind storms turned the land into a moonscape and drove dirt into exposed flesh. Clayton could grow nothing to feed the cattle that the family now depended on, so he spent his days collecting tumbleweed to drag back to give to the starving animals.

Finally, it was time to leave. The truck was dead so Clayton rented space on a boxcar heading east. The family and the cattle spent the next week in that wooden car, doubling back, hungry, broken and defeated by weather, dust and macroeconomics. Not far from the tracks in Orton, Ontario, they found a marginal piece of land and set to work surviving.

Fifty years later Archie and my mother were invited to walk across the road from their weekend farmhouse for a celebration. All of Clayton and Georgie's children and grandkids were there, crammed into the small, insulbrick-sided wooden structure. It was a big day. Thanks in part to the money my parents had paid Clayton to build an addition on their place, they'd been able to pay off a mortgage that had been in place since the darkest days of their lives.

They wept as the mortgage was burned.

Memories are fading

Today, memories of the Great Depression are passing with the generation that endured it. But the events of the 1930s shaped my parents' value system and dominated their adult lives. If it happened once, they knew, it could happen again. That possibility underscored the naked danger of exposing yourself to too much debt, or of investing hard-earned dollars in risky and speculative ventures. It meant that frugality, simplicity and preparedness were virtues. Buy with cash. Retire the mortgage as quickly as possible. Trust only guaranteed investments. Expect adversity.

Years after Archie's death, my mother, in her mid-eighties, quietly and against my best advice, kept tens of thousands of dollars in a savings account paying her less than a half of 1% interest a year. But the rate of return was inconsequential to her. Growing money had never been a priority. Preserving it was everything. All she had to do to silence me was to look straight into my eyes and say, "But what if something happens?"

For her, it had. She knew.

JUBILEE YEAR, 1927, was a good one in Canada. Archie was 16 and it was the 60th anniversary of Confederation. There were celebrations everywhere—even a parade down the Talbot Highway through Fingal, Ontario, with Clydesdales pulling wagons covered with Union Jacks and bunting. Of course, the big year for marking the country's birth should have been 1917, the 50th anniversary, but then Canada was deeply involved in a foreign war that it was close to losing, so the bands, banners and fireworks had to wait a decade.

In 1927, people across North America could also give thanks for a newly found prosperity and a roaring economy that was creating fortunes and lifting the standards of living. Even the farmers were doing well, on their way to a bumper crop in 1928, although soon that overproduction would result in falling prices and depressed wheat sales.

Phenomenal growth and technological advance south of the border were whetting an appetite for Canadian exports. Governments were pouring money into building roads. There were more than a million passenger cars in Canada, up from just 5,000 two decades earlier. Cities were growing. In Montreal, the Royal Bank was building its new national head office on St. James Street, while Bell Canada was topping off a 20-storey skyscraper. In Toronto, the tallest building in the British Commonwealth—the Bank of Commerce head office—was being built, along with the Royal York Hotel. In Ottawa, Canadian National was doubling the size of the Chateau Laurier, sitting on prized real estate across the Rideau Canal from the historic East Block of the Parliament Buildings. Bigger, higher, grander. Even war was about to be "abolished" in the public's mind by the Kellogg-Briand Pact of 1928, a whimsical treaty that, in the end, meant nothing.

Capitalists, entrepreneurs and the captains of new technologies were celebrated. Companies grew wealthier, not always by manufacturing or selling more, but often just by refinancing. In 1925, Simpsons issued a massive amount of new stock, followed a few years later by Canada Cement.

Investors were eager to snap up the new shares then, just as they over-subscribed to initial public offerings in the 1990s. Other hot companies included International Nickel, Noranda, Massey-Harris and Imperial Oil.

In the late 1920s, everyone knew this was a modern, progressive society on the move, celebrating technology, peace, wealth, rising markets, ubiquitous communications devices like the telephone and the prospect of more to come for decades. Everybody was coming to watch the same movies, eat the same foods from new chain stores and share a commonality of everyday experience. It was, in many ways, just like today. It was cool.

All eyes were on the Dow Jones index

Between early 1928 and September of the next year, the average price of stocks in New York rose by 40% and the Dow jumped from 191 to 381. Trading volumes almost doubled, and huge new amounts of cash flowed in. Confidence abounded. In Ottawa, Prime Minister Mackenzie King would come to be a pillar of stability. In Washington, the American president had come to office saying, "The business of America is business." And it was. Henry Ford was a living god.

Yet within three short years, life had been shattered. The pivotal event came in October, when the stock market crashed as few believed was possible and erased $16 billion in wealth in a single month.

In hindsight, it should have been easy to see coming. Prices started to waft lower in early September but the pundits said it was nothing, and new money kept pouring in, despite warnings that the market was simply overvalued. Many corporations were making more money selling pieces of themselves to speculators than actually producing goods. By late 1929, U.S. companies had realized more than $6.5 billion doing so—money backed more by the promise of future valuations than by economic reality. On the third Monday in October, the decline accelerated and many investors panicked, and bailed. Things stabilized mid-week, before a new wave of selling was unleashed as the market opened Thursday morning. It was an ugly day, which came to be known as Black Thursday in New York, Toronto and Montreal.

As author Doug Fetherling described the session in his book, *Gold Diggers of 1929*:

> In Montreal, on both the senior exchange and the curb, the panic was almost unrestrained. The greatest chaos was caused by brokers emptying their customers' portfolios. Total sales would reach almost 400,000 shares on the MSE, an absolutely unprecedented figure; by noon almost every stock on the board had lost anywhere up to twenty-five points. In Toronto it was almost impossible to get a bid. Losses went up to ten, fifteen, and even twenty points in a few cases. Among the hardest hit were Loblaws, Steel Company of Canada, Consolidated Bakeries, and Canada Gypsum—all the tried-and-true safe stocks. Even Brazilian and that old standby, International Nickel, dropped markedly in a few minutes; Massey-Harris sank to within a point of matching the lowest price in its history, and some sellers were not even that lucky. At noon, the Toronto Stock Exchange's own ticker was running behind, a rare occurrence.

At the same time in New York, officials were clearing the public gallery above the New York Stock Exchange, ostensibly for fear of collapse under the weight of scores of panicked observers.

A group of prominent American bankers tried to save the market on Friday, but by Monday the selling sentiment overwhelmed all else. On that day, October 29, the Dow lost 12.82% of its value—a crash that would be eclipsed just once (October 19, 1987), but a loss that shattered the confidence of an entire society. The selling continued on Tuesday and the next morning the headline in the *New York Times* was: "Stocks Collapse in 16,410,030-share day, but rally at close cheers brokers; bankers optimistic, to continue aid." In Toronto, the *Daily Star* screamed at its readers, "STOCK PRICES CRASH EARLY; SLIGHT RALLY LATER."

But optimism would be in short supply for a long, long time.

The glory days were over. This event would mark the beginning of the Depression that swept across most of the western world. Between that Monday in September and the end of the year, entire U.S. industrial production fell by 9%. The job losses started and a huge credit crunch rolled over North America.

But even before that, there were ominous signs the economy was not the titan most thought it had been.

• Car sales, the engine of growth, had fallen by a third in the nine months before the crash.

• A recession had technically started in August, with construction, wholesale prices and personal incomes all declining.

• The economy had become too dependent on just a few industries, like autos and radio.

• There was too wide a gap forming between rich and poor.

• Too few corporations, after a wave of merger mania, controlled too much of the wealth.

• Investors speculated on stocks, snapping up shares in companies that were not making much, if any, money. RCA stock, for example, soared during 1928 even though the company had paid no dividends—shades of Amazon.com 70 years later.

• Consumers were chalking up too much debt through the newly devised instalment payment system.

• And as society modernized, people became more dependent on others and less reliant on themselves. Cars got complicated, and needed mechanics to fix. Investments become complex, and investors needed advisers. Food became readily available canned or frozen, so people stopped growing it. Electricity at the flick of a switch meant the end of worrying about oil lamps or once-popular (and dangerous) gasoline stoves. Self-sufficiency was surrendered to the new "experts" in all fields.

When the Depression hit, most people were completely unprepared, shocked and vulnerable. At first, governments and business leaders insisted that the market crash had nothing to do with economic fundamentals, which they pronounced as being solid.

But by the winter months of 1930, central bankers in Canada and the States had cut interest rates to try and stimulate the economy, but it did not work. In the U.S., the federal government passed the Smoot-Hawley Tariff, erecting trade barriers to foreign goods, and inadvertently taking a bad economic situation and turning it into a global disaster. Protectionism was the last refuge of a system now in full retreat.

It was not until banks started to fail all across the United States that policy-makers realized the extent of what they were dealing with.

First bank panic in 1930

The first bank panic hit in late 1930. Across America, it would be followed by two more—in the spring of 1931 and March 1933. People hoarded cash money as faith in the financial system crumbled, and as they withdrew cash, banks closed their doors.

The Depression all but destroyed the American credit system. When it started, there were more than 30,000 U.S. banks, many of them with pitifully small capitalizations, compared with the Canadian system that was then, as today, dominated by a handful of large players. When people began demanding their money back, banks that had taken large commercial mortgages suddenly worth pennies on the dollar, simply did not have the reserves. They closed their doors.

When it was all over, more than 10,000 U.S. banks had collapsed and more than $2 billion in deposits had been lost. Central banks stumbled in not ensuring that the banks had enough reserves in the form of newly printed money to cover their deposits (a lesson both the Bank of Canada and the U.S. Federal Reserve learned as Y2K approached at the end of 1999).

At the same time, unemployment was becoming a societal disease. In the States it rose in 1930 from just 3% to 8.7%. In 1931, it climbed to 15.9%. The next year the gross national product dropped by 13% and the jobless rate became 23.6%. In Canada, it became an unbearable 30%.

President Roosevelt deals with a run on the banks by simply ordering them closed in March 1932.

The market, between 1930 and 1932, lost 80% of its value

The money supply contracted by about a third and in Canada and the U.S. more than 16 million people had lost their jobs.

Farm prices collapsed by half between 1929 and 1932 while 66% of all the people in Saskatchewan went on relief as the provincial income dropped by 90% in two years. All the western provinces were technically bankrupt after 1932 and unemployment relief camps were set up to house single and homeless men. Food shortages were widespread and so was scurvy.

In March 1932, President Franklin Roosevelt ordered American banks closed, trying to stem the third panic.

Recovery came as governments became more interventionist. In the U.S., it took Roosevelt's New Deal and massive reconstruction projects, along with a lot more regulation of the economy. Washington created the FCC (Federal Communications Commission) to regulate radio, and the SEC (Securities and Exchange Commission) to ride herd on the financial markets. In Canada, the government created the Bank of Canada (1934), the Canadian Wheat Board (1935), the CBC (1932) and Trans-Canada Airlines (1937).

The lasting effect was to vastly increase the size and role of government in North American society; making citizens far more dependent upon policy-makers than they had been in the past, as a trade-off for the creation of a social safety net. Some would argue, and I would agree, that the Depression bred big government, which led to the deficit/debt crisis that would materialize 50 years later.

Then, of course, came World War II. Massive public spending created virtually full employment and wiped out the effects of nine years of economic hell. But the hell of war was about to begin.

IN A COMMON hospital room in London, Ontario, in the spring of 1940, my father was talking to his wife, now pregnant and about to give birth. The Great Depression had ended, and it was finally safe and hopeful enough to get married and plan a family. But then the world turned again, so sharply. Canada was at war and there was talk that the Germans and the Japanese could invade Canada from both coasts, while the Americans remained neutral and determined not to get involved.

My parents devised a plan to reunite, should disaster strike and they be separated. They would meet down at the river.

The Ominous Parallels

Why did North America go from having a great economy to a Depression? How could things have turned so quickly without any real warning? How did so many jobs come to evaporate? How did deflation spread its poisonous declines without warning? How could investors have been happily pushing money into financial markets mere hours before those markets collapsed? How could respected politicians and business leaders speak to people in reassuring tones when things were going to hell? Did they deceive, or did they simply not know? Most importantly, could it happen again?

Many people, observers, market analysts, even some economists, are struck by what they see as the ominous parallels between life in the early millennium years and society seven decades ago. Unfortunately, this anxiety and dread has driven many people into the false safety of cash fixed-income, and high-cost guaranteed investments.

What were the causes of the Great Depression, and are they echoed today in any meaningful way? As you read the next few pages, you will see that there are many parallels. Indeed, imbalances are building up in society that will probably lead to a sharp reversal of our economic fortunes, and affect the lives of every Canadian who is not prepared.

Study the parallels closely, but do not panic. There is at least a decade to go before history is repeated—a decade that could well end up being the most important of your life.

Polarization of Incomes

Then:

The 1920s was a decade of prosperity and amazing economic growth. The overall income of North Americans soared by 20% between 1923 and 1929, but the gains were very unevenly distributed as the gap between rich and poor grew wider and wider.

The top one-tenth of 1% of Americans, for example, had a combined income equal to almost half the entire population. They controlled a third of all savings while eight in ten people had no savings at all. And as the disposable income per capita rose 9% during the decade, those with the top 1% of incomes enjoyed a 75% gain. In Canada, the average savings per capita in 1925 was a meagre $185, but even that number did not reflect the fact that most of the country was rural, and most outside the cities had no cash reserve whatsoever. When the price of commodities, and farmland, plunged, they lost almost all their net worth.

Symbolizing this income polarization was Henry Ford, the farm boy who in the space of a single generation created an empire, revolutionized society with technology and amassed incomprehensible wealth. Ford paid himself $14 million a year, the equivalent today of about US$345 million. The average personal income for Americans at the time was $750 a year. For farm workers, it was $250. Fewer than 10% of Canadians were middle-class and less than 3% of the Canadian population owned non-interest-bearing securities like stocks.

This income gap, serious and destabilizing and growing, was masked by the overall prosperity of the era, and the massive media attention given to the new class of industrial and technological millionaires and their spending habits. Meanwhile, most people had zero financial reserves, and no ability to withstand the financial firestorm that was coming.

Now:

The 1990s turned out to be another decade of unprecedented prosperity, income growth and astonishing technological advance. Deep federal deficits in Canada and the United States in the 1980s turned into surpluses of $9 billion and $73 billion respectively by the end of the decade as inflation dissipated, interest rates collapsed and the cost of carrying debt slid. Unemployment declined modestly in Canada and dramatically in the United States, while the ranks of the millionaires swelled.

But the income gap is once again very much in evidence. According to the Vanier Institute of the Family, the wealthiest 20% of Canadians control a stunning 67% of the national income. The average Canadian family now earns about $60,000, a number that has been essentially stagnant for the last 20 years.

Meanwhile taxes have exploded higher and the amount people have saved has declined. Most working Canadians today could survive about a month after their paycheques stopped coming. As noted, the personal savings rate has collapsed, from about 12% to about zero. If it were not for forced savings plans (Canada Pension Plan contributions, for example), the national savings rate as the old millennium ended would have been negative.

Only half of Canadians have any money in an RRSP. The other half has an average saved of just $37,000. And the numbers in the United States are even more alarming.

Consistently, since 1969, according to the U.S. Census Bureau, the proportion of families that are low-income has been rising—to about 24% of the population. Meanwhile, the number of families that are high-income has been expanding at exactly the same rate. The personal savings rate has, astonishingly, declined at the same time the stock market has soared in value, doubling between 1990 and 1995, and then again by 1999.

And then there is the Henry Ford of modern life—Bill Gates, founder and chairman of Microsoft. His personal net worth in mid-1999 was just over US$100.5 billion, with his wealth growing at the rate of more than $1 million an hour, or $300 a second. At that same time, the average annual U.S. income was slightly more than $18,000.

As in the 1920s, despite the obvious income gap, people are drawn to wealth as moths to a flame, looking for the sage advice that will enrich their lives. When Warren Buffett, worth US$36 billion, presided over the 1999 annual meeting of his company Berkshire Hathaway, in a hockey arena in Omaha, Nebraska, he stared out at a sea of 15,000 people, a significant number of them having just flown in from Vancouver, Calgary and Toronto. J.P. Morgan would have been amused.

Overcapacity

Then:

The polarization of income in the 1920s started to make the economy unstable. As more wealth flowed to the top, into the hands of people who spent just a small fraction of their incomes, less was put into the hands of middle-class consumers. Without their demand for goods, an oversupply developed, leading to lower prices, lower wages and even less demand. The seeds of deflation had been planted, even as monetary authorities worried about excessive market valuations and inflation.

People with incomes of less than $2,500 a year—about 75% of Americans and 80% of Canadians—spent almost everything they had buying essentials. The wealthy—the top 25% who had 55% of all income—spent far less as a percentage of their incomes. That money went into savings and securities, and out of circulation.

Meanwhile, rampant technological advance made industry far more productive. The Ford assembly lines in Windsor and Detroit could turn out cars in 90 minutes that previously took 14 hours to build. Productivity went up, but without a corresponding increase in jobs or income. The imbalance that developed between supply and demand was masked in part by a dangerous new trend: buying on credit.

Overcapacity was also made worse by slumping commodity prices, which reduced production costs. Commodities peaked during 1920 and entered into a 12-year slide, bottoming along with stocks in 1932. No commodity, it turned out, even gold, proved to be a safe haven from the Depression and the asset deflation that engulfed society. There was, literally, nowhere to hide.

Now:

The North American middle class has continued to spend, and prop up demand for domestic goods, but at the expense of savings and also through additional debt. The Canadian savings rate has plunged and household debt levels now equal about 100% of annual income, at the same time as car makers, for example, are reporting record sales on both sides of the 49th parallel.

But the problem of overcapacity has spread far beyond our borders. It's become a global concern, as the Asian flu showed when it collapsed financial markets in the second half of 1998. Asian economies simply burned too hot for too long, spawning hyper-inflation and unbelievable real estate valuations until the inevitable meltdown occurred. As early as 1995, according to Brookings Institute economist Nicholas Lardy, China reported that production capacity of 900 major goods was twice the demand. And as the nineties ended, the slowdown in Asia caused a worldwide slide in commodity prices, leading to oversupply and economic hardship for loggers in northern British Columbia and coal miners in Cape Breton.

Oil prices retreated in 1999 to levels of 20 years before. An ounce of gold was changing hands at less than US$260 an ounce, compared with $800 an ounce in the early eighties. One Friday alone in the spring of 1999, it dropped by US$10 an ounce. The price of lumber, coal and base metals were all sliding as they did during the 1920s, and at precisely the same moment that stock markets were marking historic highs.

Technological unemployment

Then:

It was a new phrase coined during the 1920s—the concept that as technology got better and companies more productive, turning out more goods for the same overhead, machines replaced workers.

In the U.S. and Canada, as many as 200,000 workers a year during the second half of the decade lost their jobs to automation. Ironically, as the assembly line replaced the work station and trucks replaced wagons, and as the continent was electrified and tied together with telephone cables and miles of highways and ribbons of steel track, work became more scarce, not more plentiful.

This helped fuel the polarization of income, because the wealthy families owned the industries that were profiting from increased productivity and lower wage costs. By 1929, the richest 1% owned 40% of all the wealth in the United States. The bottom 93% actually experienced a 4% drop in real disposable income between 1923 and 1929. And this took place while the productivity of the individual worker soared an incredible 43% between 1919 and 1929.

Now:

This must be the golden age of technological unemployment. Voice mail replaces receptionists. Telephone and Internet banking replaces tellers. Self-serve gas pumps replace service-station attendants. Banking machines replace whole branches. Desktop publishing programs in newspapers replace layout artists, typesetters, camera operators and proofreaders. Robots replace highly skilled auto workers. The Internet replaces travel agents, librarians and perhaps, soon, teachers. Online trading replaces brokers. Email replaces postal workers. E-commerce replaces stores and their employees.

Of course, other jobs—for webmasters, IT workers, couriers and others supporting the new technologies—are created or augmented. But the net effect on society is gripping. Home offices are replacing centralized places of work. People talk less and communicate more. Entry-level jobs require more and more training and education. Virtual corporations spring up and immediately carve out market share from traditional ones.

Once again, worker productivity soars thanks to the new technologies, and yet unemployment in Canada remains essentially unchanged. Youth unemployment is epidemic. Incomes continue to polarize with the top 20% earning, on average, $114,000, a level that is increasing annually. The bottom 20% earn $17,000, an income level that is steadily decreasing.

Deflation

Then:

A massive decline in values was the most depressing aspect of the Great Depression in North America and Europe. Wages went down; prices fell. The value of commodities crashed. Real estate slumped. Stocks cratered. Deflation, which had been mild in the late 1920s, became virulent starting in 1929 and continued right through the next 10 years, becoming most painful around 1932.

The effect on the economy was catastrophic. Between 1929 and 1933 Canada's economic output fell a staggering 42%. It took until 1937 for government and consumer spending to return to 1929 levels, but because of a plunge in exports and investments, gross domestic product (GDP) remained far below previous levels. Less economic activity meant fewer jobs. More than a third of the workforce was unemployed—an even bigger human disaster than in the United States, partly because our economy then (as today) was more dependent on commodities, which suffered a huge price decline.

One in five Canadians had to surrender their sense of self-reliance and depend on government relief programs. The Canadian unemployment rate never fell below 12% until the outbreak of the Second World War.

But deflation was not even across the economy, and prices fell faster

than wages. That meant that anyone who could hold on to a job fared
much better than those who could not. Farmers and small business people were particularly devastated. Those with savings and little debt were
the best off—in fact, some personal fortunes were started then by people
who could buy up real estate for pennies on the dollar.

The four western provinces, along with hundreds of municipalities,
became bankrupt, unable to provide relief to unemployed workers. Finally,
in 1932, Ottawa set up relief camps, run by the Department of Defence,
where single and homeless men were paid 20 cents a day to do hard labour
in the bush. Conditions were appalling, and led in 1935 to a riot in Regina,
in which a police officer was killed and dozens of people were arrested
or injured.

Deflation started as an economic phenomenon and quickly became a
social one, stealing jobs, wealth, dignity and opportunity, and leading to
violence, disease and even death. It profoundly shaped the personalities of
those who endured it, and many seniors today are haunted by an experience
that they constantly fear will be repeated in their lifetimes.

Now:

As the 1990s ended, the North American economy was in a state of mild
deflation, but most economists were predicting that it would not turn
into a 1930s-style disaster. In Asia, however, there was no question about
deflation, as the unemployment rate soared, commodity prices caved and
economic output collapsed. Once again, a severe asset decline was causing
human misery.

In Japan, the government pushed down short-term interest rates in
1999 to zero in a desperate attempt to stave off a serious deflationary spiral. It was believed to be the first time in history that a central bank had
pushed overnight rates down to nothing in an attempt to rekindle inflation. There were calls from government critics for interest rates to turn
negative. Some economists said it was only a matter of time before Tokyo
would have to start buying up its own bonds in order to create inflation. And the move appeared to work, with the Japanese stock market regaining huge chunks of lost ground in 1999, and Asian mutual

In 1999 Japanese officials tried to turn deflation into inflation by dropping interest rates to zero.

Source: The National Post

Japan takes rates to zero

Bank of Japan takes radical move to reflate economy

BY GILLIAN TETT

TOKYO • The Bank of Japan pushed effective short-term interest rates down to zero yesterday in an unprecedented new attempt to stave off an economic downturn and deflationary spiral in Japan.

The overnight call rate or the market short-term rate dropped to 0.02% during trading, as the bank flooded the money markets with 1.8 trillion yen ($23-billion Cdn) of surplus liquidity.

The 0.02% rate means money is being provided for free, as brokerage commission in the call money market is currently 0.02%. The bank said the average rate for the day's trading was 0.04%, down from 0.07% on Tuesday.

This is probably the first time a major central bank has pushed nominal overnight rates to zero in a bid to reflate its economy. Switzerland briefly introduced what were, in effect, negative interest rates in the 1970s, but the purpose was to deter inflows of flight capital.

Yesterday's measures boosted long-term bond prices as some investors removed money from the call market and sought out yields. However, the yen also fell to 121 yen against the U.S. dollar, two yen weaker on the day, as some economists concluded the bank was poised to use even more radical methods to stimulate the economy. Kazuo Ueda, a member of the

bank's policy board, denied it was now seeking negative interest rates. However, he said the bank would introduce "further credit-easing steps" if they were needed to reflate the economy.

The bank has so far rejected suggestions that it should directly underwrite Japanese government bonds, or purchase more JGBs from the market to create inflation.

It has also opposed suggestions that it should pump enough liquidity into the markets to achieve a specific target for monetary growth, in a policy known as "quantitative easing."

Instead, it has sought to guide overnight rates into a band: Last month, for example, it announced it would guide them down from 0.25% to 0.15%.

Mr. Ueda said the bank was now seeking a "middle way" between targeting interest rates and quantitative easing.

Some economists believe the bank may soon be forced to buy more government bonds or government-guaranteed bonds to create inflation.

In particular, the bank is locked in negotiations with the Deposit Insurance Corp., the government body organizing bank reform, about how to finance a 7.45-trillion-yen injection of public funds into the banks' capital bases.

After insisting it would not provide the funds, the bank is now considering supplying the DIC with about four trillion yen for a limited period, a step economists say would amount to an unorthodox expansion of the money supply by the bank.

Financial Times

funds becoming the darlings of global investors.

In Canada, officially, it was borderline deflation, with the inflation rate oscillating between zero and 3% annually. Were it not for increases in the price of government-regulated commodities, such as cable TV, air transportation, tobacco and telephone service, the entire economy would be tasting deflation.

The official numbers were probably wrong. The Bank of Canada has admitted that its official inflation rate is probably overstated by a half a percentage point, meaning that at several points there was none. Meanwhile, sharp declines in the value of the Canadian dollar in the late 1990s meant imports were made far more expensive, masking the fact that Canadian prices overall would have been in a significant decline were it not for the dollar's effect.

As the Royal Bank reported, even without these factors being taken into consideration, the four Atlantic provinces were already deflationary in 1998 for the first time since the Great Depression. And the situation deteriorated significantly in British Columbia during 1999 with a massive decline in the forestry industry as commodity prices collapsed, causing a corresponding drop in the value of houses in distant Vancouver.

In fact, residential real estate itself is a deflator. The price of an average home in Toronto finished the 1990s at around $225,000, or $50,000 below the level a decade earlier. A 1930s-era, seven-storey office building in the downtown core that sold for $22 million in 1990 was worth just $5.25 million when it was brokered by Royal LePage in the fall of 1998. A 30-foot lot in the financial district with a 100-year-old building on it that changed hands for $22 million in 1989 sold in 1999 for $1.2 million.

Other commodities, like computers, have been in a price freefall. In 1998, the overall price of computer equipment declined by 20% and in 1999, the decline averaged 2% a month. By the end of 1999, it was possible to purchase an Internet-accessing computer for what consumers paid for a printer a year earlier. Even new vehicles were falling in value, with the sticker price of a 1999 Ford being less than that of the previous year's new model for the first time in 30 years. Seventy years earlier, founder Henry Ford, facing similar deflationary pressures, slashed the price of a standard coupe by $50, to $500.

And then there were wages. After-tax earnings fell steadily from 1990 to 1999. According to Bruce Campbell, director of the Canadian Centre for Policy Alternatives, "When incomes aren't rising, all sorts of things happen—and one of them is weakness in demand." That situation, of course, inevitably leads to falling prices—the kind of cycle that turned vicious in the 1930s.

Stock market speculation

People are dealing in illusions and dreams and I am afraid that there has been a replacement of analysis and fundamental thinking. Those illusions and dreams are going to end up in a disaster for some people,

NED RILEY

CHIEF INVESTMENT OFFICER

BANK BOSTON, 1999

Then:

In the 1920s many believed in a "new era" just as investors today put faith in a "new paradigm," a belief that history would not be repeated and economic boom times not be destined to turn into an economic bust.

The most famous man of his time, Henry Ford, put it well when he said, "History is bunk."

Millions of investors believed him. In 1929, the U.S. and Canadian economies felt great. Corporate profits were on a roll—ahead a stunning 20% from 1928 in the States. Real wages were increasing as was productivity, and the stock market mirrored the relentless optimism of the day. The Dow Jones Industrial Index soared an incredible 700% between 1920 and 1929—eerily, almost exactly the same advance as between 1990 and 1999. There were corrections along the way, but they were all brief, and turned out to be just great buying opportunities.

The investing public looked at all of this—at the new technologies, the apparent prosperity everywhere, the magic of radio and the power of the automobile industry, the stock market wealth being created—and wanted in. There was mass speculation and in 1929 more than 1.1 billion shares were traded in New York. The Dow doubled between early 1928 and the third day of September 1929.

Many people bought on margin, which meant they need only raise 10% of the stock price in order to buy it, borrowing the rest from their broker. By the summer of 1929, there were outstanding broker loans of more than $7 billion, and by September, that rose to $8.5 billion, despite the fact the interest on those loans ranged as high as 20%.

Canadian market advanced 299%

Coming out of a post–World War I recession, markets in Canada and the States were electric with excitement. Between August 1921 and September 1929, American markets in total gained 394%. In Canada, the advance in the same time was 299.8%. North American society was being flooded with new products and services and new wealth at the same time Europe remained in a post-war state of chaos. Why wouldn't you invest and grow rich?

In August 1929 an article appeared in the *Ladies' Home Journal* spelling out how people could build wealth over the next two decades by investing in the stock market. Just $15 a week, said author and capitalist millionaire John Raskob, could earn you $80,000 in 20 years. It sounded like an absolutely sure thing.

Well, the bubble burst, of course. From its high on September 3, the Dow retreated and it looked an awful lot like another of those buying opportunities. Money continued to flood into the market. On Monday, October 21, 1929, things began to unwind faster, followed by a meltdown on Thursday, a rally on the weekend and then a disaster on Monday and Tuesday. It was over.

Within two years, the market had lost close to 90% of its value and the Dow, which had hit 381, bottomed at just 41. Not until 1955 did it achieve the level hit back in the beautiful autumn days of 1929.

In Toronto, stock investors lost, on average, 80.1% of their market wealth between September 1929 and June 1932. The best-performing stocks of the 1920s became the worst performers during the ensuing bear market. Henry Ford had been proven wrong. This time, it was no different.

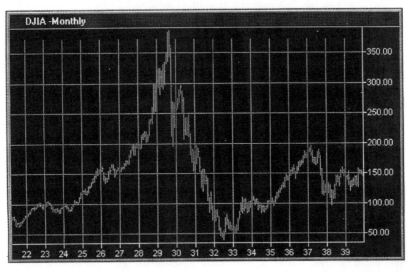

Source: New York Stock Exchange

From its high in 1929 to its low in 1932, the Dow lost almost 90% of its value.

Now:

Buys 100 AWEB (Autoweb.com Inc.) shares at 22⅜. Now the real run on AWEb stock starts. She's intensely focused on her computer screens, watching numbers jump in front of her, and on the monitor to the side, the lines of a buy and sell graph wiggle up and up. Her fingers drum the table, her chair shakes; she impatiently taps the enter key. She's made $262 so far. '$30, $30. My goal is $30.'

—ACCOUNT OF A DAY TRADER IN TORONTO

AS REPORTED IN THE NATIONAL POST, MARCH 27, 1999

Day traders. Mutual fund madness. The Dow at 11,000. National governments in Canada and the U.S. committing billions in public pension money to the market. For the worriers, all the signs are there.

In 1999 it was estimated that five million North Americans actively traded securities online. Three years earlier, there were virtually none. The advent of online, Internet-based discount brokerages suddenly offered the potential of turning everyone into a trader, removing the filter of an experienced professional, and exposing the market to the full frontal reality of ebbing and flowing human emotion.

In the U.S., intensely worried about the new volatility day trading could bring, the National Association of Securities Dealers started drafting rules to curb it, warning day trading could be extremely risky, could result in large commissions and that trading on margin or short selling could result in losses far beyond the initial investment.

By early 1999, in Canada, a country of just 30 million people, there were 42.1 million mutual fund accounts opened, an 18% increase in a single year. Total investment fund assets hit $346 billion by mid-year, representing an 1,100% increase from the $27 billion Canadians owned in similar assets in 1991. The number of investment funds available climbed to the 2,000 mark.

Meanwhile, the personal savings rate declined to the lowest point ever reached in the previous 24 years. Personal debt increased at the same time, with total debt and liabilities representing 112% of personal disposable income. The poorest 20% of Canadian families recorded no personal net worth, only debt. The number of young Canadian families falling below Statistic Canada's cut-off level for low income doubled from 20.4% in 1980 to 42% in 1996. What, exactly, was this market speculation being based upon?

Total Net Assets February 1991 to 1999

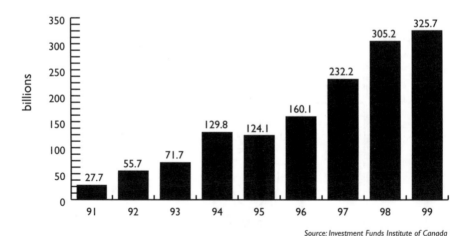

Source: Investment Funds Institute of Canada

The explosive growth in mutual fund investing during the 1990s. Thirty million Canadians owned 41 million accounts by 1999.

On the markets, Internet stocks led the charge higher. Bid.com, a Mississauga, Ontario, online auctioneer, rose from 56 cents in October of 1998 to $17 in March of 1999, then on to $30. Legendary Amazon.com did in three years what Wal-Mart took 27 years to achieve. Its market capitalization exceeded that of Ford. Of course, neither Bid.com nor Amazon.com were profitable.

Merger mania

Then:

The 1920s saw a massive consolidation of North American industry that was actually encouraged by governments that believed that bigger was better and that rapid technological advance required deep corporate pockets.

In the U.S., between 1919 and 1930, 8,000 businesses just disappeared, with a major consolidation going on in the newly bustling electric light and power industry. More electric power generation capacity was created in the decade between 1920 and 1930 than in all the years that had come before. And with that growth came monopolies.

Likewise in the banking sector, as large banks swallowed smaller ones. In 1919, there were 80 bank mergers and in 1927, there were more than 250. National chain stores flourished, destroying the local competition posed by mom-and-pop outlets across North America. The number of A&P stores grew from 400 in 1912 to more than 50,000 by 1932, and accounted for 10% of all the food sold in the United States. One massive company, Drug Incorporated, owned almost 12,000 drug stores, including 10,000 Rexall outlets, along with Bayer Aspirin and Bristol-Myers.

In 1928, Chrysler Corporation merged with Dodge Brothers, as 70 years later Chrysler would merge with Daimler Benz. Colgate merged with Palmolive-Peet. By 1929, only 200 corporations controlled about half of all the corporate wealth in America. Four tobacco companies manufactured 94% of all cigarettes.

But while this spectacular consolidation was going on, some industries were falling by the wayside, particularly as commodity prices started to

When "Everyone's getting rich!" on technology stocks, maybe it's time to bail out? Has a 1928-style mania reinvaded North America? Or, is it different this time?

deflate. Farm prices were plunging, and the cost of food fell about 70% because of overcapacity and a huge surplus. Other sick industries included coal and textiles.

Now:

Announced mergers in the United States alone totalled $1.6 trillion in 1998, the fourth consecutive year that a record was set. In 1999, another 50 deals worth an additional $1 billion would close, and in the first three months of that year U.S. companies announced $260 billion worth of acquisitions; $50 billion more than announced in the same period a year earlier.

In the auto industry, Daimler merged with Chrysler, Nissan merged with Renault, Volvo merged with Ford, which also merged with Jaguar. In the energy sector, Exxon and Mobil came together in a staggering $80 million deal that actually reconstructed part of the Standard Oil dynasty of decades earlier. MacMillan Bloedel was swallowed by Weyerhauser in a $3.6 billion deal. In banking, the 1990s saw an unprecedented consolidation in the U.S. and Europe. Deutsche Bank AG merged with Bankers

Trust in a $9 billion deal. Fleet Financial merged with BankBoston in a $16 billion arrangement. Canada Trust became a target of a major Canadian bank. In the Internet sector, America Online merged with Netscape, worth $4 billion.

In Canada, Quebecor swallowed Sun Media. Loblaws swallowed Sobeys.

The deals were non-stop, and wall to wall, and helped to propel financial markets to record-high levels. But at the same time, slumping commodity prices, asset deflation and weak Asian markets were causing major problems in industries like forestry, mining and agriculture.

Reliance on too few industries

Then:

North America was rolling, and it was tuning in. The 1920s was a decade of rapid technological advance, and nothing epitomized that better than the car and the radio.

In 1900, 4,000 cars a year were manufactured. By 1929, production in the U.S. was 4.8 million vehicles annually. Henry Ford was revered as the industry's greatest man, and, as an extension, the one person most people could thank for the prosperity that surrounded them. In 1928, Ford announced a new car, the Model A, and 500,000 people bought one without having seen the vehicle or knowing its price.

By 1929 there was one car for every five Americans, or one for just about every family. In Britain, there was a car for every 43 people. The booming auto industry was the chief engine of the economy, consuming 15% of all the steel output and assuming an equal importance to producers of nickel, lead, glass, leather and textiles. The rubber industry boomed, as did the fuel business.

Construction companies reaped the windfall from contracts worth $1 billion a year, every year of the decade, to build miles of new roads. The car brought urbanization, and that resulted in the construction of suburbs, apartments and offices. And a more mobile population travelled as never before, prompting the construction of new hotels and motels across North America.

Concurrently, radio won the hearts of consumers and investors.

Radio gained its credibility on November 2, 1920, when a Pittsburgh station broadcast the U.S. presidential election returns. That year, as William Leuchtenburg reported in his *Perils of Prosperity*, $60 million worth of radios were sold. Within seven years, sales had mushroomed to $852 million.

By the end of the decade four in ten households had one, and by 1926 the first of the big networks, National Broadcasting Company, emerged. Suddenly advertisers had a huge, growing and intensely interested audience for their messages. The medium of radio led to a surge in the growth of the whole communications, advertising and public relations sector. At the same time, radio stations were being established in every centre, electronics stores were springing up to sell radios and the demand for electric power surged.

The spread of radio also meant the continentalization of popular culture as everyone listened to the same entertainers and the same advertising messages. On Wall Street, investors clamoured to get their hands on radio stocks. RCA shares soared fivefold in 1928, before crashing to earth in 1930.

Now:

The North American economy appears to be diverse and thriving, and in many ways, it is. But there are now simply more people who do things than who make things. The service sector is worth about $2 trillion and supports a payroll of almost $500 billion. Extremely sensitive to consumer confidence, business conditions, interest rates and public perceptions of the economy, it is immensely vulnerable to a slowdown or potential dive on financial markets.

At the same time, the growth of the Internet in the 1990s has been akin to that of radio in the 1920s and 1930s. If it continues on its current path, it could be ubiquitous within a decade, which is the only possible logic behind the frothy excesses of Internet stocks. Companies with meagre sales and no profits, like Amazon.com, eBay and Bid.com have been bid higher by investors in purely speculative plays. As the market capitalization of Internet stocks grows so does the danger that investors have gambled on many companies that will not exist years, or even months, after their investments were made.

The manufacturing base of North America has been eroded in a globalized world where cheap labour attracts investment dollars. It is an inevitable and probably inescapable result of trade barriers crashing down, leading to an overdependence here on sectors—the service industry and information technology—which are intensely tied to shifting consumer confidence.

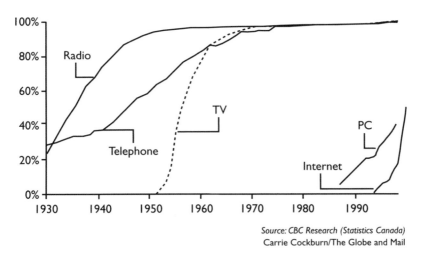

Source: CBC Research (Statistics Canada)
Carrie Cockburn/The Globe and Mail

Radio and TV became ubiquitous much faster than did the telephone. The growth in PCs and the Internet in North American households is repeating the pattern of both radio and television.

Personal debt

Then:

Along with prosperity and an unbridled faith in what lay ahead in the 1920s came the idea of being able to telescope the future into today through the use of instalment plan purchasing. The idea of buying—and enjoying—now and paying later became very fashionable, and it had a huge impact on the economy.

By 1929, two-thirds of all cars and a massive 80% of all radios were bought on instalment credit. Sixty per cent of all furniture was purchased the same way. In the five years leading up to the crash of October 1929 on stock markets, the amount of outstanding instalment credit in the U.S. grew from just over $1 billion to $3 billion. It all helped create an artificial demand for consumer goods and ate into future earnings, which would ensure an inevitable downturn if wages did not keep increasing relentlessly.

In the end, instalment buying made the economic collapse of the 1930s far worse than it might have been otherwise. When markets fell and the economy started to shrink, deflation set in and wages began to recede.

Anxious consumer debtors were quick to start defaulting on their interest payments, and were only too happy to return their cars and radios and cancel out their unrepayable debts. Suddenly manufacturers had an inventory problem, which led to faster production shutdowns and more job losses than would have been the case without the use of instalment credit. Ironically, what led to rapid growth, humming industries and prosperity, was at the heart of the coming social and economic collapse.

Now:

Instalment debt in the United States passed the $1 trillion mark in 1996, and has been climbing ever since. In Michigan and Illinois the average debt carried by someone seeking counselling assistance in 1998 was just over $60,000. The average income of that person was just over $30,000. In Canada, outstanding credit card debt routinely tops $9 billion, while Canadians are now the heaviest users of debit cards on the planet.

The total number of bankruptcies in the States during 1998 was 1.4 million, breaking the record set the previous year—a similar experience to that in Canada. In fact, bankruptcies across North America set a record in each of the three years following 1995. "This third consecutive record year of bankruptcies correlates closely with the increased debt load carried by American families," said Samuel Gerdano, executive director of the American Bankruptcy Institute. "The same consumer spending that helps to sustain the national economy can put households at risk of needing bankruptcy relief."

Statistics from the Administrative Office of the U.S. Courts show personal bankruptcies between 1990 and 1998 increased 94.7%, while business bankruptcies declined by about a third over the same period. In Canada, every year in the decade of the 1990s, with the exception of three, saw a record set for personal bankruptcies.

It gets worse. Credit-card delinquencies in North America are at a 15-year high. The average 50-year-old American in 1992 had $2,300 set aside for retirement. As noted above, the Canadian savings rate has plunged to nothing while family debt has rocketed higher. Almost 20% of family income is now devoted to paying instalment debt, or 10 times more than is being put into savings.

Personal debt levels have never been greater, nor have been the number of people who are living paycheque to paycheque. And this is after a decade of substantial economic growth and expansion. What happens if the bubble bursts again?

Loss of self-reliance

Then and now:

Life continues to get more complex as society becomes more progressive and technology more sophisticated. The advent of chain stores meant it was no longer necessary to grow a garden. Suddenly we were dependent on the stores. Cars became better, faster, more advanced, and so it became impossible to fix them or even routinely service them ourselves. We became dependent on dealerships and technicians in white coats to do that. Investments have become too complex for most investors to fully comprehend, so we are dependent on advisers, bankers and brokers. Even paper money has largely disappeared from everyday life, as we use direct deposit, credit cards, debit cards, cheques and pay bills over the phone or the Internet. We have become dependent upon technology as money in our pocket is replaced with so many electronic pulses.

Perhaps at no time, and nowhere, was our modern loss of self-reliance so much in evidence as during the ice storm that ravaged Eastern Ontario and the Montreal region in January 1998. Without a single service everyone was used to—electrical power—life virtually froze. No heat. No light. Almost no water. No job. No functioning bank machine. No cash. No gasoline. No transportation. And what became the currency of that time? What was really valuable? Batteries, candles, firewood and generators.

When the good times of the 1920s turned into the hell of the Great Depression, a lot of people regretted their intense loss of self-reliance in a similar way. All of a sudden, a garden was of incredible importance, as was a working gas well on a farm, or a horse.

Does this foretell another Depression?

The parallels between the end of the 1920s and modern times are disturbing, fascinating and deeper than many people like to admit. But they undoubtedly exist, and should be taken seriously.

Does this mean another Depression could be close on the horizon? No, it does not. Here is why:

• Financial markets are high, but there are more reasons to believe they will go higher still, rather than collapse. However, expect lots of volatility.

• Personal finances across North America are a mess, but it does not look like the house of cards will start to collapse until the Big Generation —the baby boomers—faces its own retirement crisis.

• Deflation stalks the global economy, but Asian economies have been able to bounce back and growth in North America has been robust enough to compensate for falling commodity values.

• Interest rates will probably decline over the next few years, stimulating more consumer demand and postponing an inevitable credit crunch.

• Those boomers are just entering their peak earning-and-spending years, which should stimulate the economy.

• The push is on across North America for lower tax rates, as governments move into huge surpluses, and that will stimulate both spending and the financial markets.

• Inflation will be a non-issue for years, maybe decades. Corporate profits should hold up well in this low-inflation, low-rate, low-tax environment.

So, it is not a time to hunker down and prepare for the next storm, but rather to do just the opposite. Doubtless, another storm is coming, but the best defence against it will be personal wealth. Pursue the tax and investment strategies that will give you this.

Soaring Dow holds 10,000 – at last

SURGES 184 POINTS

Jubilant applause as benchmark ends 1.9% higher

BY IAN KARLEFF

After flirting with the magical 10,000 mark on three occasions in the past two weeks, the Dow Jones industrial average yesterday finally closed above that landmark.

The trading floor of the New York Stock Exchange broke into a jubilant applause at 4 p.m. when the closing bell tolled for what has taken 102 years, nine months and 25 days to reach.

"I'm ecstatic," said Charles Crane, chief investment strategist at Key Asset Management. "The way in which we passed 10,000 is just as significant as the fact we did it.

Strong gains in technology, oil and financial stocks helped the Wall Street benchmark surge 184.54 points, or 1.9%, to close at 10,006.78.

At one point the average reached an intraday high of 10,040.4.

New York mayor Rudolph Giuliani, NYSE chairman Richard Grasso and John Prestbo, markets editor at Dow Jones & Co., cautiously awaited the official close before showering the floor traders with hats reading 'Dow 10,000', after having to repossess them on March 18 when the Dow ended the session above 10,000, only to settle after trading to end at 9997.62.

Although some market watchers were calling the break over 10,000 a huge psychological milestone

that is bound to lead to further gains, others were less enthusiastic, preferring to remain cautious about earnings, growth fundamentals and increased hostilities in the Balkans.

Others pointed to the fact that the Dow is only a small indicator of the broader market with a limited breadth of stocks responsible for this year's gains.

"[It's] what 30 stocks have done," said Alan Greenberg, chairman of Bear Stearns Co. "You have to own the right companies, and I don't think it's that significant."

First launched as a 12-stock market measure with a value of 40.94 on May 28, 1896 by journalist Charles Dow, the only stock in today's basket that was also in the original dozen is General Electric. International Business Machines Corp. (IBM/NYSE) was the

catalyst behind yesterday's gains, adding 24 points to the index with a rise of $57⁄16 (US) to $1779⁄16 (US).

The computer giant got a boost from comments in the *New York Times* by the markets most persistent and accurate bull, Goldman Sachs & Co. investment strategist Abby Joseph Cohen. She said IBM deserves to be selling at a higher price-to-earnings multiple because it is trading at a lower PE than the Dow.

While the Dow is now trading at 25.5 times earnings, and the Standard & Poor's 500 index has a PE of 33.7, the Nasdaq composite index trades at a whopping 71 times earnings.

Financial Post

Hooray for 10,000: Page D3
Eight milestones in '90s: Page D3

A trader celebrates Dow 10,000 on the floor of the New York Stock Exchange yesterday. The average rose 184.54 points to close at 10,006.78.

ADAM NADEL / AP

It is clear that another difficult time is coming. Perhaps it will approach the intensity of the Great Depression. Perhaps it will be worse.

But just imagine if, in 1909, you knew what the next 20 years would bring—an unexpected world war, complete with the horrors and opportunities every war contains; a post-war era of unprecedented prosperity and technological achievement; the greatest bull market in history; and then the greatest collapse.

Today it is quite possible to foretell the future. In fact, there are many predictable things about the future. To ignore them is to take the greatest single gamble of your lifetime.

The Next Depression

THE ARGUMENT

Canada has a unique, and aging, population. The number of seniors will soon start exploding, while pensions dwindle and personal savings stagnate.

By 2020 the economic drain will be immense, and the investment boom will have abruptly ended. It is now already too late for governments to prepare for what is going to happen, but not too late for you and your family.

The spectre of the Great Depression, together with the stock market crash of October 19, 1987, has understandably raised concern about the possibility of another major economic collapse.

Nevertheless, the similarities should not be exaggerated. The economy today is quite different—institutionally, structurally, cyclically—from that of 1929.

GARY H. STERN

PRESIDENT, FEDERAL RESERVE BANK OF MINNEAPOLIS (1987)

The burst that follows the boom will be every bit as devastating as the upturn will be salutory—starting around 2010, when the height of the baby boom passes through its spending peak. That's when I predict the onset of the Mother of all Depressions—as opposed to the multitude of forecasts for the Great Depression of the 1990s.

HARRY S. DENT

THE GREAT BOOM AHEAD (1993)

This bull market, when it comes crashing down, may pose a whole new threat to the economy. With such a significant percentage of American and Canadian households owning shares directly or through mutual funds or pension funds, the coming bear will wipe out the wealth of a far broader segment of the population than any previous crash. This will devastate not only retirement savings, but also consumer spending.

ANDREW SARLOS

FEAR, GREED AND THE END OF THE RAINBOW (1997)

FOR THE LAST SEVEN DECADES, people have been trying to predict when the next economic crash will occur—plunging stock markets, toppling investment portfolios, rampant job loss, collapsing retail sales, waning consumer confidence and many consecutive quarters of negative growth. Or maybe worse. Maybe a rerun of the 1930s. So far, all the predictions have been wrong. But one day, someone will be right.

As the millennium ends and a new one begins, some people see danger signals flashing all around us:

•   Stock markets in North America have repeatedly hit all-time highs, with companies vastly overvalued relative to their earnings, by all traditional methods of valuation.

•   Personal incomes are down, debt is up, bankruptcies flourish.

•   North Americans now have more money in mutual funds than in real estate equity. Wealth that doubled in a few years could be erased in a few hours.

•   Corporations are laying off unheard-of numbers of people, many of whom, in their fifties, will never really have a decent job again.

•   Most investors have never experienced a bear market, where assets can fall in value for years. They could panic and sell. Investment fund managers pushed by those same investors for higher and higher returns, who were reluctant to have much cash on hand, could be overwhelmed by a tidal wave of redemptions. Selling would just beget more losses.

•   Globalization has tied all economies together, incredibly increasing the risk of a mutual collapse.

• Speculation is rampant in our society as investors gamble billions on shares in companies that are essentially worthless, who have never turned a profit and yet have huge market capitalizations.

• Day traders flourish. They are the electronic equivalent of gamblers streaming into the casinos of Kelowna, Niagara Falls or downtown Halifax. Losers almost always; optimistic despite it; blind to the risk.

Yes, you should be concerned about these factors. Any major negative economic event—another deflationary crash in Japan of the kind that gave us the Asian flu, an ethnic war in Europe, an extended computer malfunctioning—has the potential to crash overextended markets and wipe out the assets of an entire generation. But the odds of that happening in the first decade or so of the new millennium are, in my estimation, about zero.

Expect growth and volatility

This does not mean there will be no serious stock market corrections, however, which the media and many others will misinterpret as crashes, as happened in the second half of 1998. The market will be volatile, frightening and dangerous for short-term investors. But for those who buy, and remain in for a decade, the danger is minimal. In fact, 10 years from now you should expect stock values to have at least doubled, if not quadrupled.

But this will not go on forever. As I said earlier, imbalances are clearly growing within the system. Most people are building their financial lives on foundations of debt, and on the wrong kinds of assets. When the glory days at hand are over, the crash to earth will be truly painful.

After 2015, the odds of crisis should grow quickly. By 2020, a massive downturn would seem to be all but inevitable and baby boomers could find themselves reliving the experiences of their parents in the 1930s. Younger people will be experiencing a nightmare—staring into an economic crater right in the middle of their working lives. This should alarm and preoccupy those people who are today in their twenties.

Here is why we appear destined to experience this crisis:

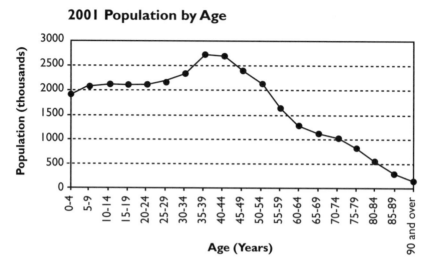

2001 Population by Age

All you need to know about demographics: The peak of the population today are people in their forties—eight million boomers entering their peak income and spending years, which will keep the economy and financial markets robust.

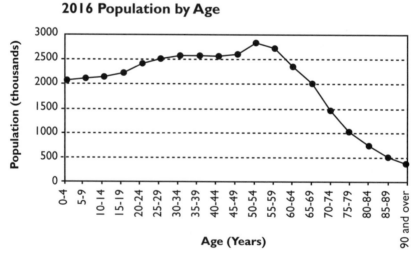

2016 Population by Age

By 2016 there will be almost 40% more seniors than there were in just 1996. The peak group in the population will be over the age of 50.

We have a unique population

It has been responsible for the boom. It will be responsible for the bust.

Canada has the biggest generation of baby boomers in the world, relative to the size of our population. This group, born between 1947 and 1967, was responsible for the baby-food boom in the 1950s, the school-building orgy in the 1960s, inflation in the 1970s, the real estate phenomenon of the 1980s and the mutual fund mania of the 1990s.

Boomers like me have set the social, political and economic agenda for decades. Even as we turn 50, the music we listened to 30 years ago still dominates the mass media. It's the trigger that advertisers use to get our attention. Now as the baby boomers age, the top medical stories are impotence and menopause. The top-selling products and services are things like Viagra, progressive lenses and laser vision. The cars we craved as young adults, like Mustangs and Beetles, Jaguar roadsters and convertibles, have been re-created. Our children-hauling minivans have morphed into SUVs—sport utility vehicles—and are morphing again into luxury sedans.

Baby boomers competed for real estate, and drove prices to artificially high levels. They caused a huge demand for borrowed money to finance those homes, and drove up the cost of money. Mortgages topped out at an incredible 22% in the 1980s.

The boomers were expensive to raise and educate. Governments responded with new programs and new taxes. The federal debt exploded higher and today sits at almost $600 billion—an unrepayable amount that we can only hope to pay the interest on while the economy is good.

The boomers were born into the best medicine to date in history. They smoke less than their parents. They exercise more. They eat less meat. They have seen cloning, genetically altered foods and miracle cures. The incidence of heart disease is rapidly falling.

This generation will live longer than any that has ever come before. It will cost more to care for than any other. It will be the biggest burden.

In fact, in its sheer size and vitality, the baby boom carries the seeds of its own downfall. It's too big for its own good. In the 1960s it was pretty cool that so many people at the same time shared the same naive idealism of youth. We were going to end war, free love and buy Canada back from the Yanks. In the 2020s it won't be so cool that so many people at the same time will share the same bitterness with their lives. But, unfortunately, it seems destined to come.

When most boomers were in their teens, there were six Canadians like them, under the age of 20, for every person over 65. Today there are about three young people for every senior. By 2020, the ratio will be even more frightening. This will have profound consequences on our entire society.

As the 1990s ended, Canada was spending $55 billion a year on seniors, in elderly benefits, Canada Pension and Medicare, while the same three million people contributed only about $10 billion in taxes. That shortfall of $45 billion is paid for by those who are working, when seniors account for just 16% of the population. Imagine what things will look like when 24% of the population has retired and fewer workers are supporting them.

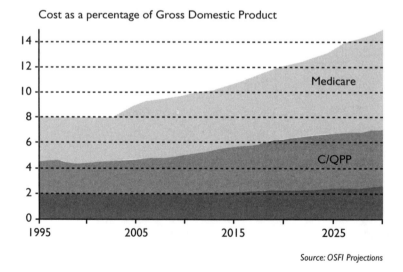

Cost as a percentage of Gross Domestic Product

Source: OSFI Projections

Senior subsidies: The combined cost of looking after people over the age of 65 today is $55 billion. By 2030 it will be about $100 billion.

Our unique population mix guarantees that the number of seniors will about triple within the next three decades, at an additional burden to the public purse of close to $50 billion a year. And already the Canada Pension Plan does not realize enough in the way of contributions and earnings to pay benefits to those currently retired. As mentioned here already, in the government's own estimation, the CPP's cupboard will be bare in 2016.

Between now and 2030 the retirement age population will jump by more than 140% while the country as a whole grows by just 15%. By 2015, half the Canadian population will be over 40 for the first time ever. By 2040 the number of people over 85 will increase by 500%. The fastest-growing group of people will be those over 100.

So, how will Canada finance the awesome future burden of pensions and health care for the baby-boom generation when all those people want to retire? Will those still working be willing to pay far more in taxes than their parents ever did to finance those millions of seniors? After all, that's what is happening today as Canadian boomers enter their peak income-earning years and face tax rates as high as 54.2% of their incomes. Will their children pay 60% or 70% tax rates to help out their aging moms and dads?

Are you kidding?

The result is obvious: There will not be universal public pensions for everyone. There probably will not be first-rate universal public health care for everyone. There certainly will not be free drugs, income supplement programs or 15% seniors' discounts at the dry cleaners.

As Canadian actuary Robert Brown has pointed out, if baby boomers get all the benefits in retirement that today's seniors receive, tomorrow's workers will have to transfer 60% more wealth to us than is being transferred today.

And that is not going to happen.

Annual Cost of Health Care By Age Group

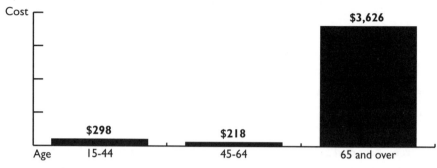

Source: Talvest Fund Management

Health emergency: The lion's share of health care costs are consumed in the last years of life. Given our aging population, this is a recipe for disaster.

Meanwhile, consider the effects on the Canadian economy when there are more than eight million seniors and far more old women than young girls. The cost of operating a public health care system (if it survives) will rise from about 8% of the economy to 15%. That means a $70-billion-a-year system that is a huge burden on taxpayers today will turn into a $120-billion-per-year colossus that will have to be supported by even fewer workers than there are now!

Can the future be any clearer?

• The number of retired people will explode by 300%.

• The costs of public pensions will rise, from about $22 billion a year to more than $60 billion.

• Health care costs could double.

• For every retired person there will be just one working taxpayer.

2030 Population by Age

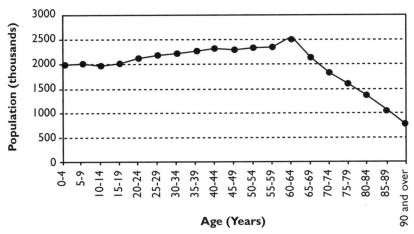

Canada's population in 2030: The peak group is now over the age of 65, and the number of retirees has increased threefold from the 1990s. There are more old people than young people.

• Life expectancy is surging higher. Boomers will spend decades in retirement.

Given these facts, what can we expect? Either future taxes will erupt higher, or the level of services Canadians receive will plunge. But, of course, there is no room for more taxes, nor will there be the political will to raise them once the baby boomers' grip on the House of Commons is loosened.

Demographic changes will have a major impact on the ratio of retirees to workers; the ratio of the number of people ages 65 and over to the number ages 20 to 64 is expected to grow from about 20% in 1997 to 41% in 2050.

—CANADA PENSION PLAN

SEVENTEENTH ACTUARIAL REPORT

And just consider what all this spells for our economy. A rapidly aging population is both costly and ultimately less productive. In the future, there will be a huge transfer of wealth from workers to retirees, unless public pensions and universal health care are allowed to collapse. And if these safety nets do not survive, what kind of social wreckage will be left behind? Already the system is starting to work quickly against younger people. According to the Institute for Research on Public Policy, today's 20-year-olds will pay hundreds of thousands of dollars more in taxes than they will ever receive in government benefits. Today's seniors, in sharp contrast, will get $120,000 more than they contributed. Baby boomers will be in a slightly negative position.

This is unfair and unsustainable.

But, incredibly, the news gets worse:

There is going to be a retirement crisis

Of gigantic proportions. Most people are unprepared and unsuspecting. Seventy per cent of all the retirement savings accounts in Canada contain less than $50,000. At the current contribution rate of about $4,000 per year, the average baby boomer will have put aside about $95,000 in his or her RRSP by age 65. According to economists, that is 10% of what will be required to maintain personal lifestyle.

A survey released by CIBC in January 1999 had a chilling message. This was the question:

Thinking about where the money is going to come from for your retirement, how much would you say that winning money in a lottery is part of your financial plan?

To that, 14% of the people responding in British Columbia said "very much" or "somewhat." In Ontario and the Atlantic, 12% agreed, and nationwide 11% of Canadians said winning a lottery was important to their retirement plans. Meanwhile, the odds of winning a lottery, at least in Ontario, are about 14 million to one.

Another 1999 survey, conducted by Hart & Associates Management Consultants, found about half of Canadians believe their current retirement fund will not give them enough money to live on, and half of those people say they have absolutely no idea how the situation can be rectified. Meanwhile the 50% of Canadians who are not worried about retirement perhaps should be, if they are counting on CPP benefits to pad their after-work incomes.

Reasons for not contributing more to an RRSP

Too much debt	47%
High income taxes	24%
Job instability	18%
Wages fallen behind	17%

Source: Canadian Association of Insurance and Financial Advisors

Canadians, especially baby boomers, are headed for a retirement that could last well over 20 years and is now just 15 years away. The dangers posed to the economy, government finances and society in general are crystal clear and compounding them is the fact that most people today in their forties and fifties are acting like there is no problem at all.

What, exactly, are you going to live on in retirement?

If the CPP is still around in 20 years, and still paying 1999-style benefits (two dangerous assumptions), the maximum you can collect is $9,020 a year, and the most the Old Age Supplement will pay is $4,929. For a couple, the most Ottawa will give you is $27,898, which, of course, is taxable income.

That means that a couple earning the average family income of just under $60,000 will have to get by on 50% of their income in retirement, if they do not have savings or a corporate pension.

But the situation gets far darker for those people who have higher incomes. If you and your spouse bring home $100,000 and want to have 70% of that in retirement, the shortfall per year after collecting the CPP and OAS is $42,000. If you live 20 years in retirement, from age 65 to 85, that shortfall is equal to $840,000.

Where are you going to get it?

Pre-retirement Income	Retirement Income	CPP/OAS	Shortfall	Over 20 yr.
$100,000	$70,000	$27,898	$42,102	$842,040

Just to die broke, with no money left in the bank on the day you expire and no estate passed on to heirs, you need to have savings equal to 15 times your required income. According to pension expert Malcolm Hamilton, of William Mercer Ltd., to live a decent life in retirement, a person today earning $100,000 should be saving at least 10% of his or her gross income, and at $150,000 income, that should rise to over 12%—or $18,000 annually, from the age of 30 on, to retire at age 60.

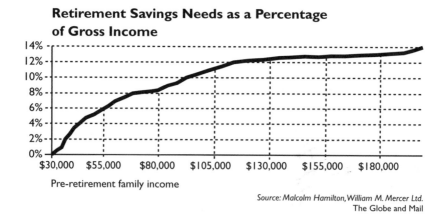

Retirement Savings Needs as a Percentage of Gross Income

Pre-retirement family income

Source: Malcolm Hamilton, William M. Mercer Ltd.
The Globe and Mail

Curse of the middle class: The more income you have, the more you need to replace in retirement.

Corporate pensions are a thing of the past

My father retired on a pension of about $6,000 a month—a huge amount of money at the time, and indexed to inflation. It was the culmination of his long career with the same employer at a management level. It turned out to be a good thing he received it, as every cent eventually went towards his care as an Alzheimer patient for 24-hour supervision, for years. Without that pension, my mother would certainly have been forced to sell the house and watch the proceeds dwindle to zero in just a few years.

Today there are few pensions around of the kind that Archie received. In fact, only 5.1 million Canadians have any kind of working pension at all, either being paid now or coming in the future. That means most of us are on our own, hoping the CPP survives because if it does not, there will only be what we have saved ourselves.

The union or company-sponsored defined-benefit pension plan is dying a wretched death, and many of those that still exist are pathetic. The most you can hope for is that the plan will pay you about 2% of your top annual salary for every year you worked.

But today just one in three Canadian workers has a defined-benefit plan and the number of companies offering plans is sinking fast. At the same time, in the new economy, fewer people are working long periods of time for the same employer, as my father did. Big companies have laid off more than 38 million people in North America in the latest wave of downsizing, and there are many more layoffs to come.

Do you know many people who have worked 25 or 30 years with the same company—long enough to get their maximum pension benefits? Do you know *anyone* like that?

Today the economy is being built on the World Wide Web; in home offices across the continent; and in small companies employing 10 or 50 people—not the kind of enterprises that will ever set up a company-operated pension plan.

The bottom line, I hope, is becoming clear:

• The vast majority of Canadians do not have a corporate pension now and will never get one.

• Most middle-aged people have saved about a tenth of what they will need to retire in comfort. Most young people have not even started.

• The Canada Pension Plan is underfunded and being abused. Without a miracle, it's out of money by 2016.

• The number of seniors in this country is about to explode.

Most people have no idea what is in store for them, and I almost hate to spell it out. But, let's face it. The long-term future is quite dark. In many ways, it's terrifying:

• Twenty years from now there will be about eight million 70-year-olds who are newly into a retirement that is rapidly turning into a nightmare.

• Public pension benefits will no longer be universal—just available for the destitute.

• Health care certainly will not be free, but laced with user fees to keep the system functioning.

• The economy will be slowing quickly, dragged down by a huge tax burden on employers and employees.

• Residential real estate values will have plunged because there are millions of desperate sellers and far fewer buyers. This loss of equity and net worth will dash consumer confidence and further drag down economic activity.

• Financial markets will be in crisis as boomers with no choice pull money out of mutual funds and stocks to live on. A tidal wave of selling will occur as redemptions force fund managers to cash in their holdings, driving unit values lower, triggering more panicked redemptions.

• Those who loaded up on segregated funds, believing their principal was guaranteed, will get a nasty shock if they panic and cash in before holding them a full decade—not realizing that guarantee was worthless until 10 years had passed.

This is the breeding ground of deflation and Depression.

Sadly, I've come to the conclusion that both are now inevitable. But it is not immediate. This is an early wake-up call. But while it is not too late for you and your family to survive what is coming, it's probably too late for society.

It's already too late to prepare

Inflation-Adjusted Tax Bill and Consumer Tax Index, 1961–1998

Year	Tax Bill (1998 $)	Percent change in taxes since 1991
1961	9.719	—
1969	14,453	48.7
1974	18,940	94.9
1976	17,486	79.9
1981	21,054	116.6
1985	21,460	120.8
1990	23,738	144.3
1992	22,092	127.3
1994	22,576	132.3
1996	23,238	139.1
1998	23,218	138.9

Sources: The Fraser Institute, 1998; Statistics Canada, The Consumer Price Index, catalogue 62-001

Taxes cannot rise. In fact, they must fall.

One solution to finding the money necessary to cope with a 300% increase in the number of Canada's seniors is to raise taxes. But the consequences of doing so would be worse than the cure. Canada already is vastly overtaxed compared to most countries, especially our chief competitor, the United States. Our top tax rate is over 54% and the top American one is less than 40%, and it does not kick in until an income level of well over $200,000, compared with $60,000 here.

Higher Canadian taxes—income taxes, payroll taxes, property taxes, sales taxes or user fees—would make us less productive and less competitive, leading to slower economic growth than already is in the cards.

Successive governments have gone back to the well of taxation too many times in the past, so that now personal income taxes are almost 140% higher, even after adjusting for inflation, than they were in 1961. High taxes have increased the cost of doing business in Canada substantially, raising the price of a litre of gasoline far above that in the U.S., inflating levies for the ownership of property and swelling employers' payrolls.

High taxes are also a huge disincentive to saving and investing. After-tax income has not been growing for almost a decade, which makes it difficult for Canadians to put aside enough money for their retirement years. In fact, the growth in taxes has been completely disproportionate to the growth in other costs that families face, like shelter, food and clothing.

Higher taxes are not an option. Any move by government to increase its revenues would be destructive and counterproductive, deepening the crisis that is coming. Both taxes and government expenditures must fall, not rise.

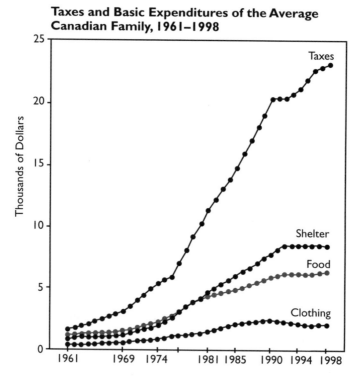

Taxes and Basic Expenditures of the Average Canadian Family, 1961–1998

Source: The Fraser Institute

It's the 11th hour for the pension plan

About 2.5 million Canadians now draw money from the Canada Pension Plan. In 1999 they took out about $11 billion. Two-thirds of that money went to people who were retired, a growing number of them between the ages of 60 and 64. In fact, almost 60% of everybody in that age group now takes CPP money, compared with 45% of the 60–64-year-old crowd in 1988.

This is partly because of an overall trend to earlier retirement by people who probably completely underestimate the length of time they will not be working. It's also because millions of people have lost their jobs, and have no choice.

Another 20% of CPP pensions go to people with disabilities, and the rest go to the survivors of deceased contributors. Upon death, a survivor gets a lump-sum payment of $3,540 and after that, about $400 a month.

CPP Expenditures

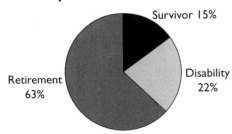

Source: An Information Paper for Consultations
of the Canada Pension Plan

Every few years the federal and provincial governments get together to review the Canada Pension Plan, and the premiums that support it. When the CPP was created, its founders estimated that the contribution rate paid by employees and employers would never be more than 5.5% of earnings. It is now planned to raise that to almost 10%, while the plan's own chief actuary says something like 14% is more like it.

Raising the rate from less than 6% today to more than 14% by 2030, however, would constitute a massive tax increase. This increase would be so massive, in fact, it would probably crater the economy. It cannot happen, and everyone knows that.

But without some kind of radical reform, the CPP will be out of money far before 2030. Of course, there are solutions, but it is too late to implement them since the huge debate about pensions reform that must precede these changes hasn't even really started. Why? Because ...

There is no political will to face this issue

To date, no political leader who values his or her job has had the nerve to tell the House of Commons: "Mr. Speaker, the public pension plan is now some 140 months from collapse, a point at which the government will no longer be able to support Canadians in retirement. I call for an emergency debate, right here and right now, as this is the most serious, dangerous and socially disruptive issue in our country's entire history."

You won't hear that, because most Canadians would react with a fury deep enough to sweep away any government. Most people believe that all the money they ever paid in CPP contributions has gone into a big pot somewhere with their name on it.

Of course, it just went into the pockets of people already retired—the wealthiest generation of retirees ever, of which my father was a member, and the last one to collect vastly more in benefits than they ever paid in contributions.

Now, we will see change, or we will see millions of people retire into poverty. But will change come soon enough? I do not think so.

To save the CPP as a government-run universal pension system would require substantial changes:

- Vastly higher contribution rates for employers and employees.

- A higher return on the money the CPP invests once contributions are increased. That would mean putting public retirement funds into the stock market and other securities.

Both of these changes are in the works. In themselves, though, they will not be adequate to keep the pension system afloat. Other changes that might be required:

- Reducing retirement benefits. The money people receive would have to be cut by about 10%, reducing the monthly benefit from $727 to $654 —not enough to rent a two-bedroom apartment in Kamloops.

- Making people work longer to qualify for a pension.

• Making beneficiaries wait longer to collect their pension. One plan is to raise the age by a few months a year until it is 67 or 68 years by the time the baby boom hits 65 in 2011.

• Chopping disability and survivor benefits.

• Giving people incentives to keep on working, delaying retirement until at least age 70. That is a far cry from the dream of "Freedom 55," where financial independence allows you to choose voluntary retirement. It's also at extreme odds with large employers' penchant for tossing out workers when they pass the age of 50, usually with meagre benefits. But already we are working longer. A 1999 Statistics Canada survey found a big jump in the number of men working past 65, most dramatically for the self-employed, from 26% to 60% in the previous decade.

How would today's voters feel about increasing the money everyone pays into the pension plan, then telling them that they will have to wait years longer to get thousands of dollars less?

You can see now why the CPP is cooked. Nobody has the stomach to even start the debate.

But there are models Canada could follow, like that of Chile, where the pay-as-you-go pension plan, like ours, was scrapped. Older people could still get a government cheque, but others were allowed to opt out, as long as they saved and invested 10% of their incomes in approved assets. It has worked.

Canadians are in deep denial

The coming retirement crisis could bring an economic depression simply because most Canadians are sleepwalking into it. The national savings rate is zero. People continue to put billions of dollars into residential real estate that could well be worth less in 10 years, instead of financial assets like stocks, bonds and investment funds that will certainly be worth more. Others worry about the wrong risks—the temporary and inconsequential risk of market volatility as opposed to the crushing risk of living decades in retirement without enough money—and so they put what they have in absolutely the wrong places.

We are still living and investing by the old rules that worked for my father, but do not work for his son. Blind faith in the system, optimism in a sunny future and faith in your employer, along with a loonie, will buy you a coffee at Tim's.

Surveys consistently show that while about half of Canadians are uneasy about their retirement plans, the other half don't really think about it. The fact that close to 70% of people eligible to make an RRSP contribution in 1999 did not, speaks volumes about where we are going. In that same year, six million Canadians put money into their retirement plan, but only a scant 12% of what could have been contributed. Meanwhile we removed $5 billion from our RRSPs—a dollar for every one put in—with half that money taken out by people under the age of 45.

Just imagine the shock and the outrage that is coming in 12 or 15 years, when people close to retirement realize they cannot retire. When there is no corporate pension; when they have to wait until they're 68 to get a reduced government cheque; when their house is virtually unsaleable; their kids are having trouble minding their own finances; and after they spent all those years paying down the mortgage and buying depreciating minivans.

Imagine with how much envy people in that situation will view you— you, who realized 15 years earlier how to scramble onto the path of self-reliance. You, who learned the new rules your father never imagined.

Is the future bleak?

Far from it.

While the future two and three decades from now is most troubling, there are powerful reasons to believe that the next 10 years or so will bring a substantial rally on financial markets and a booming economy in Canada and North America. An immense opportunity to create wealth is at hand —a second chance for the baby-boom generation.

If you know what to do now and in the immediate future years, you can avoid the crisis that seems inevitable later.

New Rules for the New Age

THE ARGUMENT

The path to financial peace starts with you embracing a new set of rules, governing the accumulation of wealth, your work and your personal life.

The story of the last thousand years can be summarized in a word: progress.

The story was repeated over the last century; all but 15 years of it witnessed by my father. He worked building a highway across Ontario with an iron scraper pulled by a horse. The hearse carrying him back home used the same highway, now 16 lanes across. As a kid he thrilled watching the stagecoaches thunder into town. The same eyes watched the moon-walk and the Internet.

Archie started out teaching in a one-room school. He finished his career authorizing construction of massive buildings housing thousands of students. As a young man he devoted everything to helping his elderly parents survive the Depression. As an old man, his pension was his guardian. As a suitor, he courted a woman whose father crashed his brand-new McLaughlin-Buick, pulling on the steering wheel and yelling 'Whoa!' As an executive, he piloted his white Cadillac and its 400 horses through the fields to his country retreat.

It was a life of constant, unrelenting change. But, almost always, change for the better. Progress. In his world, the rules were pretty clear, and if you played by them, respected and remembered them, your life also would progress.

I'll bet your father shared some of these rules.

Archie's Rules

(a) Be loyal

It went without saying that this applied to your spouse, your marriage and your family. Divorce or separation were social taboos and signs of fundamental personal failure. But loyalty went a lot further, right into where you worked.

During my father's time it was a badge of honour to be a long-time employee, and worker loyalty was rewarded with money and position.

TODAY: Workers who have been around a long time are likely the first to go in corporate layoffs and restructuring because they make too much money. Experience is expensive, so it is dispensable. Fifty years old and making more than $50,000? Watch out. The bigger and more impersonal the company, the greater the odds of that Friday afternoon visit.

One on-air television broadcaster I worked with was an absolute icon of the industry, working for the same station since it was founded in the 1950s. His face and voice were known by millions of people, but after four decades of service and salary increases, he was simply too expensive. The new CEO, who was in diapers when this man first stared down a TV camera, fired him. So much for experience. So much for being an employee.

(b) Shun risk

In a world of relentless progress, rising prices and expanding opportunity, you just didn't need to stick your neck out to have a decent life. It was safer to be an employee than an entrepreneur. It was better to buy bonds that were predictable than stocks that were a gamble. It was better to buy a house that certainly would go up in value than an investment that was speculative.

The real risk was losing your capital in a bad investment or your job in a failed venture.

TODAY: In a deflationary world where jobs are unsure, a decent pension is an illusion and assets as likely to fall as rise in value, risk is a necessary and important tool you must master. You must embrace it, trusting that over the decades, financial assets, like equities and investment funds, will outpace real assets, like gold or real estate. Today, more people face the risk of running out of money than they ever do losing it in a bad investment. Too bad they do not know this.

(c) Trust the system

And it would look after you. Pay your taxes, and you were assured of having first-class, immediate medical attention and a guaranteed pension when you retire. Pay off your house and someone would come along and buy it for more later. Send your kids to university and they would end up with professional jobs and happy lives. Work hard and you would be rewarded. Respect elected officials and they would toil nobly for the public interest. Admire presidents and hockey players and corporate leaders because they would have ethics and be worthy role models.

TODAY: The system is as likely to bite you as feed you. You can lose half of all the money you make in taxes and still have to line up for medical care and worry whether you'll have any pension at all. You pay off a house, and it declines in value. Your kids are geniuses, but there are no jobs. Professional athletes are as likely to be cross-dressers or profanity-spewing brats as they are overpaid. Corporate downsizers are rewarded with insanely rich compensation for laying off thousands of people. Political leaders have been charged, tried and convicted. Looking for something to trust? Trust yourself.

(d) Save your money

Saving was a virtue. Saving was patriotic. During the war, people saved lard, string and tinfoil. They bought savings bonds. They saved on gasoline and rubber. They saved with rations and coupons.

The Saving Generation kept it up, because that was about all you needed to do. Savers in the 1980s got 15% returns on the investment certificates. Saving was safe; it was the opposite of investing. My father kept most of his liquid wealth in a savings account because, well, why wouldn't you?

TODAY: Saving is insane. Bank savings accounts routinely pay one quarter of 1% interest per year. Interest rates have collapsed, so after taxes and inflation, many savers are making absolutely nothing. For the Dow

Generation there are no alternatives to investing, no certainty, no safe havens. All the rules have changed.

We may not like it, but there it is—a new world. This is one where you have to be fluid and flexible, taking on multiple careers, always learning and never coasting, always ready with a resume and a survivor's attitude. Gone are the days when you could actually trust your employer, especially if it's a large one. You probably stand a very good chance of being replaced by a machine and, if not today, then within five years. It's a world in which, to your father's utter amazement, it probably does not make sense to pay off the mortgage. It's probably unwise to trust the government. The government, in fact, will take half of your earnings and provide less service. And it's a new world in which even your privacy is not assured, where paper money is disappearing and people run pieces of plastic through machines to get their groceries.

If an investment is safe today, it pays you next to nothing. If you buy something, you have to be prepared for it costing less next year. If you call somebody where they work, they probably won't be there anymore.

Sure, it's still a world of progress, and an exciting one. Opportunities still abound, and it is completely possible to have a fulfilling and wealthy life. Maybe, in many ways, it's even easier than it was for my father because while the old rules were a crutch, they were also a straitjacket.

New times, new technologies, new realities, new risks. They all make it necessary that we all know the new rules by heart.

The New Rules

A. Wealth rules

(1) KNOW REAL RISK

The real risk is running out of money. It is not losing money in an investment that declines in value. Most Canadians will never experience that. But most people will run out of money, or be forced to drastically alter and reduce their lifestyles and expectations to match the amount of capital and income that they have.

This is the polar opposite of what my father considered to be the risk he must avoid. He did not invest in stocks or other financial assets because they were "a gamble." Instead, he saved his money in interest-bearing investments, and bought real estate. He survived in this environment because inflation continuously boosted the value of houses, and kept interest rates high.

He did not start businesses or take on employees, because the perceived risk of failure was just too extreme. Instead he was a steady and loyal and long-time employee who was able to grab the brass ring—a sizeable, life-long pension, indexed to inflation.

Today both inflation and pensions are gone, or going. Do not expect the cost of living to rise in any meaningful way for at least a dozen years, perhaps longer. Residential real estate is a gamble. Interest rates have collapsed. Life expectancy is rising quickly and the savings rate is dropping.

Living Longer
Life expectancy at birth of both men and women has increased dramatically since prehistoric times

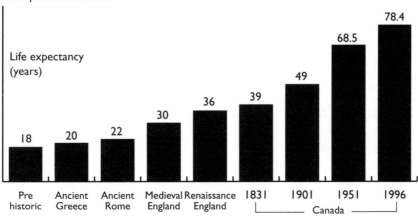

Source: The Urban Futures Institute
Toronto Star Graphic

Life expectancy: While the average ancient Roman lived to be 22 years old, and the average Canadian died at age 65 in 1951, people today will be long in retirement.

Many people will actually be longer in retirement than they ever spend working. The notion of retirement itself, within a decade, will have changed drastically. Today, those people who view risk through my father's eyes will fail. Regrettably, most Canadians are doing exactly that.

The real risk is growing. The ability of your government, or your country, to look after you in 15 or 20 years is being diminished quickly as each day passes with little or no long-term planning.

Face it: we elect people to give immediate results—cut taxes, boost medical spending, reduce tuition fees or create instant jobs. Nobody is even talking about what Canada will look like when there are five million more senior citizens than there are today.

Obviously, there is trouble ahead. A CIBC survey found 62% of Canadians now expect they'll have to work in retirement. More than 70% of your friends, neighbours, relatives and co-workers do not have a financial plan. Shockingly, the bank found that more than half of all Canadians have saved less than $30,000.

Amount saved	% of population
Less than $30,000	51
more than $100,000	30
more than $400,000	7
amount needed to live in retirement	
from age 60 to 80 on $51,000 a year:	$544,787
% of Canadian population who, at this point,	
will achieve that goal:	2

As individuals, we have to build a defence against this risk, and that is wealth. It is only prudent to do so, and wealth comes through the successful combination of investing and avoiding tax. Never apologize for making money, but never flaunt it. There is risk in that. Society will surely break down further in the future as the gulf between the "haves" and "want-to-haves" grows.

I fully expect social upheaval lies ahead. The polarization of wealth and income in this country will continue and the pressure on governments to step in and solve the retirement crisis will be intense. But struggling with falling tax revenues and rising social program costs, at the same time as the economy is slowing and the burden of debt growing heavier, governments will be powerless to change things.

What happened during the last Depression, when millions of people were suddenly thrown into an unexpected financial situation, and faced hardship for the first time in their lives? Riots and death. Remember your history.

(2) INVEST AGGRESSIVELY

It's probably the most difficult thing for you to do, but also the most necessary. For a combination of reasons detailed below, financial markets in North America, Europe, Japan and other places are headed vastly higher.

The Dow at 10,000 is just a stepping stone to a market that could achieve 30,000 or even 50,000 by 2015.

Of course, the journey higher will not be without trauma or decline. In fact, the higher markets go, the greater the stumbles will be. You should expect corrections that can erase up to 30% of the market's value in a matter of weeks, perhaps even days. The time when the Dow can go down 1,000 points in a single trading session, between 9:30 a.m. and 4 p.m. Eastern time, is now at hand. The media will go nuts. The Internet will come alive with speculation that this is The Big One, but it won't be.

Why will markets recover, and rise? Because they mirror economic activity. As long as the economic fundamentals are good and positive, markets will advance. But they can often get ahead of themselves, or be panicked by false or misleading news, and fall steeply, before recovering again.

Just remember that in times of crises and declining markets, the people who are guaranteed to lose are those who sell, and lock in that loss. The ones who hold on will inevitably see a rise and with the macroeconomic conditions as they are today, that recovery will be almost as swift as the trip down. Remember the basics: no inflation, cheap rates, governments living within their means, globalization and free trade and the positive impact of demographics. Declines will be terrifying yet temporary.

Each, at least for a decade, will be followed by an advance. Logic then tells you to buy when others sell.

But this runs counter to human nature. As I write this, fear stalks the land. Despite solid gains in the market, people remember the gut-wrenching and overly publicized declines, like the 32% drubbing that the Toronto Stock Exchange 300 index took in the autumn of 1998. The human reaction is to act immediately to preserve your capital, and flee to safety.

Siren call of guaranteed investments

That has helped explain the phenomenon of guaranteed investments, like segregated funds, in Canada. Most major mutual funds companies, insurance companies and lately the banks have brought products to market that promise to return the investor's capital at the end of a certain period of time, regardless of whether markets rise or fall.

Segregated, protected, insured and guaranteed products have gained a large amount of market share in a short period of time. In the opinion of some experts, these funds will even eclipse mutual funds in terms of total assets within a few years. For reasons explained more fully later in this book, I feel this is a lamentable development.

Investors are required to pay a premium to get this guarantee, in the form of higher management fees, which impact on the fund's performance. As well, many investors do not realize that segregated funds and others that promise to return your capital carry no guarantee whatsoever before the maturity date. They will rise or fall in value, just like mutual funds, and cost you more in fees along the way. Only after an average of 10 years does that guarantee click in.

And, if I am right in my assessment of where markets are headed, and if history is any guide, the guarantee is simply not required. Ten years from now markets will be higher. Vastly higher.

Be highly exposed

Investing aggressively means having a high degree of exposure to those markets. The younger you are, the greater that exposure should be. The less money you have to invest, the more risk you need to shoulder. So, equity mutual funds, stocks and index funds, along with other products based on overall market performance, like TIPS and SPYDRS, are ideal ways of participating in long-term growth.

Use other people's money

Investing aggressively can also involve using borrowed money, whether that is employing a margin account at your broker's, using existing assets, like mutual funds, to pledge against investment loans, or taking a home equity loan against your residential real estate. I have no problem with any of these strategies, as long as you understand that as you leverage up the rewards, you also leverage up the risk. For short-term thinkers who will be blown about by the fickle winds of media opinion, this is not recommended. For long-term thinkers who understand the sweep of decades, using other people's money to build wealth is a hugely valuable thing to do.

Buy during the panics

Investing aggressively will also mean going against the tide, and actively buying when others are selling. Expect more market panics, and expect them more often. As the Dow hits 10,000, then 15,000 and 20,000, some investors will get nosebleeds and be very susceptible to the inevitable blowouts that will follow the overly frothy advances. Great companies and mutual funds will be jettisoned by people who need to bail out at any cost. That happened in 1988, in 1997, in 1998 and it will happen again at any moment. In a market panic, the only losers are the sellers. The buyers are the winners. Those who do not sell lose nothing.

Be fully in the market

Investing aggressively means being fully exposed to the financial markets. It does not make sense in an era of cheap interest rates, readily available credit and rising markets to have six months' worth of cash salted away in case of a household emergency. That may be the standard investment advice of magazines for homemakers, but it's worthless. Simply, establish a line of credit for $10,000, and use it when necessary to deal with a crisis. It also does not make sense to divert your precious investment capital into paying off the low-rate mortgage on a house that is depreciating (or soon will) in value. All of your cash, if you are serious about building wealth over the next decade, should be working for you. All of it.

Buy the future

There is nothing as certain as the ascendency of technology. In fact, it appears we are entering a golden age of post-industrialism where there are billions of dollars to be made anticipating what looks inevitable. The Internet will be ubiquitous by the middle of the first decade of the millennium, and it will be as useful and used as the telephone. In fact, we are headed directly for the convergence of the Internet, the telephone and radio and television.

Examples are already all around us. My Investment Television show began broadcasting on the airwaves in January 1999 and on the Internet a month later, to a huge www audience. My daily radio commentary appears on the Web as it hits the airwaves across Canada. The truest, fastest, most comprehensive source of information was once the newspaper, then the radio, then TV news, and now the Internet—where news organizations scramble to break their stories first.

The 2000 Mercedes S-Class cars have two buttons, a screen in the dashboard, dedicated cellular service and uplinks to positioning satellites. Push one button and you are connected to a "living owner's manual"—a live technician who will help you understand the car. Push the SOS button and you get emergency help, live and immediate. If you are unable to communicate, the car relays back its position, speed and direction, so you can be found if you run off the road. If the car is stolen, it uplinks and tells Mercedes where it can be found. And the screen on the dash displays a map showing where you are, and tells you how to get to where you are going, thanks to a CD-ROM, dedicated software and the satellites above.

All this in a car that is obviously better than the previous year's model, and selling for about 10% less. Yes, deflation and technology go hand in hand.

Then there is e-commerce, which has only started to revolutionize the way goods and services and customers interface. Amazon.com opened many eyes to this, providing customers with more titles of books than a store could possibly carry, and next-day delivery, along with the convenience of web-based credit-card orders. Here was the Internet helping to power two ancient technologies—the printing presses turning out the books and the wheels of the courier trucks speeding the order to your door.

As I write this, many Internet and e-commerce stocks are wildly overvalued compared with historic measures of corporate valuation, and most certainly prone to correction. But, this is the future. You will make long-distance calls on the Internet, listen to radio and watch TV over it, order your groceries, glasses and clothes over it, bank and invest through it, earn your living on it or because of it, be offered video-on-demand and countless other services, at a fraction of the cost of today's phone and cable bills. Deflation and technology. And a better life. Buy it.

Buy demographics

The other inevitability is an aging population, as I have already made detailed mention of. The opportunities for the aggressive investor are clear as the baby-boomer generation comes into its peak earning years with more mortgages paid off and increased disposable income. This will result in vastly more money flowing into financial assets, powering stock markets higher and making index fund investors look like geniuses.

According to Calgary-based People Patterns Consulting, spending by middle-aged people (aged 35-54) will peak in 2011 at $352 billion, and then start to decline. Spending by mature people (55-plus) will rise by 75%, from $129 billion in 1996 to $226 billion by 2016, and then start to trail off.

These dates are memorable because they signal the points at which the economy will start to degrade. But between now and then, an aging population poses great opportunities for investors who aggressively target the sectors and companies that will benefit. For example, spending on dentures will rise 52%, says retail consultant Roger Sauve. There will be a boom in the sale of retirement homes, as people bail out of their multibedroom real estate and downsize. Spending on hotels and gambling will jump as millions more retirees travel. Drug and pharmacy companies will be obvious winners.

Then, an explosion in nursing homes and long-term care facilities, as the over-75 crowd climbs 75% higher in 2006 than it was in 1996.

Learn the strategies

If you are a dedicated aggressive investor, determined to make risk work for you, there are many options, products and strategies. Learn about common and preferred stock hybrids like convertible securities, including convertible debentures. Learn about using leverage to make money trading corporate and government bonds.

You can sell things you do not own, and make money doing it. This is called short selling, a technique that lets you profit just as much in markets that are going down as ones that are rising. In this instance you would borrow stock from another investor (typically your broker) and then sell it in a declining market, only to buy it back later at a lower price, pocketing the difference.

There are also calls and puts, index options, derivatives—many strategies for those investors who are both sophisticated and driven. They are complex, compelling and exhilarating, but certainly not for everyone. If you are intrigued, don't do anything before you read *Aggressive Investing* by Richard Croft (Prentice Hall, 1998).

Don't be stupid

There is accepting risk as a tool and working with it, and then there is gambling, which is synonymous with stupidity. A great example of the latter is day trading, as mentioned earlier, a phenomenon that appeared across North American in the late 1990s. Day traders make their money from exacting dozens, or hundreds, of trades a day. Corporate and economic fundamentals play no role—only momentum and human emotion (mainly greed) are important. It was estimated by mid-1999 that about five million people were taking part in this insanity, either through online brokerage accounts or day trading operations like Swift Trade, in Toronto.

Day traders, typically, have no idea of the inherent worth of the stocks they are buying and selling, and make money on the small spreads that open up minute by minute between bid and ask prices. It's a rush, and some people have made huge amounts of money. But the similarities to playing the ponies or the slots is obvious. This may be aggressive, but it's not investing.

(3) HARNESS DEFLATION

For the first time in a generation, the value of a dollar is rising. A dollar will buy more commodities today than it did last year or 10 years ago. This is new to most people. It's revolutionary.

It means that as long as deflation, or even disinflation, continues, you want to have more of your net worth in dollars than in commodities. The value of commodities, or real assets, is in decline while the value of dollars, or financial assets, is rising.

This should not surprise you. Instead, it's inflation and the last 25 years that should surprise you, because that experience—the one my father profited from—is the historical aberration.

The Dow this Century

00   10   20   30   40   50   60   70   80   90

Source: The New York Stock Exchange

The markets since 1900: The direction is clearly up, despite the collapses experienced in 1929 and 1987.

Refer back to the 200-year chart of commodity prices on page 00, and see clearly that real assets have been heading relentlessly downward. The inflationary spikes occurred after the Industrial Revolution, after the two world wars and then again during the formative years of the baby-boom generation in the 1980s. Inflation happened then as supply and demand went out of whack with each other, for example, through the stimulus of war or a demographic bulge.

Now look at the direction of financial assets over the last 100 years, as measured by the Dow Jones Industrials.

In a deflationary world, these are the new realities:

• Debt becomes far harder to pay because it actually increases in size relative to the value of the asset that secures it. In other words, the dollar amount of your mortgage will stay constant, while the worth of your home declines.

• Wages and salaries are more likely to decline than increase.

• Your purchasing power increases, because things cost less, but you may be earning fewer dollars.

• Stocks of companies developing new markets or increasing market share rise in value. Mild deflation can cut the overhead of efficient companies, offsetting the decline in the selling price of their products and services.

• Interest rates decline, and remain low.

• Non-income-producing residential real estate is negatively impacted.

• Gold and other commodities fall in value.

How can you harness deflation? Simply, by abandoning the old rules. Your income could well be lower in five years than it is today, along with the value of your house. But interest rates will also be cheap, and consumer prices will have declined. Therefore, it would be wrong to have most of your net worth tied up in your house, or to have borrowed on the expectation of a salary increase in the future.

Conversely, it would make sense to borrow at low rates to buy investments that will rise in value, like stocks or mutual funds. It would make sense to take equity out of declining real estate and put it into financial assets. It would be smart to aggressively reduce the tax load on your static income. It would make sense to invest in bonds, which rise in value as the cost of money falls.

(4) BE A GLOBAL THINKER

Canada is a puddle. Our markets represent just 3% of those around the world. Our currency has been under attack and is only a few pennies off its all-time low. Trade barriers are falling all over the globe and there have been exceptional investment opportunities opening up in Japan, Europe and emerging markets. Asia was discounted hugely by the meltdown of 1998, and will be undervalued for years. Europe in the age of the Euro is poised for strong growth based on free trade and currency union, and emerging markets are just that—emerging to a developed state, which means more potential for growth (and, yes, more risk) than with established economies.

In this context, why would you have all of your wealth in Canadian dollars? Why would 80% or more of your RRSP holdings be in Canada?

In the new millennium, there will doubtlessly be a global shrinking as national and regional economies continue to integrate. The introduction of the Euro in 1999 was a landmark step. Eleven countries adopted a single currency in a bold move that was a triumph of common sense. The Euro will strengthen all of those national economies, and make the European free trade zone that much more dynamic and prosperous.

The same will happen in the NAFTA zone. The logical and next step in the North American free trade area is the adoption of a single currency, which will be the U.S. dollar. I think people should be preparing for this eventuality today.

Let's face it, there is no stopping the American dollar. The Mexican peso in 1998 dropped by about a third against the greenback as interest rates rose by about half. During the 1998 global currency meltdown, it took 150 Japanese yen to buy a single dollar and the Canadian loonie swooned to 63 U.S. pennies. The Russian ruble was essentially worthless. Smart money all around the world bailed out of currencies that were devaluing, and into the American dollar.

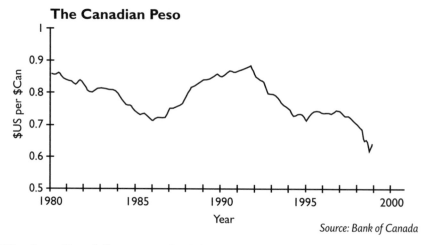

The Canadian dollar: A steady slide over the last 15 years. There is little reason to believe this trend will stop, increasing the argument for putting more of your wealth into something more stable, like the U.S. dollar.

When free trade is denationalizing economies around the world, then it's only a matter of time before currencies are also denationalized. The Euro has epitomized that. The Yankee buck will take it to a new level, and the benefits will be tangible, levelling out economic activity without the distortions of national political interference.

If you look hard into the future, you will see the U.S. currency as the new gold standard. As McGill University professor Reuven Brenner has commented, "Region after region would then adopt the currency and the world would get back, step-by-step, to a viable successor to the gold standard. Countries with an unstable monetary history would especially benefit, while those that eschewed the standard and did not make their banking and financial systems transparent would signal their laxity, and the international capital markets would extract the appropriate price."

No country on earth has a more compelling reason than Canada to make this move, although it would not be a painless one. Our current low dollar masks a productivity problem by making our exports cheap. The antidote to that is lower taxes, less regulation and more free enterprise, all of which will come as governments become less able to control the national economy in a free-trading world.

Monetary union with the States is no longer a pipe dream, having even been discussed at the federal Cabinet level in Canada just six months after the Euro combined 11 European currencies. The idea has also been heavily promoted by think tanks like the C.D. Howe Institute. In a landmark 1999 paper, authors Thomas Courchene and Richard Harris concluded that our existing floating exchange rate makes markets more unpredictable, as evidenced by the run on the dollar in 1998, and may even be hurting the economy.

"Floating rates make real exchange rates more volatile, do not appear to offer effective buffers against external shocks, and can result in prolonged currency misalignments, as the current period of pronounced weakness relative to the U.S. dollar demonstrates," it concluded. "Such weakness or volatility may tend to discourage productivity improvements in Canadian firms that export or compete with imports; bias investment toward U.S. locations and thus away from Canadian ones; and discourage the development of human-capital-intensive industries in Canada."

The Institute also argued that as trade with the States intensifies, so does the benefit of having exchange rate certainty with the U.S. How can we measure competitiveness clearly without it? The conclusion: pegging our dollar to the American currency, as was done during the 1960s, would be better than today. Unifying the two currencies would be even better. And I am certain it will happen.

The implications for you are clear:

•   Hedge against future fluctuations and devaluations of the Canadian dollar by investing in U.S.-denominated securities.

•   You can buy preferred shares of Canadian companies, like the banks, that will pay you dividends in American dollars.

- You can buy bonds from Canadian issuers, like Ontario Hydro, that will pay you interest in U.S. dollars.

- You can buy the shares of companies that earn the bulk of their incomes in American currency, like Bombardier.

- You should have at least one U.S. dollar account.

- You should increase the foreign content of your RRSP. You can purchase mutual funds that hold other funds with foreign content, effectively doubling your content. For every dollar you invest in labour-sponsored venture capital funds, like Working Ventures, you can triple your foreign-content investment to 40%. And you can buy foreign index funds, to achieve 100% foreign content inside your RRSP.

- You should buy international equity funds. You should also buy into Asia, and especially Japan, which is clearly on the rebound. Latin America is also a very attractive long-term buy.

- You should clearly try to earn income in the new gold standard, the U.S. dollar.

Of course, the journey to a North American currency union will be rough and charged with 19th-century-style political and economic nationalism. There will be many people who believe that adopting the U.S. currency will mean a loss of sovereignty, and indeed it might. But it will also likely result in more economic growth and opportunity, with fewer currency crises of the kind the western world suffered through in 1998.

I think this is coming over the next decade, and the sooner you move wealth out of a currency whose days are numbered, the better off you will be.

(5) UNDERSTAND DEMOGRAPHICS

Murray Legate and his twin sister, Muriel Johnson, were born in Fort Saskatchewan in 1898. They both feel great.

The oldest person in the world until recently was a Quebec woman who died at age 128. And this could be just the start. "We know we can extend the lifespan of mammals," Dr. Judith Campisi of the U.S. Berkeley National Laboratory told *The New York Times*. "There is no reason to believe that we couldn't do the same today in humans."

A 1999 conference held in Los Angeles among scientists specializing in aging came to the inescapable conclusion that soon, maybe in a generation or two, people will routinely live to be 150 or 200 years old.

Already consider what's happening:

• By 2025 every single Canadian baby will have a life expectancy of more than 80 years.

• In that year, more than 20% of the entire Canadian population will be over the age of 65, most of them women and most in need of expensive and prolonged health care.

• Now and every year in the foreseeable future, Canada will need to add another 1,000 to 1,500 nursing home beds, in the opinion of Barry Reichmann, who heads the country's fastest-growth nursing home real estate investment trust.

• Ontario has pledged to add 175 new nursing homes, with about 20,000 beds, by 2006.

• According to separate reports by the World Health Organization and the U.S. Census Bureau, growing life expectancy around the world threatens to outpace nations' abilities to care for an elderly population. And science may be about to make that a lot more difficult.

"There are a huge amount of aging people and they don't have 10 kids each to shoulder the load," Dr. Larry Libranch of Toronto's Mount Sinai Hospital was reported as saying in the *National Post*. "My interest is that people don't die miserably."

ARCHIE TURNER FIRST developed signs of Alzheimer Disease in his late seventies. My family watched helplessly as he started to forget life's cues, struggled to decipher jumbled thoughts and suffered bouts of debilitating frustration at the inability of his mind to clear of this impenetrable and suffocating fog. Treatment was hopeless. Home care turned into a nightmare. By the time my mother admitted she could no longer cope, she was practically dead herself. Her body was deeply bruised from trying to guide him up stairs and through doors. She suffered acute sleep deprivation from lying awake all night, anticipating the next time Archie would bolt upright, put on his clothes and want to head off to an office he had not seen in two decades or visit a relative who had been dead for 50 years.

One day, he narrowly missed driving over her with the car on the driveway. His last Christmas dinner at home, he was full of demons. A few days later he fell, struck his head on the coffee table that held the Royal Doulton figurines he'd bought my mother, and never came home again. His long-term care came in a retirement home with a special floor for Alzheimer patients, where they and staff were locked in and Archie got 24-hour attention. It was not a happy place, despite the heroic efforts of everyone. It cost $6,000 a month and, in the end, Archie was too sick and too much work for the staff to stay there. He went to a nursing home, stopped eating and died.

My father was a fortunate man. Had he been his own father, without a pension and living in rural Depression-era Ontario, there would have been no care other than that of an exhausted spouse. Certainly no pension to cushion the crippling financial blow.

Now, ironically, the generation just reaching middle-age could be considerably at risk once again. Increasing longevity means vastly more cases of dementia, including Alzheimer's. I know my own family history puts me at great risk of reliving my father's senior years. But a huge increase in the number of old people in 20 years will stretch resources to the breaking point. Meanwhile, most people today do not have the kind of ongoing financial security that Archie enjoyed. It makes you wonder, what's going to happen?

The demographics of Canadian society are unalterable. And they made certain things predictable.

• The public health care system will not stay public forever. It can't. There are not enough taxpayers or tax dollars around to sustain it when the baby-boom wave hits. This means you will have to pay for a huge amount of care yourself. Old age in Canada will be expensive and if you do not have the money, you will be out of luck.

• Medical insurance will grow in importance as the public health care system deteriorates. Budget for adequate coverage.

• Millions of aging people will constitute a massive market for personal care products and services. Dentures, graduated glass lenses, absorbent undergarments and hair dye will bring in billions in sales. Pharmaceutical companies and drug store chains will prosper.

• Already big money is moving into the retirement and nursing home business. Central Park Lodges owns 74 homes in Canada and the United States, with another 23 under development. CPL Long Term Care REIT is now the country's biggest retirement home owner and operator. Investors have seen the company's unit price jump from $10 at its initial public offering in 1997 by a factor of almost three. By mid-1999, CPL had 75 homes with more than 10,000 beds and contracts to build 15 more facilities in Ontario. This is an industry with unlimited potential for investors.

The aging of our population is unstoppable. It will put severe strains on government and social support programs, and on families who will be shocked to learn their only alternative is to take an elderly parent in, or be bankrupted by the cost of outside care. But at the same time, the demographic reality of Canada means a bonanza for certain industries and sectors and individual investment vehicles.

Investors would do well to stay invested in science and technology funds and high-tech ventures. Also of obvious merit are funds that focus on demographics.

(6) AVOID TAXES

No, I did not say evade taxes, but avoid them. This is completely legal and, in fact, completely necessary. Canadians shoulder a crushing tax burden, giving over up to 54.2% of their incomes.

If you make more than $60,000, you are rich—at least in the government's eyes. You must surrender half your income to help look after those who make less, to pay interest on the national debt and run the country. In addition, you pay user fees, sales taxes, payroll taxes, land transfer taxes and property taxes. Most of the price of a litre of gas is tax. Most of the price of a bottle of wine is tax.

You are taxed on the money you earn, and when you invest the money that is left over, you are taxed again on it. We are now paying almost 8% more of gross domestic product (the value of the entire economy) in taxes than the Americans do. In the last decade, our taxes have risen by a quarter.

And if you are middle-class, you are paying most of the freight.

Every federal budget removes more and more lower-income people from the tax roles. Meanwhile record numbers of people have just walked away from their financial obligations by declaring personal bankruptcy. That leaves most of the tax bill in the hands of the steady Eddys. In fact, just 30% of Canadians pay more than 60% of all the taxes. It's people like this—collecting a paycheque with taxes deducted at source, supporting a family and earning a little income in interest—who are being nailed.

But there are things you can do to avoid paying more than your fair share—lots of them.

Top tax rates

Country	Rate	On Income above (Cdn$)
United States	39%	$200,000
Canada	54%	$60,000
Germany	53%	$117,000
Japan	65%	$325,000

Here are the steps to follow:

- Avoid excessive taxation.

- Pay only your fair share, on time and in full.

- Concentrate on the tax-free compounding of what you've got.

- Be aware before you invest that different kinds of income are taxed in different ways.

- Maximize credits and deductions.

- Split income within your family.

- Be creative with your RRSP.

- Make interest tax-deductible.

You will find simple instructions to implement all of these strategies in the next two chapters of this book. Saving a substantial amount on your tax bill is not overly difficult, but most people never even try. They just accept the fact that up to half of what they make they simply never see, because it is deducted at source.

Remember: it does not need to be that way. In fact, there are dozens and dozens of methods you can use to reduce the amount of money extracted from you. There is nothing unpatriotic or unseemly about this, and I say that after having been in charge of the Canadian tax system myself. Millions of Canadians overpay their taxes unknowingly, mostly because they were trying to save two hundred dollars trying to fill out the tax return themselves. That is a false economy, indeed.

The new millennium will probably bring more tax pressures, as governments try to cope with the age crisis and the inevitable squeeze on resources. The easiest targets for politicians to hit are the retired and middle-class employees. If you fall into either of those groups, then it is essential that you take action. For example, you can make monthly RRSP contributions and then use them to have less money taken off your pay-cheque. You can use a self-directed RRSP to make assets you now pay tax on, tax-free. You can pay your spouse a salary, and deduct it all from your taxable income. You can convert some of your real estate equity into growth mutual funds, and reduce your taxable income at the same time. You can earn up to $23,000 in income and not pay a dollar in tax if you take that income in the form of dividends.

Pay your fair share, but do not pay more. Let the other guy do that.

(7) IGNORE THE MEDIA

Most people in the Canadian media, it seems, subscribe to some very dangerous myths:

- Stocks are risky investments that are inappropriate for most people.

- Real estate is a safe haven of wealth.

- Financial advisers are commission-driven salespeople in disguise.

- The best investments are those with a guarantee.

- Financial markets could crash at any time, and probably will.

- If you pay your taxes and work hard, you'll be okay.

- Average people can't become rich people unless they break the rules.

Because many media commentators are blinded by these assumptions, they misinterpret events. The stock market correction of 1987 was described as "Armageddon." The correction of September and October 1998 prompted observers to trot out comparisons with 1929. The correction of October 1997 was a "market meltdown" in headlines across the country. All of these events turned out to be the same—temporary stumbles, and huge buying opportunities.

Without a doubt, the next rapid decline will be painted in exactly the same colours, and that negativity will deter a lot of people from taking full advantage of the great 10 or 12 years that lie ahead of us.

In the new millennium, you need to act on good information that has not gone through the biased sieve of individual commentators. That means having professional advisers to help you with investment and tax planning. It means using the Internet to access all the research, historical data and expert opinion you need to help reach decisions. It means seeking out the advice of successful and wealthy people who, I can guarantee you, do not get their strategies out of the columns on the business page.

(b) Work rules

(8) FORGET LOYALTY

Have you ever been fired, laid off or unexpectedly lost your job? At the time, it's like a kick in the head and a knee to the stomach. Because so many people take their personal identities from "what they do," the loss of a job can be totally debilitating.

More and more people have been having this experience. More and even more will. The pace of corporate mergers, acquisitions and restructurings will only accelerate in the context of a globalized economy. Soon there will be just a handful of global banks and auto manufacturers and communications conglomerates.

For example, as the 1990s end, just 14 car manufacturers account for 94% of the world's vehicle production and by 2005 Ford will dominate in a way it has not since the Depression-era 1930. Corporate marriages have transformed this industry, as they are transforming others. Ford owns Volvo and a third of Mazda. Chrysler and Daimler have merged, as have Renault and Nissan. GM owns half of Isuzu and an equal piece of Saab. And there is more consolidation to come.

In the new millennium it is a lot more dangerous working for Boeing or General Motors or the CBC than it is the start-up advertising agency with seven people working from their homes in a virtual corporation. GM and the CBC have massive overheads to feed, complicated and costly personnel problems and often crippling levels of benefits to pay. They are slower to move to changing market conditions; even to make decisions. A speedboat can turn much faster than an oil tanker.

You can be loyal all your working life to that massive multinational giant, and yet the decisions that will affect your life will not factor in a single day of your loyalty. It just doesn't matter. It's all too big. They don't care.

Some people claim this attitude is changing. "Before we said loyalty is dead. Now we realize it isn't dead," said the Royal Bank's Blair Pollard, in commenting on a 1999 study on employee commitment. "It's just a different definition of loyalty. It isn't a job for life but it certainly is a strong relationship with employees."

This study found employees today are looking for five things from their employers:

- A recognition of personal and family life.

- Opportunity for personal growth.

- A commitment to satisfy customers.

- Competitive pay.

- The need to upgrade skills.

But most companies are not giving these things to the people who work for them. Often, the reality is that shareholders come first and everyone else comes last. Where managers and executives also have stock options, then maximizing shareholder value can translate into minimizing employees. There is no quicker fix for an ailing stock price than for a company to reduce overhead. Work for somebody else? Then you're considered overhead.

Today you have to work hard to protect your income, your future options and, most of all, your dignity and self-respect. If you surrender your identity to your job, and you do not control that job, you have done an incredibly dangerous and reckless thing. You are setting yourself up to

be brutalized by anyone from the chairman of the board to your immediate supervisor who just had a fight with her boyfriend.

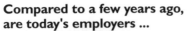

Source: Wirthlin Worldwide

*A survey of workers found two-thirds feel employers are now less loyal to
employees. Among people aged 55 to 64, almost 80% believe it.*

I am not saying that you shouldn't be an employee. Working for somebody else is just fine. But don't turn it into your life, nor make that the
sole source of your income stream. And don't give freely what you cannot get back. Remember, the old rules simply do not function anymore:
Doing your job well is no guarantee that you'll keep it. Working for one
employer for years is no guarantee that you will be promoted or get more
money. Rising to a management position probably puts you at more
danger of being sacked, not less.

These are the danger years for baby boomers.

There are more than eight million people my age. We are all approaching,
or past, 50 years of age. That puts us in the prime of our careers, making
the most money, soaking up the most in benefits and at the same time

probably less educated, less technologically competent and certainly less pliable than our grown children. If you were running the company, whom would you trim, and whom would you hire?

Exactly. These are the danger years for baby boomers. Compounding the problem is that many people today hitting 50 delayed having families and now face a lot of financial pressures. The number of Canadian men with both bald spots and kids less than three feet tall is staggering. They may be enjoying their children, but they are also entering the danger years without the financial security to withstand what may be coming. You need to be ready at all times for that knock on the door, that memo or those telltale signs that something unpleasant is about to happen to you. It might be co-workers who don't engage you the same way. Meetings you were once a part of go on without you. Superiors are evasive. Messages go unanswered. Suddenly you start hearing the four worst words possible when you check voice mail, "Your mailbox is empty."

In the new workplace reality, North American workers can expect to move to a new job seven times during their careers. And as the pace of technological change picks up, upgrading job skills will be a constant challenge. On average, companies now have to replace half their workers every four or five years. How can either employee or employer have a lasting commitment given such constant change and flux?

There is no loyalty in the workplace anymore. Companies do not hire for life. Employers are not paternalistic. There is no family at work. Studies consistently show the younger workers—especially people in their twenties—understand this perfectly. They have seen all those job losses decimating their parents' generation, and they have learned the lesson well. No loyalty. Don't extend it. Don't expect it. So, in the millennium, you must think differently, and act differently. Here are eight rules to protect yourself.

• Assume the job is a temporary one, and make the most of it. You are in a position to interact with hundreds, or thousands, of other people and organizations. All could have something to offer you. Network. Build contacts. Circulate your name and your card. Don't put down roots, emotionally or physically. Join work-related associations outside the office. Build a web site for your own career purposes, updating it constantly and using it as a tool to help slide from one position or company to another.

• Become an intrapreneur. Leverage up your position and contacts to create other situations that you do control. For example, as a personal finance columnist for a daily newspaper, in my thirties, I struck a deal to buy advertising space near my column to promote a newsletter I wrote (and owned). The paper was happy to take my money, and I was happy to leverage the same audience that read my column into subscribers who wanted more detailed information. Within a year my newsletter income was double the money the paper was paying me, and I'd turned into a client giving over tens of thousands of dollars a month to my employer.

• Develop multiple income streams. Start a home-based business. Free-lance in your area of expertise. Turn a hobby or an enjoyable pastime into a money-making venture and maybe even into a career. Imagine doing something every day that you loved!

My friend Christine was a bookkeeper, working first at an accounting company and then for a lawyer. She was good at it, but she hated wearing makeup and stockings, and she had an absolute passion for German shepherds. When I first met her and husband John, they had two of them, Rocky and Baron, both grand champions. Within a few years they owned about a dozen, living with them in their bungalow. They were well into the breeding business and travelled extensively attending shows.

Christine was very curious about my companies, as she worked on my books, and I encouraged her to strike out on her own, getting into the breeding and boarding business to supplement her other income. She did, borrowing to construct a state-of-the-art kennel, which was soon full of boarders, and went seriously into breeding, advertising her pups continent-wide.

The last time I visited her and John, after an absence of several years, the bungalow had turned into a magnificent new house, the kennel was palatial and she had quit her day job for good. And there was not a stitch of makeup on that sunny face.

• Establish a new relationship with your employer. You'd probably be better off supplying exactly the same service to your company as a contractor than as an employee and, ironically, have more job security. That way you'd earn income in a less-taxed way, you'd be able to deduct more expenses from that income, and you'd be able to supply services to other companies. I also bet you'd be respected more. They might even send you a Christmas basket. Remember: employees are expensive since the employer must make CPP and EI contributions, as well as other payroll taxes. In addition, there could be pension and health care plan contributions, not to mention the cost of providing a desk, chair, phone, computer and everything else an employee might need. Ironically, you may have work for a lot longer as a contractor than you would have a job as an employee.

When I was a network television newscaster I faced the classic employee dilemma—stay in the chair in front of the camera every night and make the TV gods happy, or hit the road and earn much more money, since I was in heavy demand at the time as a public speaker.

The solution was forging a new relationship that was fluid, flexible and satisfied everyone. I became a contract worker, supplying services on an annual basis, and hired a seasoned broadcaster to fill the chair when I was travelling across Canada. The network got a newscaster, I got to make a lot of money, and my replacement got a good job when I had to move on entirely.

• Get equity. If your company has a share purchase plan, subscribe to it. Then if your job evaporates, you will still own a piece of the company that you can sell. If you work for a smaller company, ask if you can purchase an equity position, either with cash or with your labour—giving over a portion of your salary or wages for shares. Equity is far more important than regular compensation. I have certainly worked for free on many occasions to become a stakeholder in something I believed could have a future.

• Always remember that the most precious thing you can lose when it comes to work is your self-reliance. The most dangerous thing to acquire is dependence. Loyal workers are dependent workers who are playing by the wrong set of rules—Archie's rules. They are setting themselves up for a big fall in a workplace that has no justice anymore. Preserve your self-reliance by following the guidelines above.

• Never, ever have just one option for income. Instead, work at developing multiple income streams within your family. Take your job skills and freelance them. Take your interests and develop them into companies. Start a home-based business. Start a web business. Expand your knowledge base and value by learning new skills and new technologies. Hire your kids or your spouse and pay them tax-deductible salaries.

• And always be careful about *who you are*. Yes, I mean your identity and the way you describe who you are to others. If you're at a neighbourhood party and someone asks you what you do, don't say, "I work for Nortel, in development." True enough, you may do that, but next month you may also be on Nortel's downsizing list. What do you say then? Besides, that's not really who you are. You're actually an electrical engineer, or a marketer or a webmaster—you just happen to be at Nortel right now.

And you have more to your life, in any case, than what company you hang around with. If you don't, you should.

Intrapreneurship

As mentioned above, there is a space between employee and entrepreneur, and it could be for you. It has certainly been a comfortable place for me whenever I found myself between projects, and working for someone else's corporation. It's being an intrapreneur.

While an entrepreneur creates new ventures, jobs, opportunities and wealth, an intrapreneur adds value to an existing structure. This can happen in a few ways for employees:

• You piggyback on your employer's resources to make more money. For example, a major Canadian television broadcaster allows its camera operators to rent the company's equipment, including cameras and trucks, to do freelance work. This is a major source of additional income for the employees; the company has happy workers without having to pay them a lot; and the broadcaster's trucks are rolling public billboards when they'd otherwise be parked. It also enjoys getting revenue from equipment that otherwise would generate nothing. Everybody wins.

• Or, you create opportunity for yourself by creating opportunity for
your employer. For example, one of my assistants who handles subscriptions to my newsletter, *The Turner Report*, surprised me one day with a
detailed and insightful report on the subscription base, the renewal rate,
the content and powerful ways in which it could generate more income
and become a better product. I realized I had not paid enough attention
to this property, and was vastly impressed at the initiative.

Within a few weeks I had promoted her to general manager of the
newsletter, with a substantial budget and on a profit-sharing basis. She
proved her ability to be an effective intrapreneur, and it was clearly in my
interests to let her fly. If she meets her revenue targets, she has an immediate opportunity of increasing her compensation package by 50%, and
my company's bottom line improves. Everybody wins.

Being an intrapreneur usually will not earn you equity in the company,
but it is a major improvement over being an employee. You can give
yourself hope. You can create another income stream. You insulate yourself a bit from all of the uncertainty and lack of loyalty that comes with
working for a corporation today. You certainly make yourself more valuable to your employer, increasing the odds that the next career move will
be your decision, not that of your boss. Other benefits:

• It's easier to add creative value to an existing job, or network, than start
something from the ground up.

• That means there is inherently less risk. And usually no startup capital is required for an intraprenurial project. Often it's your employer's
money at risk, not yours.

• You can maintain your existing workplace friendships and contacts,
instead of having to leave the building to find opportunity.

• The company has already established a brand in the marketplace, so
you just build upon, enhance or use that image. That was the situation
when, as a newspaper columnist, I sold newsletter subscriptions to readers

of the paper. They bought it every day anyway because of brand loyalty. I augmented that for my employer by bringing more advertising revenue to it, while I added value to myself, through those subscriptions.

• You can find a shared corporate vision with your employer, making you much more valuable, and maybe even restoring some employer loyalty.

Of course, there are some risks. Your idea or project could fail. It could lose the company money, or otherwise discredit you. You will then pay the price for sticking your neck out and daring to be more than just another employee. Or you might engender some mistrust or jealousy among your co-workers. After all, an intrapreneur is a corporate hybrid. You will annoy others because you have more freedom and opportunity. You may arouse managers' suspicions as to whether you are putting your employee interests first, or those of yourself (was there ever any doubt?).

In fact, the better you do and the more you stand out in the herd, the more you must expect, and endure, resentment and even hostility. As an intrapreneur in the media job I had before entering politics in 1988, I always drove the only new Mercedes in the employee parking lot. I had a home in the city and a stone farmhouse on an acreage for the weekends— all impossibilities on the salary my employer was paying me. This did not endear me to the other newsroom types. When I announced my intention to run for Parliament, there was a movement (that succeeded) to throw me out of the building. Six years later when I lost my seat, the editor of the paper (still toiling away for his five-figure salary), editorialized that the election had been a disaster, "but the golden lining is that Garth Turner was defeated."

At the time, the jab found its mark. Today I know that is exactly what those who seek freedom must anticipate.

But do not let any workplace emotion deter you. At the end of the day, any employer that does not reward you for showing ambition or initiative is not worth working for. Any resentful colleague is best left in the dust. You are taking a solid, positive step towards creating a superior, more independent future.

The intrapreneur's 10 commandments

1. *Come to work each day willing to be fired.*

2. *Circumvent any orders aimed at stopping your dream.*

3. *Do any job needed to make your project work, regardless of your job description.*

4. *Find people to help you.*

5. *Follow your intuition about the people you choose, and work only with the best.*

6. *Work underground as long as you can—publicity triggers the corporate immune mechanism.*

7. *Never bet on a race unless you are running in it.*

8. *Remember it is easier to ask for forgiveness than for permission.*

9. *Be true to your goals, but be realistic about the ways to achieve them.*

10. *Honour your sponsors.*

Source: Gifford Pinchot, Intrapreneuring

---

(9) WORK FOR YOURSELF

Being on your own is exhilarating and terrifying. But this is the real, true key to a secure future as our society changes fast. It all comes down to one thing: control. If you control your own job, you control your hours and your salary, your environment and your destiny. You can maximize opportunity and minimize wasted time. You live and exploit every day for yourself, not someone else. At the worst, your business may fail, but nobody will ever fire you, dismiss you or lay you off. And there is a huge difference.

Are there considerable risks to working for yourself? Of course, and most small, startup businesses fail within the first five years. And most Canadians will never even attempt this, because they fear those risks— of insufficient sales, cash-flow problems, personnel hassles, lawsuits, of a loan being called or a competitor crushing your enterprise. Running your own show takes a huge amount of effort and time. To succeed simply takes more guts and adrenalin than most people can produce.

The good news is, more and more Canadians are taking the plunge. As the nation's unemployment rate fell by almost 2% to the 8% level by 1999, the number of self-employed as a proportion of all workers was rising to almost 18%. In fact, Canadians now have more entrepreneurs per capita than any other country outside of the United States. We're learning one of life's most cherished lessons quickly.

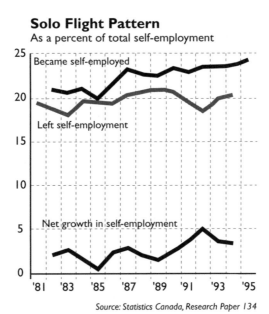

Solo Flight Pattern
As a percent of total self-employment

Source: Statistics Canada, Research Paper 134

But being an entrepreneur has always been admired, and never so much as today or, I believe, in the years to come. Once, most people were entrepreneurs, without really thinking about it. The generation that spawned my father was massively entrepreneurial, because there were not that many jobs working for others. In 19th-century Canada we had an agrarian society, where every single farm family was on its own. There were no government pension cheques, no universal free health care, no denticare, no disability assistance.

We also had a large merchant class, because before the advent of cars, each town, village and hamlet had to have essential services—a blacksmith, a veterinarian, a school, a general store, a feed mill and farm supply depot.

Then, it all changed. Canadian society began to develop a terrible dependency that has brought us to our current dangerous point. But you certainly could not blame people for what they did, which was crave a financial security their parents never knew.

That was exactly what Archie did, clamouring to become a professional, not a farmer. He sought out education that would have been worthless to his parents, but that was his ticket into the big town. He took few chances, always looking to cut the odds against failure. He made my mother wait seven years to get married, until the economic rubble of the Depression years was clearing, and when he had the job security that was all-important to him.

Eventually, he became an executive. In fact, every cell of his being was an executive cell. He wore executive-length socks, always bought a gleam-

ing white car, had his suits handmade and was impeccable and vainglorious. My father came to breakfast dressed in a white shirt, tie and cufflinks. He came home, napped at noon, and worked every night chairing meetings. I cannot imagine him wasting executive time taking his kids to hockey games, working on the lawn or building a deck. That was just not on.

And, it worked. He succeeded, got the top job, took early retirement, joined the exclusive, executive golf club, and had no financial worries. Neither did my mother, until the day we went, early in the morning, to arrange Archie's trip from the hospital to the funeral home. On his casket would sit my mother's favourite picture of him—not at the cottage, with his children, or smiling mischievously at the camera—but the professional photograph of an executive, in suit and tie, posing with his pipe among the books that symbolized his journey from gritty rural survival to suburban superiority.

Today being an executive is a dangerous thing. Legions of companies are waging war on their overheads by thinning the ranks of the executives. Following every merger, acquisition and takeover, there is executive blood-letting to address issues of duplication and overlap. Today those who are dependent on their larger corporate masters are at extreme peril, having surrendered so much in the tradeoff for the perceived security my father attained.

People become entrapped with a single income source, a single identity and a future singularly dependent on decisions they cannot control. Employees. Fifty-year-olds who long ago lost the self-reliance and stomach for risk that satisfied their grandfathers with every crop that they sowed.

Entrepreneurs are revered again now. Bill Gates, starting out building computers in a garage, is an icon of the age, his story having been relived countless times by countless others as the Internet age dawned. Ted Turner, turning a second-string TV station in a secondary market into a global empire. Michael Cowpland, flourishing his software company in the unlikely town of Ottawa, with a trophy home complete with a car wash in the basement and a trophy wife.

Today every major media outlet follows the entrepreneurial class breathlessly, as it should. This is the future. The entrepreneurs stand out so much because they are in stark contrast with the kind of society we have built, which eschews risk and rewards subservience. It's a society heading for a financial meltdown, which will be made all the more dangerous and traumatic because most of us have lost the self-reliance that allowed our grandparents to survive. Imagine the 1930s. Could you make it?

But working for yourself is not easy. It is all-consuming and dangerous. Everyone attempting it should be very cautious or very driven. I learned that early on.

DOROTHY AND I MARRIED young and were well-educated, upwardly mobile employees by our early twenties. I was a newspaper editor. She started out as a high school teacher, hated it and went on to be the promotions manager of a major shopping mall. At 25, we quit our jobs, sold everything we had, borrowed $10,000 from Archie, hired eight people and started a weekly newspaper in competition with an established daily in an Ontario city. We had enough money to meet payroll and operating expenses for six weeks. After that, I had no real idea what would happen, but I was saucy and confident.

The paper succeeded because we worked day and night, kept overhead down and sold like hell. Enough advertising revenue came streaming in to keep the doors open. We eventually expanded, starting two other papers, buying a couple more, getting a press and moving into our own building. I bought a new Oldsmobile and put a phone in it—unheard of at the time. We built a new house in the country. I wore white suits. When there were 60 employees, and we were 28, we retired. The new owner paid us a lot of money for the company, which was to be doled out in annual payments. The first year's payment was lost entirely to the government in capital gains taxes, and then the company abruptly went bankrupt. We were forced to end our early retirement.

There were many lessons in the first experience, which we have never forgotten.

• The risks involved in a startup operation are huge. Foolish, naive, idealistic young dreamers can afford to take them. Wiser and older investors should cut the risks as much as possible before even starting, through market research.

• The rewards involved in working for yourself can also be huge. The potential for true wealth is almost always closer for the entrepreneur than the employee. The only way employees normally can accumulate wealth is through an equity ownership position that may or may not be offered. For the entrepreneur, equity is there, in spades, from the get-go.

• Independence is addictive. At the end of the day, being free to chose your own path and walk down it is more valuable than money.

- Employees are an emotional drain. The burden of responsibility is indeed almost unbearable at times. Meeting payroll is not a business necessity, but a moral and social obligation. People are dependent upon you for paying their mortgages, feeding their children and running their lives. You must remember that you made them dependent. Ironically, you need and expect their loyalty.

As employers in our twenties, we felt that burden intensely, knowing we were responsible for that single mother's ability to clothe her boy; for the new immigrants who desperately needed money to buy an old car at the Toronto Auto Auction; and for the middle-aged woman earning extra money to support her newly disabled husband.

But every entrepreneur must remember that employees think like employees, not risk-takers. I was shocked one day at my first business to be summoned into a room and confronted by all the people working for me, demanding to be given three weeks of holidays, instead of the two that the law stipulated. It was a huge task for me already to sustain the business while people took time off, and the move angered me. With typical entrepreneurial arrogance and impatience I said everyone was free to quit and work someplace else, and stormed out. Nobody did. If they had, we would have been financially destroyed inside a week. Employees can be a pain, but you cannot build a business that will sustain you or give you wealth without people. They should be inspired by you. I came to learn that.

- Financing is everything. You must build a healthy, respectful relationship with the sources of money, typically your bank. Make your banker a partner, involving him or her in your plans and seeking advice. Get used to the idea of having to pledge your personal assets to secure financing. If you do not show that level of commitment, the bankers won't, either. Nor should they. But be careful about accepting capital you don't really need to survive. One of the greatest lessons to learn is that money is always far easier to get than it is to return. The line of credit is a wonderful business tool. It is also the entrepreneur's equivalent of crack cocaine.

The first business and the first employees

• If you have to do something, usually you can. In fact, as an entrepreneur working for yourself, you will be amazed at your resilience and ability to accomplish things you never tried, or even contemplated. But there is no choice. You must. You are far richer for it happening.

The first time I ever stayed up all night, working, was getting the first issue of the first newspaper to press. Dorothy and I and the others spent it in a dank, freezing composing room, working with second-hand equipment and make-shift work spaces, eating hamburgers and wondering how we managed to create a crisis. At dawn, just minutes before the deadline to get to the printers, I stood at the door with the finished page flats in my arms. Everybody cheered. I cried.

Two years later we had a million-dollar press in our own building and Dorothy and I worked again all night. This time we had to manually insert a fat, profitable advertising supplement into thousands of newspapers as they streamed off the press. We'd hired a bunch of high school students to help. They showed up after the school prom, the boys in tuxedos and the girls in their party dresses. The kids kicked off their shoes, turned on the boom box and danced and stuffed through the darkness as the presses roared. It was one of the best nights of my life.

• Work is a bond. Not for everyone, of course, but for my wife and myself, it is. The depth of experiences we have shared in creating opportunity and wealth and problems is a glue that keeps us close and makes us stronger. Most married people who are employees never have the opportunity of sharing their work experiences. In fact, most companies and employers pretend their workers don't have personal lives because it is irrelevant to their goals. Families and spouses are messy, complicated and expensive.

But for entrepreneurs, work is your day, not just a piece of it. Work does not start or end at a defined time. When you are both involved, you wake up and go to sleep discussing some aspect of work. It is inseparable from the other things you do. When it is going badly, the worry and anxiety oppresses your house. When it is going well, the buzz and excitement and enthusiasm turns you into infatuated teenagers. Work is a complete turn-on.

In the future, entrepreneurs have the best shot at building wealth, achieving financial and emotional security and avoiding the massive problems that now appear inevitable in the second decade of the millennium. The most successful class of people will, without doubt, be the entrepreneurial class. Working for yourself will be increasingly important as the economy restructures. And because of the new technologies, it will be easier and less expensive to get into your own business. Anyone with a good personal computer system and an Internet presence can look like an established corporate entity, no matter what your location. The opportunities are boundless.

Over the course of our marriage, Dorothy and I have operated commercial real estate, published newsletters, magazines and newspapers, owned stores and today run a book publishing company, television production company, financial products company, newsletter and several television programs. In addition, I write books and newspaper columns, speak across Canada and do daily radio broadcasting. We have made sure we always have multiple income streams and diversification of activities. We have learned that risk can be our best friend and the accumulation of experiences is far more important than the amassing of wealth. It was our early experiences with risk that led to other actions affecting our lives, like my decision to run to be a Member of Parliament, and subsequently as a leadership candidate. In this country you need to be either daft or truly free to contemplate such things.

After his death, my mother told me how proud Archie had been of my time as an MP, and how envious. It had always been his dream, she said, to stand in the House of Commons. But he had not taken the risk.

(10) BUILD BRAND EQUITY

In the future it will be very rare to have one career with one company. For both entrepreneurs and employees, therefore, expect competition at every stage of your life—for jobs, for contracts and opportunities.

You will enhance your chances of success by building your own brand equity. Who you are is equal to what you do. Star mutual fund managers, like Kiki Delaney, have brand equity. She is known for her ability to make funds grow and reward investors, so *she* becomes the focus of attention rather than the funds she manages. Kiki Delaney, like Peter Lynch in the U.S., has brand equity. That gives her freedom, flexibility, money and choice.

Athletes and media personalities work very hard at building equity because that has an all-important impact on the money they command. Politicians also have to build equity because it translates directly into the only thing that matters in politics—power. Star lawyers, like Eddie Greenspan, have brand equity. It turns into media attention and attracts high-profile clients and cases. It helps sway juries and judges and win those cases.

You can build brand equity in any line of work, and you should. In the future it will become increasingly important as the world becomes more wired and the media more pervasive. With the convergence of television and the Internet, the reality of a 500-channel universe and the ability of anyone to become a broadcaster or a publisher, it has never been easier to become a brand.

Broadcasters Pamela Wallin and Peter Gzowski are brands. Astronaut Roberta Bondar is a brand. Soldier Lewis Mackenzie is a brand. Joe Clark and Preston Manning are brands. Pamela Lee Anderson is a brand. Veronika Hirsch is a brand. Brokers Paul Bates and John See are brands. Bankers like Peter Godsoe and Matt Barrett (even in retirement) are brands. Columnist Jeffrey Simpson is a brand. Economic nationalist Maude Barlow is a brand. Wayne Gretzky is a brand.

Do you think for a moment that this happened by accident? Of course not. All of these people devote time and attention to making sure they are recognized not for where they work or what title they have, but instead for *who* they are. In the new millennium, this brand equity will only become more valuable, and critical to personal success. It is worth a lot of money, in some cases, millions.

How to build brand equity

• Name your company or product after yourself. This is simple and cost-effective. It could be the Ballard fuel cell, Key Porter Books, the Bronfman Foundation or Garth Turner's Investment Television. You have to call these things something, so you might as well use them to brand yourself.

• Seek out as much publicity as you are comfortable with. In our media-drenched world, people that others have "heard of" are inherently (but not necessarily) more important than people with no equity. Having a recognized name will open a surprising number of doors, bring you contracts and clients and lead to more opportunities.

• Develop media skills. Target the media outlets that speak best to the audience you want to reach. If you're in provincial politics, then it's the regional newspapers and television stations. If you're running for prime minister, it's the national networks. If you are building a restaurant supply business, seek exposure in the trade magazines. If you're a mortgage broker, get quoted in the homes and real estate sections of local newspapers.

Always promote yourself or your business with each new accomplishment. Learn how to write effective news releases. Get to know some key media people—a TV reporter or newspaper editor or columnist. The media are always looking for interesting and new stories, especially in competitive media cities. Be helpful as a source of expert information in your field, offering your comments on current events and developments.

Never, ever, ask for payment from a media organization for any service you provide. Just be happy to help and humble to receive promotion. Always return media calls immediately. Always make yourself available for interviews. Always tell the absolute truth even if it is unflattering because if you do not, and it comes out (and it always does eventually), you're dead.

Find media channels you can use. If you're a financial adviser, offer to host a weekly phone-in show on money, and do it for free. If you're a veterinarian, offer to write a weekly pet-care column for the local paper, without charge. If you have a clothing store or a hair salon, contact the local television news anchors and offer to make them look pretty, in return for an on-air credit. Then you can use your new status as a "preferred" or "exclusive" supplier of goods and services to the TV station in your advertising and promotional materials. Suddenly some of the media glam is transferred to you, which you can use to help build your business.

• Maybe you should hire a publicist, if your business is dependent on a public profile. News coverage is always more important to building brand equity or your business than advertising. People believe what they read in the columns and see on the news more than the commercial messages that accompany them. A publicist can help you get that kind of attention and, at the end of the day, cost you a lot less than what you would have spent on advertising to achieve a lesser result.

(11) LEASE, DON'T BUY

Leasing means renting and using something while it's useful to you, and then giving it up. You rent things that depreciate. Owning means making a commitment to hang on to something and tying up capital, then selling it when it's no longer important or has risen in value. So, you buy things that appreciate.

It is evident that it makes more sense today to lease cell phones, computers and other things that are rapidly depreciating in value. It makes sense to buy artwork and niche real estate that will maintain or increase its worth. Run-of-the-mill real estate, which will not rise in value, should be rented or purchased with a minimum of cash—as long as mortgage rates remain low. More on that in the pages that follow.

Lease your job

But it's also wise to think about your job in the same terms, if you are not self-employed. Because there is little or no workplace loyalty anymore, and no vertical job ladder to climb, then there's no reason to invest heavily in a job that will probably disappear. Instead, lease it. Use your office as you would a hotel room. Don't look for your friends among your co-workers, because when your job goes, so will they. But do spend a lot of time networking with people who you believe may lead you into the next position. Don't invest emotion in your company, unless you own it. Keep a current resume, and keep it in circulation. Network all the time.

Keeping in mind what I will lay out in Rule 18, I believe that any ambitious person should always carry a mobile telephone and always keep it on. The cost of celltime is falling steadily and today you cannot afford to be out of touch, anytime, anywhere. Use the infrastructure of your employer to build your own network. Your voice mail message at work should direct callers to your pocket or car phone, not to your company-paid assistant. Wherever possible, live out of your car and work out of your briefcase. Trust nobody that you work with unless you are prepared for disappointment. Definitely find your friends elsewhere.

I used to respect one television network executive whom I had known for a long time until the day he was dumped on by his superior for failing to have his department file adequate sales reports. And while it was clearly his problem, as manager, he blamed his assistant for not having prepared the reports properly. Without any sign of remorse, he fired her, despite eight years of loyal service. That move cost the company 18 months of severance pay. It cost him his heart.

Lease your people

If you are an entrepreneur, lease people instead of buying them.

• Use contract workers, temporaries or commission-driven salespeople. Especially in Canada's high-tax environment, employees can be incredibly costly with all of the current and future payroll taxes. You are responsible for withholding and remitting income taxes, topping up CPP and EI contributions and even paying a punishing health tax in Ontario when you have employees. Use freelancers.

• Lease office space, don't buy it. Lease computers, copiers, phone systems and databases. With the cost of technology falling, it is wise to rent and misguided to buy. With the pace of technology rising so quickly, you need the ability to upgrade equipment frequently.

• Shun overhead you cannot easily slip out from under. In many cities, you can lease all the business services you need—secretarial support, word processing equipment, mail and reception—right along with your space.

• In almost all instances, it makes sense to lease your car instead of buying, especially if it's new. If the car is a few years old, and one that holds its value well, like a Lexus or BMW, then buying can be the preferred option, depending on prevailing interest rates. If you are an entrepreneur, then get a nice car. It is your rolling business card and one of the few social cues as to how you are doing. Nobody is going to ask you about your $95,000 S-Class when you drive up, but everybody is going to notice.

(12) RESPECT PEOPLE

All the technology in the world cannot replace them. And yet it is so easy to use technology to abuse people. I worked out of a television station for a few years where the vice-president of news actually fired an on-air personality by voice mail. Being fired, of course, is bad enough, but not even having someone look you in the eye when it happens is unbelievable—and inexcusable.

If you don't watch it closely, in the future technology will increasingly isolate you from others. In fact, it's already happening.

• Don't use e-mail as a substitute for conversation. Sure, it's fast, conve-
nient and addictive. But e-mail is also vastly more impersonal than speech
and without all the inflections that we use to communicate effectively. I
have had e-mail conversations with people that have deteriorated rapidly
into acrimony and misunderstanding. I suspect if it had been in speech,
that would not have happened.

• Never use e-mail to reprimand, scold, punish, lay off or fire anyone.
But use it lavishly to praise and encourage people. The bad news must
come from your lips. Good news can come from anywhere.

• Voice mail is another great tool, but the purpose should be to set up
physical meetings and real phone conversations. Pay attention to your voice
mail message, so you encourage positive feelings in those who hear it.
Make it brief and upbeat. Nobody has time to listen to what you're doing
today. Never use humour on your voice mail message. It may be amusing
once. The second time it's tedious. After that, people will stop calling you.
And the kiss of voice mail messaging death is to have your children record
the message.

• Don't mistake the Internet as a substitute for real life. It's not. It's a
tool, not a religion. Use it for entertainment as you would the TV. Use it
at work as you would a book. Do not let this seductive, never-sleeping,
ever-expanding and alluring medium charm you too much. You will truly
regret it.

• If you are an employee, recognize that one of the best chances you've
got of keeping your job is to work well with others. That will help you to
task better, to succeed and to avoid knives in the back. If you are an entrepreneur, then other people are absolutely critical to realizing your dream
and to creating wealth. Employees are not expenditures, but investments.
Remember how you were treated when you were an employee? Never
forget it, and do the opposite.
So, always keep personal relationships with those working for you.
Talk to them instead of sending an e-mail. The tone of your voice will convey more correctly what you really want someone to know. Don't leave

long messages on their voice mail rather a request that they give you a call. If you have something negative to convey, convey it in person.

(c) Personal rules

(13) DOWNSIZE YOUR HOUSE

Six months before my fiftieth birthday I moved from a 5,000-square-foot suburban house on 25 acres with a three-car garage, acres of decking, a forest, three ponds and waterfalls, to a one-bedroom, 1,500-square-foot stone cottage in the heart of the city. No, it was no less expensive to buy, and some of the people who know me thought I'd lost my mind, but it was the right thing to do for many reasons.

• The big, labour-intensive suburban property will steadily lose its value as the potential universe of buyers dwindles. With an aging population, fewer people want to worry about, or maintain, all that infrastructure.

• The little city property will maintain its value as the potential universe of buyers grows. More people will want to have access to health services, public transit and entertainment. Aging boomers like me will want the convenience of a home that, like a condo, requires little attention, but which also comes with a garden and a garage and privacy.

• With the drastic change in the makeup of households about to take place, large, traditional, multi-bedroom homes will be hard to unload, at any price. The average household size will drop from 2.7 to 2.4 people in 2016. The number of people living alone will rise by 70%, to almost four million Canadians by 2016, making up more than a quarter of all households. The number of two-person families will soar, doubling from three million to six million by 2016, representing then fully 55% of all families. How many bedrooms are these people going to need?

• There are about eight million other Canadians my age. Baby boomers were responsible for the explosion in real estate values in the eighties, and for the exodus to the suburbs. They were behind the monster home phenomenon. Now, as children grow up and move away, as mortgages are paid off and disposable income grows and tastes change, aging boomers will abandon those houses in favour of condominiums, upscale town homes, bungalows, niche recreational properties, and houses like mine.

Those people who do not recognize this trend, and the need to take action now—not a decade out, when housing prices will be plunging as millions try to sell—will regret it the rest of their lives.

• The economy will experience mild deflation for years to come, and deflation is the enemy of residential real estate. It will slowly and imperceptibly lower the value of houses for the next decade or more, before it becomes more virulent and attacks home equity with a vengeance. Many people will not realize that their home is a depreciating asset until they have already lost a substantial chunk of their net worth, and when the place is almost impossible to unload.

The time to act is now

For these reasons, and more, I moved. It was one of a number of deliberate steps I have personally taken to prepare myself, my family and my finances for what lies ahead. Most people are not taking similar steps, nor will they even contemplate them until it is too late. If you share my concerns, and visions for the future, then now is the time to act, while there still are buyers for your house. Most homeowners are deluding themselves, believing inflation will return and push the value of their houses higher. Media reports from time to time of bidding wars and rising prices mask what is really happening and reinforce the myth of a real estate cycle that will ratchet up home values soon.

There is no real estate cycle

Instead, housing is a commodity that's driven only by supply and demand. Demand, at least for big houses, suburban homes and multi-bedroom houses, is about to wither on the vine.

Too many people have too much money in the wrong kind of homes. That mistake is compounded when they pay their houses off, and sit on hundreds of thousands in home equity. With the twin threats of demographics and deflation, it is a losing strategy. In fact, it's no strategy at all.

I am not arguing against real estate ownership. In fact, I love real estate. Owning a unique property gives me great pleasure. Living in a nice place is a big part of an enjoyable life. But if your goal is financial independence and to wisely prepare for what is coming, then you must pay attention to the new rules.

Rules for home ownership

Buy when it decreases your living costs. The name of the game is cash flow. When you have it, you can invest it in those assets that will rise in value, like stocks and investment funds. If buying a home rather than leasing a similar one increases your cash flow, then go ahead and buy. Today, with stable prices and cheap mortgage rates, that is exactly the case in most Canadian cities.

• Use somebody else's money. If I am right, and real estate turns out to be a consistently deflating asset, then the last thing you want to do is spend the next 15 years paying off something that will be worth less than you have invested in it. And if the financial markets perform for the next decade as I suspect they will, you will have missed opportunity by putting your money against your mortgage instead of into rising assets. So, be happy to let the bank own your home. You be happy owning a growing portfolio of stocks, bonds and investment funds.

• Never cash in RRSPs to buy a house. The homebuyers' plan allows for up to $20,000 per person or $40,000 per couple to be removed from an RRSP, tax-free and interest-free, for a home purchase. But don't do it. You are taking money from a tax-free environment where it can grow wildly and putting it into something that, at very best, will just maintain its value. Does this mean some young people will not be able to buy a home? Sure it does, but if they have to raid RRSPs to do it, then they probably should not be homeowners. More Canadians should rid themselves of the outdated belief that buying a home is better than leasing one or that paying it off is a mark of financial success. It could be the sign of a financial idiot.

• Borrow short. Low and declining interest rates have been a feature of the last few years and will be a hallmark of the first decade of the new millennium. Borrowing short has been a winning strategy for years, and will continue. Just as you do not need to pay the premium for a segregated fund to insure against falling financial markets, so is the premium for a long mortgage to insure against rising rates equally unnecessary.

• Sell real estate with no future. Buy real estate that has one. I have written at length on this in my 1997 book, *The Strategy*. So far my premises have been correct. There will be strong buying interest in the next decade for recreational communities, gated communities, bungalows in traditional midtown locations, the best condominium buildings and developments, houses on golf courses, duplexes suitable for extended families and age-proofed homes. There will be declining interest in four-bedroom suburban homes, anything with a swimming pool, monster houses with Scarlett O'Hara staircases or lofts.

• Diversify. It was okay for my parents to have the bulk of their net worth in their home, but it's not okay for me. They lived their adult lives in inflationary times when the value of money was falling and the value of commodities, like real estate, was rising. That made mortgage debt easier to pay off. And because Canadian law allows tax-free capital gains on your principal residence, it was a sound strategy.

Today, it's a recipe for financial ruin. Once you have paid off your home, remove some equity and put it in quality financial assets with a better chance of growing. Diversify. In due time, your neighbours will be achingly jealous.

(14) GUARD YOUR DATA

The world is digitizing. The nature of communication is changing. The exchange of money is being revolutionized. Today, Canadians are exchanging paper cash that can be lost or stolen or counterfeited, for debit and credit and stored value cards that can be lost or stolen or accessed without your immediate knowledge. Imagine when you bank or invest by telephone or computer how many potential problems could occur. A software virus could corrupt or delete data. A criminal could hack into a system containing your accounts.

Or it could be a lot lower-tech. The receipt you get at the gas station often contains your credit card type, number and expiry date. Anyone with a valid merchant number and a cheap banking machine can put charges through on it.

Beware of the E-dangers

Then there is the Internet and its greatest convenience, e-mail.

Never assume that e-mail is like letter mail. It's not, and the law underscores that. It is a criminal offence for your co-worker to intercept and read a letter addressed to you. But your confidential e-mail is open to the entire world to peruse. Every e-mail message you send has your fingerprints permanently embedded in it. Every word you write could last forever, so you had better choose them well. And yet while e-mail is totally unsecure, it carries the same weight as if you committed the thoughts to paper and had them notarized and published.

Internal e-mails that Microsoft boss Bill Gates wrote about the competition were admitted as evidence against him at antitrust hearings in the United States. In Nova Scotia, company managers trashed a former employee via e-mail. She sued for wrongful dismissal and at the same time subpoenaed their e-mail, and then sued for libel as well.

Fingerprints on the Net

The use of the Internet carries the same embedded fingerprints. You cannot go anywhere on the Net without leaving a giant sign saying you were there. It is easy to trace everything, and everyone. The implications can be large and you should take steps to protect yourself. If you are an employer offering Internet access to employees, have a policy in place that protects you from their online actions.

If you are an Internet user, be very aware that every web page you visit will be recorded. If you are suspected of criminal activity, your computer can be seized and will reveal a record of your Internet travelling. If that makes you uncomfortable, then routinely erase this information at the end of each session. For example, in Netscape Navigator, choose "Communicator" from the tool bar, then "History," and your list of visits will appear. From the tool bar, choose "Edit" then "Select all" and then "Delete."

Trading or banking on the Web? Always ensure that the pages you are using are secure. Ditto when ordering with credit card information. If you are not completely convinced, then do not proceed.

(15) AVOID THE RETIREMENT CRISIS

As I have already detailed here, a retirement crisis of immense proportions will sweep across Canadian society in less than two decades. It is inevitable, since we cannot alter demographics and since, as a country, we are doing nothing to prepare, nothing to mitigate the effects when it hits.

The crisis will be in full blossom as millions of people my age end their career working lives and do not have enough income to maintain their lifestyles. As a result:

- The Canadian standard of living will go down.

- Consumer spending will crash, with serious economic implications.

- Governments who have billions of dollars in debt will hardly be in a position to help as their tax revenues dive.

- The real estate market will collapse as millions of listings flood in with a scant number of buyers. Many people will see the value of their homes fall below the amount of the mortgages placed upon them. They may take a walk. They may have no choice. Abandoned houses will quickly bring down the values of the existing occupied homes around them.

- Financial markets could also be at extreme risk of a massive decline as many people are forced to sell off their investments in order to finance their day-to-day lives. Being a long-term investor doesn't mean a lot when you simply need money to live on.

When the crisis actually hits, it will be too late to do anything about it. How dismal things become for you depends to a large extent on what emergency measures the federal government takes in the next few years, and when the action begins. Bold new actions to reduce personal taxes and encourage retirement investing would help a great deal. Canada could use the equivalent of the American Roth IRA, for example, which allows you to invest money for retirement, which is not deductible from your current income, but neither is the gain taxed when you take it out to live on later.

Will Ottawa and the provinces address this ticking demographic time bomb soon enough? To date, there is no evidence that it will happen. In fact, I think waiting for "someone" to "do something" is a very dangerous course of action. You should be preparing now, building wealth in the good times to sustain you and your family in the decades that will not be good. It seems only prudent.

I worry for those millions of Canadians who swallow today's conventional logic that it is enough to work hard, pay your taxes and pay down your mortgage. It is not. We are bordering on extraordinary times in which the old rules of the last generation just do not apply.

A dozen actions to take now

1. Cash in non-performing assets, like GICs, Canada Savings Bonds, term deposits, cash reserves and savings accounts and invest them for growth. Again, if you have a dozen years (or more) until retirement, put your faith in equities and equity funds. If you are more conservative, balanced funds or bonds may be appropriate. If you want no risk, pay the premium for an equity segregated fund, but realize that guarantee will surely be needless over the next decade.

2. Establish a line of credit for a reasonable amount, like $10,000, to handle any cash emergencies that might arise. All the money you have should be invested, not sitting idle.

3. Get a financial adviser and develop an immediate plan for growth, diversification, retirement and estate preservation. Stick to it.

4. Buy growth assets, like mutual funds and quality stocks. Ask your adviser about managed money products and their appropriateness for you.

5. Maximize your cash flow and reduce taxes by making regular monthly RRSP contributions and then having the taxes on your paycheque reduced.

6. Invest for the next decade, not the next month. Financial markets will be extremely volatile, so don't worry about temporary declines. The long-term direction is clearly up.

7. If you are younger than 60, don't even think about segregated funds. Do not pay the extra premium (in terms of higher management fees) to get a guarantee you won't need. Stocks will be higher in a decade than they are today. Between 1990 and 2000 the Dow went up 500%. Do you really think that between 2000 and 2010 it will go down?

8. Diversify. You should own great stocks, great funds and a ladder of bond maturities. You should pay a lot of attention to asset allocation.

9. Forget your mortgage. As long as home loan rates are cheap and houses are not rapidly rising in value, you are better off channelling your extra money into investments, not into your house. Because your house could well be lower in value by 2015, why invest in it?

10. Go for foreign content. Canada accounts for just 3% of world markets, so it makes no sense to have 80% or 90% of your wealth in Canadian dollars. Today you can achieve 100% foreign content in your RRSP, and you should. This is very easy to do with RRSP-eligible foreign funds that give you all non-Canadian content since they are derivative-based.

11. If you're comfortable with the idea, use borrowed money to invest. It could be in the form of leverage against mutual funds, a home equity loan or a straight investment loan. As long as interest rates remain at near-historic lows, and financial markets are robust, and you are liquid enough, this is a winning strategy for long-term investors.

12. Stay positive and confident. The bad news is there's a demographic bust that lies ahead. The good news is, it's at least 10 or 12 years away. If you do not panic, if you avoid the mistakes others are making, if you do not confuse short-term volatility for a long-term decline, then you will be okay. You should be able to double your invested wealth at least twice before the storm hits. That means if you have $100,000 today, you should

have $400,00 by 2015. If you have $250,000 today, you should be able to achieve $1,000,000. And, believe me, you will need it.

(16) Don't save

Today, Canadians have some $650 billion in fixed-income assets. That is a major mistake. Interest rates have collapsed and are going to stay at historic low levels for some time to come.

A $100,000 GIC today returns about $4,000 a year. For anyone making over $60,000, up to 54% of that is lost in taxes, reducing the yield to just $1,840. Inflation of 1% means the real return is less than a thousand dollars. At that rate it will take decades for wealth to be built up, and none of us has that amount of time.

If you do not already have a couple of million dollars, then you certainly cannot afford to save your money. You must invest, instead. If you are a senior terrified of the risk you might take on to get a better return on your money, then find out what your alternatives are.

• A well-managed bond fund should give you at least double the current GIC yield, and with moderate interest.

• A good balanced fund will do even better, with little more risk.

• A basket of blue-chip stocks is an excellent thing for those near retirement age to cling to for capital growth and also tax-advantaged dividend income.

• And, of course, segregated, protected and guaranteed funds are all now available, which promise to return all your money down the road if financial markets stumble. But as I have already pointed out, these are not suitable for everyone, especially younger investors.

But how can you go wrong, for example, with protected index funds, first brought out by the CIBC, which pace market growth but give you a five-year guarantee that you'll never lose your capital? You will pay a premium for this insurance over a regular index fund, but that's the price of sleeping securely at night for many people.

For younger investors, those in their twenties, thirties, forties or fifties, there is no question that saving money is a negative action. Each year that each dollar is in a near-cash savings vehicle, you are losing precious time. Change your habits. Cast off the influence of your parents and put your money to work. You should be aggressively exposed to the markets through quality funds.

If you have significant dollars, a million or so, then invest as well in quality investment-grade bonds that will give you interest as well as a capital gain as interest rates continue to decline. Consider getting your own portfolio manager. That will cost you 1% to 2% of your portfolio a year, and could be a most worthwhile investment.

Whatever you do, and whatever your level of wealth, you cannot afford to have lazy money. Get it to work.

(17) PREPARE TO BE OLD

Really old. Maybe a lot older than you want to be.

Many Canadians will work from age 20 to age 60, and then be retired for just as long as they were members of the workforce. For most of that period of time, they will be vibrant, healthy and active people. But will they be happy?

Life expectancy is soaring in a way that nobody ever expected. There is reason to believe it will continue. You should be ready. Of 13 major estimates on the maximum time human beings could be expected to live, made between 1952 and 1990, five have already been exceeded, and several other markers will soon fall. Studies also show people who are already old are lasting longer. The proportion of surviving 80-year-olds in England and Wales went up 600% between the 1930s and the 1980s.

In Canada, recent statistics on the chief killers—heart disease and stroke—offer dramatic proof of what's going on. Statistics Canada numbers show that in 1996 cardiovascular diseases killed 306 men out of ever 100,000. In 1969, the number of fatalities was 600, which means we have carved the death rate by half in 30 years.

What will be the death rate from heart disease in 2030, if the same medical progress is made? Could it be possible that the main killers of men and women will be cured? What if we then find a way to deal effectively with almost all kinds of cancers?

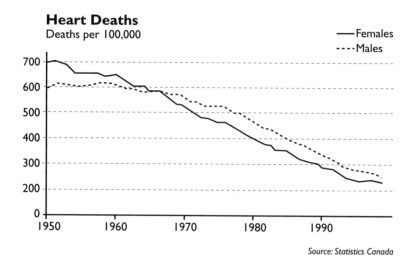

Heart Deaths
Deaths per 100,000

Source: Statistics Canada

In any case, a healthy 50-year-old man today has almost a 100% chance of living to be 80, and of feeling his Wheaties at that time. As mentioned before, this will blow the socks off the actuarial assumptions behind the Canada Pension Plan's funding and put a whole new emphasis on retirement planning. The reality of how long people are living, and the shape they'll be in, also may reverse the trend of the last few decades towards early retirement. Do you really want to work at nothing for the last 40% of your life? If you don't, those years could be incredibly expensive ones. You might not have a choice.

Young and middle-aged people today should think about this, and not just drift into it. With the fastest-growing age group now people between 75 and 100, this is also something society has to pay a lot more attention to.

Preparing to be old touches on many aspects of your life.

Housing
Decide years in advance where you want to live between the ages of 65 and 85. These will be your active and independent retirement years, perhaps stretching longer by a decade or so. After that, you could need some kind of institutional care, in a retirement home or a nursing home.

If you have wealth, you have choices. Canada or Portugal. Alberta or California. Halifax or Mexico. There are certainly cheaper places to live than urban Canada, and with better climates to boot. Just make sure you have thought through the level of social support you will want, like access to modern medical care and also family members.

The kind of housing you choose is critical. Bungalows are better than two-storey homes. Condominiums offer relief from maintenance and give enhanced security features. Age-proofed homes will become more popular, offering wider doors and hallways for wheelchairs and walkers, contrasting colours to make counters stand out and define wall junctions, more light, levers instead of doorknobs, an emergency communications system, phone and data jacks everywhere and voice-activated home management software.

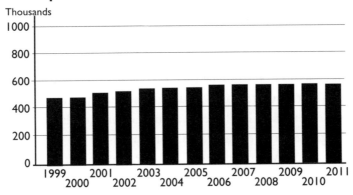

Population Growth of Over 75

Source: Care Planning Partners Inc. and Statistics Canada

Most people will want to downsize for these years, moving into spaces more often found in Europe than in Canada—800 to 1,000 square feet of living space. In fact, well-designed smaller homes will be hot commodities, perhaps equipped with their own economical source of fuel cell electrical power, stabilizing living costs. Clearly, if you are over the age of 55, it is time now that you started to make some changes in your housing, getting rid of the multi-bedroom suburban home that will be very difficult to unload in a decade from now.

Personal health

As George Burns said after he was 90, "If I'd known I was going to live this long, I'd have taken better care of myself." Well, now you know. You are going to live almost forever, so the goal is to have as many of those years as possible in excellent health.

This is not rocket science, and most of us know what we should be doing on a regular basis. Smoking anything is wrong. Today, tobacco use accounts for about a third of all heart attacks. In Canada, about 5,000 people a year die because they are married to a smoker, or inhale smoke in the workplace.

High blood pressure is a constant danger, given today's lifestyles. This can lead to heart disease and heart failure, and is preventable through weight control, exercise and eating lots of fruits and vegetables. Then, there's the big C. Steady advances are being made on cancer treatment, but it's cancer prevention that is so important.

Once again, have absolutely nothing to do with tobacco. Don't smoke it, chew it, swallow it or breathe its smoke. You will incredibly reduce the likelihood of developing cancer of the lungs, mouth or throat years from now. Fight stomach cancer by limiting, or eliminating, salt from your diet (I found it easier to stop smoking than I did to get rid of salt). Eat a mostly plant-based diet. Shun red meat and high-fat dairy products, which produce so-called bad LDL cholesterol. Don't eat junk foods which are thick with hydrogenated oils or saturated dairy fats.

Take vitamins. Vitamin C will help prevent colds and infections. Vitamin E fights your free radicals. Wash your hands after every social contact, religiously. Drink a lot of fluids. Most people, especially older people, are mildly dehydrated. Drinking too little concentrates your urine, increasing the likelihood you will get kidney stones, a chronic complaint of older people. Drink up to eight cups of fluid a day. Research is suggesting that dehydrated cells in your body may have a harder time of detoxifying themselves and removing carcinogens, leading to cancer.

And, as people age, dementia is a major concern. You can fight this by leading an active, interesting, challenged and varied life. Act like a vegetable and you may become one. Maintain hobbies and work interests and your mind will stay agile. As for the Alzheimer Disease that struck my father, research is inconclusive as to what you can do to prevent it, but one culprit seems to be the concentration of destructive aluminum in the brain.

Go right now and check out the active ingredient in your deodorant. Make sure it's not aluminum.

Sexuality is also a fundamental aspect of human health. Do not take it for granted.

Income stream

If you are going to live to be 80 or 90 or 100 or more, you will need a stable and reliable income stream. After all, you will need cash on a regular basis for up to 50 years after you receive your last paycheque.

As mentioned here before, the odds of you getting a regular monthly government pension cheque for your entire life are fading fast. Meanwhile most Canadians do not have, nor will they have, a corporate pension. That leaves just one thing: your own retirement savings and investments. For this reason, you cannot afford to blow a single year's RRSP contribution, or miss the precious tax-deferred growth that your retirement plan can give you. Find out how much you are behind, and catch up. The rules allow you to go back to 1991 and then to contribute all the money you missed between then and now. If you do not have the cash, borrow it, using your tax refund to repay the catch-up loan.

If you have unused RRSP room, and existing assets, like a GIC or mutual fund, then use a self-directed plan to slide those assets into your retirement fund. This is called a contribution in kind, and will earn you the same tax refund as if you contributed new cash.

Inside your RRSP, make sure you have growth assets. Mutual funds instead of GICs or savings bonds. Quality stocks, held for a decade or more, rather than term deposits or government bonds. Load up on foreign content. Use income-splitting techniques, like spousal RRSPs, to level out family income and reduce the overall tax burden.

Work with your financial adviser as early in your retirement planning process as possible to determine how much income you will need, and what decisions you must make today to get it. The ultimate failure is the failure to plan.

Develop alternative interests. Strengthen your marriage.

Humans have not routinely lived for as long as you are going to. The average Canadian lived to be 65 in the 1960s. You could add 30 years to that, especially if you are a woman.

What are you going to do? During the working years it may seem like sitting at the cottage doing nothing is the perfect retirement activity. But the novelty of that should wear off in a couple of weeks. Remember, at age 65 or even 75, you will feel like you did when you were 50, or younger, if you look after yourself.

Some people will dream of constant travel, seeing the world and all those things they never had time for. But that is costly. Two or three years' travel could do in 30 years of retirement savings.

For other people, especially the self-employed, there will be the luxury of semi-retirement—the best of all worlds, in which you stay involved in your business and its decision-making process, and then disappear to your other life of leisure activities. Everybody, in this age of longevity, should be involved in many activities that can be carried on almost regardless of age. Golf will be a lot more important than tennis. Walking and eco-tourism will be two of the new passions. A golden age of gardening and horticulture is at hand.

In your forties and fifties, prepare. Don't just work and mainline your career, but also branch out into other forms of work and leisure activities. Get involved in volunteerism now, because it will be of stunning important in the decades to come as governments are incapable of shouldering the burden. Volunteering is also good for the soul.

Also work on your marriage. The life expectancy of men is creeping higher and approaching that of women. As I write this, I am calculated to live another 29.7 years, and my wife 34.96 more years, but the gap is narrowing. We have been together 28 years already, and it's getting better all the time. In a world like ours, old friends and lasting friends are precious. In the years to come, with so many more older people and so many dark days to live through, a lasting and loving relationship will constitute true wealth.

(18) SET BOUNDARIES

In the world that's coming, without them, you're toast. Technology is wonderful, but it is on the verge of enslaving us. There is just no way the average person can cope with everything that's now thrown his or her way. There have to be some rules put on what you are going to notice, deal with, digest or act upon. Only you can set them, and obey them.

Maybe you're like me. I have two digital cellphones, both with voice mail, call forwarding, call waiting and call display. I have an office with staff with more phone lines, voice mail, e-mail, fax and letter mail. I receive 20 to 100 messages over the Internet each day. My web site accepts about 9,000 visitors every 24 hours. I have a big computer on my desk with high-speed cable access to the Net. I carry a little laptop with wireless Internet connectivity. I can send a fax from my car and get e-mail on my phone. I have three places that qualify as traditional offices, but I usually find myself working out of the front seat of my car. Usually at high speed. Out of time.

I have found myself spinning out of control while thinking it was progress, a forward journey. The voice mail and the e-mails become addictive. The cacophonous noise of the cellphone is somehow comforting, connecting. If it's not ringing, I check to make sure it's on. And you know you have problems when you start thinking fondly, at 7 p.m., of other time zones where people are still working that you can call.

Technology does this. It lets you be on, all the time. Voice mail never gets a sore throat. The Internet never gets tired. e-mails are always urgent. You can carry around a Palm Pilot in one pocket and a cellphone in the other, and you might as well be as much a part of your office as the photocopier. Have you ever been really annoyed at your mother because you can't just fax her a birthday card? Or send her an e-mail from a greeting-card template in your desktop program? Why doesn't this woman have a fax or a computer? Problems. You've got problems.

Technology can take work and weave its way into every little seam of your life—if you let it happen. At the same time, it has dumped more information upon us than a human mind can absorb. The Internet, for example, is a pure, unadulterated, coursing, throbbing pipeline of information that never ceases or diminishes. It just grows by the hour.

As I write this, my computer, of course, is hooked into the Net. I can flip seamlessly between the manuscript and the ocean of stuff lapping at my laptop. I do a search. Pick a name. Bill Clinton. Search results: 184,084 web sites, including Bill's own page. Search, Warren Buffett. Results: 8,180 web sites. Search, Garth Brooks. Results: 23,824 web sites. Search, Garth Turner. Results, 127 web sites. Search, Y2K. Results: 127,052 web sites.

If I were to write an article on Garth Brooks, how long, exactly, would it take me to at last spend one minute loading each of the related web sites, and three minutes scanning it? Working a 40-hour week doing nothing else, that would take 40 weeks. To do the same research on Clinton would take 5 years and 10 months.

Nobody can cope with this, or deal with it. Technology has opened the floodgates to incredibly useful information and submerged it in a sea of awesome junk. If you have to know something about Warren Buffett in a hurry, I hope you have a book with an index in it, because the Internet will drive you crazy before it drives you to the right information.

Meanwhile television now offers more than 100 channels in many locations. Cable companies deliver packages with groupings of stations and networks you did not know existed. How can the Food Network survive? Satellite TV is even scarier, with live programming, video-on-demand and, yes, the Internet. In fact, the Net is in the process of converging with both television and the radio, and the telephone and soon, your dryer.

This technological overload can make you feel stressed, out of time, behind events and constantly losing ground. It leads to what pop psychologists call "time famine," which leads in turn to people trying to cope with it through "multi-tasking" or "time deepening." That means doing two things at once (like driving and taking voice mail) or trying to make better use of time (by hiring out chores, like looking after the children).

But the only real solution is to set boundaries. How much information will you allow through the floodgates of your ears or your eyes? Do you have quiet times assigned to your days? Are you paying enough attention to your spouse or partner? Or your dog?

There are times that even the most aggressive entrepreneur must turn off the cellphone (although it can still take messages), stuff the Internet safely back down its cable (while it collects new e-mails) and go for a walk in the woods.

In the new millennium, woods will be really important.

(19) ACCEPT THE INEVITABLE

Canada has a unique population, unlike that of Europe and Asia. We have more boomers, per capita, than even the United States. This means it is about to deliver some unique problems. I have already chronicled the incredible social and financial distress that will be felt by millions of people—mostly members of the baby-boom generation like me—who will not be ready for what the coming years will bring. They have forgotten, or never asked about, the lessons their parents learned during the last lean times. They are not prepared.

There is another stress also developing, and that is an emotional one. Just as more than eight million people today aged 40 to 55 are entering the most critical years of their lives, the ones that will determine the entire success or failure of the rest of their lives, they have to deal with the decline and death of their parents.

Were this 30 years ago, late in the 1960s or the early 1970s, most parents of 50-year-olds would already be gone. If you retired in 1965, at age 65, your life expectancy was about five years. Today it is 20 years. The implications of this are enormous.

ARCHIE DIED AT AGE 85. My mother has passed that now and, as I write this, is in great shape. This story is common. It is being shared by almost all the 50-year-olds that I meet. Eight million middle-aged Canadians will be experiencing the loss of more than 10 million parents over the next 10 years. And during much of the coming decade, those parents will be aged, expensive to care for, and emotionally draining to deal with. Never before has this happened, that so many people at this stage of their lives should be so mindful of their aged parents' needs and wishes.

This preoccupation comes just at the time, as I mentioned, that is so critical for boomers to be positioning themselves for the years to come. Ahead:

• Emotionally battered by the loss of a parent, or three or four parents within a single marriage, many middle-aged people will lose precious time preparing for their own older years.

• Others will be financially drained, having to devote a lot of capital into the care of those aged parents. My father's monthly bill for the attention he required before he died was $6,000. Over three years, that cost more than $200,000, but how could it be denied?

• Some will take parents into their houses, and then have to deal with the difficult issue of home care. Having a declining parent in a room upstairs can dominate your entire space, and your life—for years, as modern technology extends human life past points we never thought possible.

But it is inevitable, and you must deal with this fact. If you are a middle-aged person now, with one or two parents still alive, then recognize that there's a good chance your own life will be substantially impacted, or changed by what you will need to cope with. As difficult as it may be, you should take several actions today, in preparation.

Actions to deal with the inevitable now

• Talk to your parent's doctor for an impartial assessment of his or her health and prognosis, and the odds of a stroke or heart attack or chronic disease occurring. This will help in your own decision-making process.

• Talk to your parents about what their expectations are. If they own a home, should it be sold before health starts to deteriorate? Perhaps a worry-free and maintenance-free condominium would be a much better choice, and this would be the better time to make the move, than after crisis strikes.

• Do your parents expect you to care for them as they age? Does that mean moving in with you? Does it mean financing a retirement home? Does it mean paying the large bills incurred in a nursing home?

• Ask your parents about their personal affairs. Do they have up-to-date wills in place, and powers of attorney for personal care?

My mother narrowly avoided a personal and financial crisis by getting my father to sign a power of attorney giving her authority over his personal care and the family finances as he sank into the clutches of Alzheimer Disease. It has been an omission, and should she have waited just weeks more, it would have been too late. She would not have been able to make critical decisions about his care, the disbursement of his pension money or even the sale of the family home.

• Ask about estate planning. Your parent may wish to pass money on to you or your children, but the tax bite will be immense on their terminal tax return if plans have not been made in advance. If they wish to gift money, do it before death. If they want their estates to survive the tax onslaught, then insurance can be purchased to pay those taxes. If you are the beneficiary of the estate, then perhaps you should be the one to pay the insurance premiums. Talk about it. Don't just let it all happen.

• Pre-arrange funerals. This can save some money. More importantly, it can certainly save emotional damage. Make decisions before a crisis occurs on the type of funeral, the costs, the service, the burial or cremation process, the death notices and every other detail that death demands.

My mother did not do that for Archie. As a result, we found ourselves sitting in a funeral home very early on the Saturday morning on which he died, my mother in tears, trying to choose a casket, a burial process and the kind of guest book people should sign when they came to the visitation.

A month later she told me she has gone back to the same funeral home and arranged every single detail of her own funeral, and paid for it in cash. "I'm sending you the papers," she said. "So you'll just have to make one phone call." I felt upset at that call, but I soon realized that having done that made her feel better. Empowered, even. It was a gift she was giving her children, which we did not want to receive and yet would be thankful for.

• Talk about your parents' finances. This, as every survey shows, is actually more painful than talking about death. But my experience has shown that after the death of a spouse comes overwhelming grief, which is itself overwhelmed by financial insecurity. The time to deal with that is before decline and death. Find out what your parents' assets are, what their income stream is, how their affairs are structured, and how the death of one (likely the husband, who is usually the source of most pension or investment income) would change things.

The house is a big issue

Your parents may be comfortable living in old and familiar circumstances, but the reality is that after the death of one of them, the other will likely have to move—because the home is too large a burden to care for, or simply because the survivor needs the cash in that house to live on.

So, not only does he or she have to deal with the loss of a partner, but that is immediately followed by the loss of the home. This is an avalanche of change and it can take years for the survivor to recover emotionally. Some never do. Better that both your parents should sell before the inevitable occurs, freeing up capital to invest for financial security, and establishing a life together in more appropriate surroundings.

Sharing of financial information

What are your parents' liquid assets? How, and where, is the money invested? Have your parents shared with each other the financial information that will be critical after the death of one of them occurs?

Dorothy's father left all that for me, in a file folder, in shaky handwriting, in pencil. His habit had always been to "handle" the family finances, which was a relief to Dorothy's mother while he was alive, and a crushing burden after he died suddenly of the complications of throat cancer, 15 years after he stopped smoking. She had no clear idea of her net worth. She worried about the sudden loss of his pension income. She did not clearly understand why their home of 40 years had to be immediately put on the market, with potential buyers coming through, invading her space and then trying to lowball the asking price because she was a vulnerable vendor.

So many of the problems that the death of a parent brings can be dealt with long before the emotional tidal wave hits. Addressing those today will make the inevitable easier to deal with. It will make the survivor feel more secure.

The same can be said for the entire aging process. We all are robust, decline, need care and expire. It has always been that way, and always will. But today the process is unique. As life is extended through 80, 90 and 100 years, children of 60 and 70 years of age will be dealing with situations that were the domain of 30-year-olds a decade ago. This changes the experience for everyone.

Today's baby boomers must take this rule to heart, lest you be surprised, diverted and delayed by the inevitability of your parents' final years. Your time to build wealth and prepare for the bleak years following the current boom is relatively short. Care for your parents. Love and respect them. Support them. But also remember that some modest planning and common sense now can ensure your own life, as well as theirs, has as much quality as possible.

(20) Be an optimist

Rather than celebrate the Dow Jones industrial average's piercing of the magic 10,000 barrier this week, investors should be quaking in their boots that the investment bubble has expanded beyond their wildest fantasies.

—FINANCIAL POST, MARCH 1999

(DOW JONES AT 10,000)

This is a financial crisis. The market is showing panic. I suspect there is a wholesale deserting of our markets by foreign investors.

—ALLEN SINAI, SHERRSON LEHMAN BROTHERS

OCTOBER 1987 (AFTER DOW DROPS TO 1,738)

If you took your investment advice from the popular media, you would never invest in anything. The operative emotion is fear. The time frame is immediate. The media—in fact, much of society and even some key people in the financial services sector—are short-term thinkers.

Every correction is treated as an end-of-the-world-as-we-know-it event, rather than the significant buying opportunity it inevitably turns out to be. The wrong advice leads millions of people to do the wrong things with their money, thinking that preservation of capital is the holy grail. But it's not, of course. And that wrong thinking has led us to where we sit today: woefully prepared, on average, for what is coming soon and will be mercilessly present within 20 years.

This is not a time for fear, but for confidence. You must remain an optimist and ignore the bleatings of those who worry about the next 10 days, not the next 10 years. The stock market and the value of your mutual funds could well take a hammering, but that should not surprise nor deter you, because it will be temporary. The lesson has been repeated over and over again, with major reversals in 1987, 1993, 1997 and 1998. They are coming more quickly, and with more intensity, like the 32% drubbing the TSE 300 took in the fall of 1998. I fully expect this pattern to be repeated, just as I suspect each correction will be misinterpreted in the next day's headlines as the beginning of the end.

Well, the fact is, the end is quite a ways off. Market declines in the first decade of the new millennium will, I am sure, prove to be nothing more than very good times to increase your portfolio at very good prices. Wise investors will remain calm and optimistic, and certainly resist the temptation to sell that so many feel when things turn south.

Over the five years between 1995 and mid-1999, the Dow in New York increased from 4,000 to 10,000. At every milepost, analysts and media commentators warned that the market's rise was unsustainable and investors could be wiped out the next day. Over that period, the Dow and the TSE 300 in Toronto suffered two major drops, in 1997 and again the next year. In New York, the Dow twice fell more than 500 points in a single day. In that same period, there was a global financial crisis that took the value of the Canadian dollar to its lowest point in history. The American Congress voted to impeach its own president. The economies of most Asian countries virtually collapsed. Russia defaulted on its external debt. There was a war in Europe.

These were not exactly days of wine and roses, and yet the markets rose and investors who stuck with their equities, their bonds and their mutual funds did exceptionally well. Those who ignored the necessary corrections after markets advanced too far, too fast, suffered no losses and enjoyed substantial gains. Those who tried to time the markets because they had no optimism in the long term, failed.

The point of this book is simple: relish the next decade and build your wealth in it, because things will go downhill fast after that. There will be a time for pessimism. But it's not now.

Before the next Depression,
the Great Second Chance for wealth
By 2010, the economy should start feeling different. From 2015 to 2020 it could be sputtering. After that, a mess. The reasons are detailed above.

But for at least the first decade of the new millennium, and for those who realize and act upon it, a huge reprieve is at hand. It will be an opportunity to create wealth—the second chance given to this baby-boomer generation that largely blew the first one.

That first chance to build personal wealth, quickly and easily, was during the inflationary days of the eighties, when you could buy commodities like gold, and especially real estate, and see inflation sweep their values higher. That was a time when you could use leverage to own properties that increased in price while the debt placed upon them stayed static.

Today, it's all changed. Today, the big money to be made is through financial assets, not real ones. Just reflect on where we are right now. There are five things to remember every time you think about what to do with your money:

• The recession of the mid-nineties killed inflation. Now we have disinflation, or deflation. This is good, because …

• It has ushered in a long period of very low interest rates and low prices.

• Governments have slashed their overheads and turned budget deficits into budget surpluses. Both Ottawa and Washington are solidly in the black.

• Corporations across the western world are joining forces and creating giants that have huge staying power and massive profit potential. Globalization will bring a stability to western economies that was previously unknown. We may not see another recession for more than a decade, until the demographic time bomb hits North America.

• And this is happening just when 80 million North American baby boomers are moving into that key 45-54 age category in which they will earn, and spend, the most of their entire lives. At the same time, these same people stand to inherit billions over the next 10 to 15 years.

Stable growth in the U.S., an increase in demand in Europe and a turnaround in Asia will all help fuel the Canadian economy into the next century.

LLOYD ATKINSON

PRINCIPAL, PERIGREE INVESTMENT COUNSEL

There are other reasons to believe that the economy of North America will be outstanding for a decade, including the technological revolution that will make the Internet ubiquitous far faster than anyone could have imagined in 1995, leading to an e-commerce bonanza, and major advances in health care. Then there is the distinct possibility of lower taxes on the continent, the direct result of the 2000 U.S. presidential election.

The most powerful generation in history—mine—is bursting into middle-age with more disposable income than any one that has gone before. Middle-aged people are close to having their houses paid off. There is more money to buy financial assets. In most cases, the kids are gone. More money for toys, like boats and roadsters. More money for trips and the cottage. And with sustained low interest rates and stable prices, everybody feels better about spending it.

Economic forecasters have been recognizing, as the 1990s ended, that Canada is in truly great shape. Inflation is conquered and interest rates should remain at historically low levels. The dollar is improving—a positive thing as we move closer towards an inevitable currency union in North America. Unemployment is falling and corporate profits rising. Millions of people are hitting their peak income years. Millions more will be turning real estate equity into spending and investing power, as they borrow against those homes or downsize.

In this environment, the economy should remain robust for at least a decade, maybe more. The path of the Dow from 1985 to 1999 could well be retraced from 2000 to 2010 or even 2015.

The best place to have long-term money will be in stocks and equity mutual funds as markets continue to rise (but definitely not in a straight line. Expect many ferocious corrections along the way.) The worst place will be in savings bonds, GICs, money market funds and other places where cheap interest rates promise terrible returns.

Too many people are clinging to the lessons they learned from their parents, whose golden days were the inflation-heavy seventies and eighties, when houses made money instead of money making money. Too many people today have too much money in the wrong places, and earning them too little return. And far too many of us pay more tax than we have to, because we just don't take advantage of all the legal loopholes that exist.

1984 – 1999

1984 1985 1986 1987 1988 1989 1990 1991 1992 1993 1994 1995 1996 1997 1998 1999

Source: New York Stock Exchange

Deja vu? Here's what the Dow Jones did between 1985 and 1999, rising from less than 2,000 to 10,000. During that time there was a serious recession, soaring interest rates, a couple of wars and a global financial collapse. The next decade should be even better.

Most Canadians have the wrong plan, and unless they change it, they will squander the precious ten years of opportunity that lie directly ahead of us. Clearly, with what is coming after that, you cannot afford to make that mistake.

If you follow the simple strategies outlined here, consistently over the next years, you will greatly increase your chance of avoiding the fate that awaits so many others.

Summary: Rules to Remember
• Be aggressive about investing. Buy when others are selling. Invest when panic reigns and values drop. Think long-term.

• Be aggressive about saving taxes. Grab every credit and deduction you can. Shelter all the income possible. Make the interest you pay tax-deductible. Earn the right kind of income and split it within your family.

• Be very careful with your real estate. Buy it the right way. Finance it properly. Sell the wrong kind and buy the better kind. Don't let it become an illiquid trap for your wealth.

• Get expert help. Today you need a financial adviser to help plot the right path ahead. There are almost 2,000 investment fund choices along with stocks and bonds and other assets. Too many people are making serious mistakes and inappropriate investment decisions because they feel they need to do it on their own. Get over it.

• Ignore the media. It is populated with Chicken Littles who will not give you good advice, if history is any guide.

A dozen reasons to love the next decade
And you should. It's going to be great.

1. Inflation is dead. For the first time in 25 years, the value of a dollar is going up as it buys more house, car or computer.

2. No inflation means no reason for interest rates to rise. The cost of car loans and mortgages remains near historic lows, increasing disposable income.

3. Cheap rates are great news for corporations, reducing borrowing costs and increasing the bottom line.

4. Rising corporate profits fuel stock market gains, lifting the value of investment funds based upon them.

5. The biggest generation in history is just hitting the peak spending years, fuelling a consumer and investment boom.

6. Tens of millions of people are about to pay off their mortgages, freeing up billions of dollars to spend and invest.

7. A wave of mergers and acquisitions is creating strong companies while reducing the number of corporations to invest in. More reason for rising stock values.

8. Technology is opening up major new investment opportunities. What happened to those who saw the future of radio and television has been happening again to Internet investors.

9. Global free trade is now firmly entrenched and even engendering a global government—the G7 (now G8) and the International Monetary Fund. International monetary policy is being coordinated, even as countries do the sensible thing, and merge currencies. Do you think they will let another Asian contagion happen?

10. Politicians finally get it. Big government has received the axe, taxes are falling (but will plunge much further in the years to come) and the back of the public sector unions has been broken. The days of damning deficits are over.

11. Financial markets will continue to drive higher on a heady mix of boomer investment bucks, institutional buying from pension funds, cheap money and the lack of alternatives.

12. Taxes have started to fall and will cascade lower. There is no choice in a globalized environment in which high taxes make Canada uncompetitive. It will happen.

Tax Strategies

THE ARGUMENT
It is far easier to save money than it is to make it.

Remember that. Tape it to the fridge. To prepare for what is coming in the future, here is the plan:

1. Avoid excessive taxation.
2. Pay only your fair share, on time and in full.
3. Concentrate on the tax-free compounding of what you've got.
4. Be aware before you invest that different kinds of income are taxed in different ways.
5. Maximize credits and deductions.
6. Split income within your family.
7. Be creative with your RRSP.
8. Make interest tax-deductible.

All of these goals are not difficult to accomplish, and I will outline some simple strategies that work. Follow them, and you will doubtlessly increase your net worth while reducing the amount you send to Revenue Canada each April.

Now, some people might question why a guy who was once in charge of the country's tax system would be writing things like this. Well, as Canada's federal Minister of National Revenue I had a crystal-clear view of the system, and I saw that middle-class Canadians are paying huge amounts of tax relative to other people. Why? Because most of us are so busy trying to live our lives, raise families, succeed at work and plan for the future that we become sitting ducks for the people who write tax policy.

Middle-class taxpayers are easy targets

The wealthy people have lots of ways to escape an onerous tax burden, like family trusts and corporate structures, and are only too willing to pay for that kind of expertise. At the other end of the income scale, there are tens of thousand of people each year who simply declare themselves bankrupt, and are able to walk away from their unpaid tax bills.

In the middle are the rest of us, who see payroll taxes decimate the cheques we bring home, and then—with what's left—we have to pay a host of other government levies.

Numbers released in 1999 showed that the pre-tax income of most Canadians were slipping, while taxes were rising. After-tax family income in the latest year for which numbers are available (1996) was $45,032, virtually unchanged from 1995. But meanwhile the tax burden had increased by a tenth, from 20% of household earnings to 22%. At an income level of $50,000, Canadians now pay almost 36% of gross income in tax, compared with 28% in the United States.

If this continues, of course, Canada will continue to lose scads of qualified people.

Just look at the balance sheet of a $50,000-income-earning Canadian today:

Total income	$49,996
Taxes	
Income taxes	8,466
Sales taxes	3,742
Liquor & other taxes	1,526
Social program taxes	4,024
Property taxes	1,884
Import duties	205
Profits tax	1,958
Other taxes	684
Total taxes	$23,218
After-tax income	$26,778
Basic living costs	
Shelter	8,528
Food	6,231
Clothing	2,120
Total basic costs	$16,879
Disposable income	$ 9,899

Source: The National Post, Statistics Canada, Fraser Institute

It's not a happy picture. And it's not going to get better any time soon. While I feel personal taxes will have to fall in Canada as we become less competitive, substantial cuts are not immediate and tax relief will be slow to come to those tax cows Ottawa depends on—members of the beleaguered middle class.

How do you pay less tax? A multitude of options are open to you, but here are the ones I think every middle-class taxpayer should be employing. If you follow only these five tax strategies, and especially if you work with a qualified financial adviser, your financial situation will improve substantially—perhaps even dramatically.

(1) Never prepare your own tax return

It is complex and confusing and, besides, you don't have the time to do a good job. This process involves thousands of dollars, and you are an amateur who only does this once a year. The margin for error is huge. The cost saving is minimal. In fact, any tax professional who prepares your return will save you five or ten times the amount of money you'll pay in fees.

(2) Claim all deductions and credits

Another reason to hire a pro to do the job. You are entitled to deduct a lot of things from your taxable income before you calculate the tax owing, and also (even better) to claim a credit against the tax that you have to pay. Examples of serious deductions:

• RRSPs. Invest up to 18% of what you make, or $13,500 a year, and you can deduct that amount from your taxable income. This is a gift, so it's incredible that two out of three Canadians don't take it. More on this a bit later.

• MOVING EXPENSES. Relocate 40 kilometres or more closer to work, and you can deduct all travelling and moving costs, the real estate commission on your old house, the land transfer taxes on the new one, legal fees and storage costs. This can amount to thousands less in tax in a single year.

• HOME OFFICE. Lots of people do lots of legitimate business from home now. In the future, it will be absolutely commonplace; in fact, employees of many corporations will be farmed out to work in their own residences, communicating via secure links on the Internet.

If you have a home-based business now, you can write expenses off your income. To qualify, your home must be your principal place of business and a separate area of the house must be devoted to earning income. Then you can deduct a corresponding portion of your mortgage or rent, property taxes, utilities, insurance, landscaping, maintenance, phone and repairs.

• YOUR KIDS. Deductions for child care expenses have been getting more generous over the years, much to the dismay of stay-at-home parents who do not get to write off the same things. That's because Revenue Canada only allows expenses to be deductible if they are incurred when you or your spouse earn an income.

If that's the case, you can write off the cost of day care, babysitters, boarding schools and camps to a maximum of $7,000 a year for children under seven and $4,000 a year for kids aged 7 to 16. If a child is severely infirm, the deduction rises to $7,000, regardless of age. The deduction must be claimed from the income of the spouse who earns the least, except when he or she is at school, in prison, separated from you or disabled.

• LEGAL EXPENSES. Any fees paid to fight Revenue Canada—to file an objection or to appeal your income tax assessment—are deductible. You can also deduct fees incurred dealing with an employment insurance problem; to collect unpaid salary or wages; to collect severance pay; or to enforce an existing right to alimony or maintenance payments.

• CHILD SUPPORT. It used to be that you could deduct child support and alimony payments from your taxable income, and the former spouse receiving them had to declare the money as taxable income. That was a good system because the tax system encouraged people to make their payments, but women's groups succeeded in having it changed since they thought it unfair that the payments were taxable.

So, now such payments escape the eye of the tax collector. The end result: Ottawa actually collects more tax because the payer can no longer deduct this amount from his or her taxable income. Any child support agreement made after April 30, 1997, falls under the new rules.

• INTEREST PAYMENTS. Yes, you can deduct interest on some borrowings. In general, where you borrow money to invest in a business or to make your own investments, the interest can be deducted from your taxable income. This can include borrowing against the equity in your home to buy stocks and mutual funds; taking out a line of credit to do the same; or through swapping non-deductible debt for deductible debt.

For example, if you had $50,000 worth of mutual funds and an outstanding $30,000 line of credit you used to buy a boat, the interest on the line of credit would not be deductible. So, sell $30,000 worth of mutual fund units and pay off the line of credit. Then borrow $30,000 and buy back your funds. Now all the interest on the line can be deducted from your taxable income. But beware, you may have to pay tax on any capital gain the fund units gave you when you sold them.

• TAX CREDITS. We all get a basic federal credit of $1,098, which means you pay no tax on the first $6,456 in earnings (the credit equals 17% of that). If you are older than 65, you get another $592 in tax credits, which is phased out if you make more than $26,000 a year and disappears at about $50,000 in income.

You also get a credit for your spouse, of $915, if he or she earns basically no income. A spouse can be married to you or just attached to you for the last year or with whom you've had a child or are separated from for less than 90 days.

If you're separated, divorced or unmarried, and if you support a child or family member in your home, you can claim the "equivalent-to-married" tax credit. That equals the spousal credit, and the child must be a Canadian under 18, or mentally or physically challenged.

If you are disabled, there's an additional tax credit of $720. You must be unable to work for at least a year, and have a certificate from your medical specialist. A dependent relative who does not work can transfer this credit to you.

Disabled taxpayers are also eligible to deduct attendant care costs, which are limited to two-thirds of your earned income. Such expenses can also be claimed as a medical expense credit, on the tax return of either spouse. Get some advice on which is the best route for you.

• MEDICAL EXPENSES. If they total more than 3% of your income, and are not covered by a medical plan, then you can claim a credit equal to 17% of expenses. If you earn over $54,000, then expenses of more than $1,614 get a credit. You can choose any 12-month period, so long as it ends during the current tax year. If you die, the credit is for the previous two years.

You'll need receipts, and lots of things qualify, like hospital fees, drugs, guide dogs, glasses, dental plan premiums and nursing home care.

• CHARITIES. Giving to registered charities can result in substantial tax savings. The first $200 nets a 17% tax credit, which is worth about 27% when the provincial tax is taken into consideration. Donations above that get a 29% federal tax credit, worth 50% with the provincial tax.

So for people in the top tax bracket (earning over $60,000), it's like having the donations treated as if they were simply deductible, while for people who earn less the credit for large donations is worth more than a deduction.

You are not allowed to claim donations for more than 75% of your income in any one year, but you can carry forward excess amounts to future years—as long as you have an official receipt. The claim can also be made by either spouse, so combine all donations and then use them against the taxable income of the one who earns the most.

Recent budget changes also make charitable giving an effective part of estate planning. You can claim donations totalling 100% of your income in the year of your death, and, if you exceed this, the extra amount can be carried back to the previous year, wiping out all of that income as well. And the rules now favour giving over assets, like stocks or mutual funds, rather than cash. Leave instructions in your will to do this, and the tax savings could seriously reduce the hit your estate will take. It's a win-win situation for both your heirs and the charity.

- POLITICS. You should give to political parties, and the tax system agrees. After all, somebody is going to be running the place, and it might as well be the person you agree with. Politics is a very expensive game, as I learned first-hand running to be a Member of Parliament, and if we don't want only millionaires to be in office, then it's up to us to support the candidate with the best ideas.

The tax credits for political giving are generous, especially at the lowest levels. You get a 75% credit for the first $100 donated, then half of the next $450 and a third for the next $600, up to $1,150. Contributions to provincial parties also earn credits (except in Saskatchewan and Newfoundland). A contribution by your spouse can be claimed by you—which is smart if you make more money. One sorry exception is that donations made to people running for the leadership of parties are not deductible, which is why few people of moderate means ever make it.

(3) Split income within your family

If you are married to someone, or live with someone, who's in a different tax bracket than you, then you can save taxes by splitting income. Ditto if you have kids, or run a small business. And while most Canadians never consider this, it is a powerful weapon in the war against excessive taxation.

Just consider the facts: a retired couple in B.C. with a single income of $70,000 coming into the hands of one spouse pays out almost $22,000 a year in federal and provincial tax. If they both earned $35,000, then total taxes would amount to $13,3170, for a saving of almost $9,000 a year.

Nine grand a year—equivalent to the after-tax yield of a $180,000 investment earning you 8%. So, what's easier—splitting income, or finding an extra $180,000?

Revenue Canada has what are called "attribution rules," which are designed to prevent you from simply giving over your assets to your spouse or kids for the purpose of splitting income and reducing taxes. For example, if you give money to your spouse or young children, then all the investment income earned will be attributed back to you. If you loan them money without charging interest, the same thing occurs. But if you loan money and charge interest at current market rates, then there is no attribution. You must be paid the interest by the end of January in the following year, which you claim as taxable income, but which is deductible to your spouse or child.

There are many other options for splitting income, and I will not mention them all here, just the highlights and the ones you can do easily for maximum savings.

• PAY YOUR SPOUSE'S TAXES. This is simple and effective, and yet baffles most people. The idea is to free up all of your less-taxed spouse's income to invest, not to pay taxes. In this way, you are shifting wealth to him or her. Here's what to do:

(1) Get your spouse on quarterly payments with Revenue Canada, which is not difficult to do, especially if he or she is self-employed or retired.

(2) Write a cheque and pay their taxes. You will not get a tax deduction for doing this, but it makes a lot of sense, because the money you use to pay the taxes is considered a gift to your spouse, and is not taxable since no income is being earned. No attribution back to you.

(3) Your spouse can now take the money he or she would have spent in taxes and invest it. None of the investment income will be attributed to you, and will instead be taxed at your spouse's lower rate. In effect, you have transferred wealth to your spouse equal to the tax bill.

• PAY THE FAMILY EXPENSES. The same principle applies here, but most families have this totally backwards. The money made by the lower-income earner is often considered the "second" income, and is used to do all kinds of atrocious things, like buy food. Meanwhile as much of the money made by the main income earner as possible is usually used to invest.

Wrong, wrong, wrong. The investment income of the person making the most is taxed the most, so it would be far better to have the investments in the name of the other person. So, the one making the most should buy the food, the other income should buy financial assets.

• LOAN MONEY FOR INVESTING. You can give your spouse or kids money they can invest, and only the simple interest earned will be attributed back to you. The compound interest—the money that is earned over years on the money already earned—is not taxed in your hands.

If you earn the most and loaned your spouse $100,000, receiving an average return of 9% over the next 15 years (which I do not think will be difficult, given what's coming in the new millennium), you would be taxed each year on an attributed income of $9,000. Over 15 years that would be $135,000 in taxable income. If the money were left to compound, after 15 years it would grow to $364,237. The total income earned would be $264,237, of which only $135,000 was taxable in your hands. The rest, almost $130,000, would be taxable in your spouse's hands, at a lower rate.

By splitting the income in half, your family saves money in taxes. If you were in the 52% income tax bracket in Nova Scotia, and your spouse was paying tax at the 27% rate, this strategy would save you more than $32,000 in tax. That is an impressive amount, on a $100,000 investment.

• GIVE MONEY TO START A BUSINESS. You can loan or give your spouse any amount of money to establish a business and all the profits that business earns, or income paid to your spouse, will be theirs. Not a cent is attributed back to you.

The only time tax could be triggered is if the company is sold for a capital gain (but then up to $500,000 can be sheltered through the enhanced capital gains exemption). The same break applies to money that you give or loan your spouse to buy into a partnership in which he or she actively participates, even if you both are operators.

Remember the business must be an active one, not a passive one. That rules out setting up a company just to manage your investments. In that case, the income your spouse received would be taxable in your hands.

• GIVE MONEY TO PAY EXPENSES. The simple return on money you give your less-taxed spouse to invest is attributed to you, but if you just pay him or her enough to cover the interest on an investment loan, it's not. So, your spouse can borrow a chunk of money, invest it and use your money to make the tax-deductible interest payments.

• GIVE MONEY FOR KIDS TO INVEST. Give or lend them money to invest in mutual funds that earn only capital gains. Those gains will not be attributed back to you, but instead be taxable in the hands of that child. But because the kid probably has no other income, he or she will pay little or no tax.

• PAY YOUR SPOUSE A SALARY. Or your kids. This is a great technique for seriously reducing your income, giving money to other family members to invest and also to take advantage of deferring taxes through RRSP contributions.

This is a great strategy for entrepreneurial couples, perhaps where one of you is working at a regular job and the other is a stay-at-home parent. Set up an unincorporated business running a newsletter, or a kennel, or a mail-order business or an Internet-based concern or anything else that has a reasonable expectation of profit. You are now allowed to pay your spouse (or children) a reasonable salary that you'd pay anyone else, and then deduct that salary from your own income from the business. That deduction could virtually wipe away your own tax liability. It gives your spouse money to invest at his or her lower tax rate, and your sweetie becomes eligible to make RRSP contributions because he or she has earned income.

• HIRE YOUR ADULT KIDS. Children over 18 are considered adults by Revenue Canada, even if they are still tender babies to you. As adults, you can give them money or hire them to perform tasks you'd have to pay for anyway, and the money will not be attributed back to you.

So, hire an older child to care for younger children or to carry your furniture when you move house (which, remember, you can deduct from your taxable income if it's a move closer to work).

Transfer losses to your spouse. It's complicated, but it can be done. Losses incurred on an investment that goes down in value can be used to offset gains your spouse makes on ones that appreciate. To make it work, sell losing assets to your spouse, who can then sell them at market value. The capital loss you incurred will be transferred to him or her, to be used to offset a capital gain.

• INVEST AN INHERITANCE PROPERLY. If the less-taxed spouse receives an inheritance, ensure that it stays in his or her hands and does not find its way into a joint account. If money is left to both of you, keep it separate, for tax purposes.

• TRANSFER THE CHILD TAX BENEFIT. The old "baby bonus" is now a non-taxable amount sent automatically to families below a certain income level. If you receive this, invest it directly in your child's name into an investment account in high-octane, growth equity funds. Not a dollar of that income will be attributed back to you. Take care to ensure there is no income stream associated with that investment—in other words, you want things that give you capital gains, not interest.

• OPEN A SPOUSAL RRSP. This is a great idea for couples in different tax brackets. The rules allow you to contribute into a spousal RRSP up to your own contribution level. You get to deduct that from your own taxable income, but the assets become the property of your spouse after three years, so he or she can cash them in and pay less tax than you would have.

Doing this does not affect in any way your spouse's ability to open his or her own RRSPs, and make contributions to them. This is a great way to split income, because none of the money you put into your spouse's plan, nor the income it generates, will be attributed back to you. This also applies to the RRIF money your spouse gets after the RRSP is rolled over at age 69—no tax to you.

Be aware that this is money you are actually giving over to your spouse. It's theirs, but if the marriage fails, then the normal situation will occur—all retirement assets are divided equally.

• SPLIT CPP BENEFITS. You are allowed to take up to half the money you receive in Canada Pension Plan benefits and stick it on your spouse's tax return, and he or she does the same with yours. If one of you is in a higher tax bracket, you're going to save money.

• SPLIT INCOME WITH AN RESP. A Registered Education Savings Plan lets you split income with your child, while salting money away for a future university stint that could cost a small fortune. You are not allowed to deduct RESP contributions from your own taxable income, but they are allowed to compound, tax-free, inside the plan. When the plan is collapsed to fund an education, the RESP money will be taxed in your child's hands. Hopefully, he or she will pay little or no tax.

You can salt away $4,000 a year, to a max of $42,000 per child. If your rotten kid decides not to go to university, then the money, plus the accumulated gains, will come back to you if the plan has been in place for a decade or more. This can be transferred, tax-free, into your own RRSP to a max of $50,000, and provided you have the contribution room. If you don't, you have to pay tax plus penalty on the extra. It's also possible to have RESP money transferred to other children if the one it was intended for buys a Harley and leaves home.

The 1998 budget made RESPs an even better deal. Now the feds will pay you a grant, into the RESP, for kids under 17 equal to 20% of the money you put in, above $2,000 per year. Whenever the government is going to give you money, take it.

In some cases, you might be better off setting up an in-trust account for your child, rather than an RESP. There is no restriction on the amount of money that can go into a trust account set up for a child, no restriction on what the money can be invested in and no stipulation on what the child will ultimately do with the money. But neither is there a government grant; you have no right to get the money back later if the child disappoints you; and income is taxable in your hands. Talk to your financial adviser about which is best in your situation.

(4) Take your income in other forms

How you make your money determines how it is going to be taxed. The worst kinds of income you can possibly receive are:

- Salary
- Pension, and
- Interest.

The bad news is that more than 90% of all Canadians get just about every dollar of income from one of these sources, and they pay the maximum rate of tax. What is that? Well, the lowest combined federal and provincial tax rate in Canada is 44.4% in the Northwest Territories and the highest is 54.2% in British Columbia. Everybody else is somewhere in between.

In Ontario, for example, above $62,000 in income you will have to give over 50.3 cents of every dollar, keeping just 49.7 cents. That applies to all income, with the exception of money earned in the form of capital gains or dividends. On that income, you get a break. Again, in Ontario, the maximum capital gains rate is 37.7% and on dividends, it drops to 34%.

You are given a break on these forms of income because the law recognizes there is more risk involved in earning it, and also that money put into investments earning you those forms of income is active money that finds its way into operating companies that help create jobs and feed the economy.

Capital gains

You realize a capital gain when an asset you have invested in rises in value above the price you paid. It could be a house, a business, a stock, a horse, a mutual fund or other things. These gains are treated in various ways. The capital gain your principal residence earns is tax-free. The gain on a rental property is taxable. The first $500,000 in capital gains you make selling a business or an operating farm is free of tax. The gains on most everything else is taxable.

The good news is that a capital gain is taxed less lightly than an equivalent amount earned in the form of salary or interest. That's because the first 25% of a capital gain is not taxed at all. This means, from a tax standpoint, you are better off ten times out of ten to earn money in the form of capital gain, such as through mutual fund ownership, than in interest, like with a GIC or bond. Here is how $1,000 in income would be taxed, as interest, and as a capital gain.

	Interest	Capital Gain
Income	$1,000	$1,000
Taxable Income	$1,000	$ 750
Federal Tax	$ 290	$ 217
Provincial Tax	$ 145	$ 108
Surtax	$ 23	$ 17
Total Tax	$ 458	$ 342

As you can see, the key is that the first quarter of the capital gain is exempt from tax. The effective rate of taxation dropped from 46% to 34%. At the same time, the return on a quality mutual fund would be far higher than that on a fixed-income asset such as a GIC or a Canada Savings Bond. If you are serious about growing your money and reducing the tax bite, then replace income-bearing investments with those that will pay you a capital gain.

Dividends

Dividend income is taxed at an even lower rate. You get this kind of income from the preferred shares of Canadian corporations, or from distributions made by dividend funds. The government allows you a sizeable tax credit on dividend income, which makes it far more attractive than interest or even capital gains.

Dividends that you receive have to be "grossed up" by a quarter of their value to reflect your proportion of income taxes paid by the corporation giving you the dividend. Then you can claim that tax credit equal to almost 17% of the actual dividend. This bit of mathematical trickery results in an effective tax rate in the 30% range. It also means if you were earning nothing but dividend income, you could make about $23,000 a year without paying any tax, which is a very cool idea.

Here is how $1,000 in dividend income is taxed, compared to that $1,000 in interest:

	Interest	Dividend
Income	$1,000	$1,000
Gross-up (25%)	Nil	$ 250
Taxable income	$1,000	$1,250
Federal tax	$ 290	$ 363
Dividend tax credit	$ 0	$ 167

Federal tax	$ 290	$ 196
Provincial tax	$ 145	$ 98
Surtax	$ 16	$ 23
Total tax	$ 458	$ 310

Note that dividend income is taxed at a whopping 15% less than that earned in interest. Now I hope you can see the logic of cashing in just about everything paying you a dollar in interest, and replacing it with investments that yield you dividends and capital gains.

(5) Be creative with your RRSP

I could write an entire book on effective RRSP strategies. In fact, I have. My annual *RRSP Guide* is chock-full of neat stuff that you can do with your RRSP to maximize tax savings and build your retirement nest egg. Anna Porter, my publisher, would love for you to buy a copy when it's published late each autumn.

RRSPs are wonderful tools, and it is hugely unfortunate that more Canadians do not avail themselves of the dozens of RRSP strategies that work so well. Others who do contribute faithfully have unwittingly stashed all their money in the wrong kinds of assets—typically GICs—which pay peanuts these days and are likely to perform no better over the next 10 years. Most Canadians, I would suspect, have no idea what an RRSP actually is, thinking it is an actual investment asset itself that you "buy" at the bank or credit union.

But it's not. Instead, it is just a process to use to shelter assets from being taxed. As a bonus, when you put an asset in your registered retirement savings plan, you'll receive a direct deduction of an equal amount from your taxable income.

So, if you earn more than $60,000, for example, and live in New Brunswick, where the tax rate would be 50.4%, for every $5,000 RRSP contribution you make, you will pay $2,520 less in tax. That, in itself, should spur you to dump money in. But it gets better, because that $5,000 will grow completely free of tax until you withdraw the money in retirement. That means growth will exceed that of money invested in nonregistered assets. And remember, you can put whatever you want inside your RRSP, as long as it is self-directed. That includes stocks, investment funds, corporate or strip bonds, mortgages and loads of other things.

I urge you to get a detailed list of winning RRSP strategies. Here is a summary of my top ten:

Top ten RRSP list

(1) Go for the growth

RRSPs are not GICs. RRSPs are instead just mechanisms for sheltering the assets in them from being taxed. So, they work really well when protecting highly taxed assets like strip bonds. For example, a government bond held for 30 years inside an RRSP would give you double the rate of return on the same asset held outside the plan, even assuming you paid the top marginal tax rate when you cashed out the RRSP.

So, rule one is that assets most susceptible to tax should go into your RRSP first. That includes strip bonds, savings bonds, mortgages and GICs. And remember, strips always beat out GICs because the rate is better, there is no risk and you can cash out anytime.

But don't stop there, by any means. Growth investments, even with a lower tax profile than bonds and the like, also belong safely tucked into your RRSP. Especially if you are, like me, a rapidly aging baby boomer, it's essential to have a lot of high-growth assets in your retirement plan. If you do not, if you stick with low-risk, low-return assets like GICs, you stand a very healthy chance of running out of money before you run out of life.

The best growth assets are mutual funds and stocks. If held long enough, I just don't see any significant risk at all in loading up on both. For example, how can investors go wrong buying into the Canadian banks? Despite the failed merger attempts, these are great companies making a ton of money. The financial services sector is clearly a winner now and in the future, so why not buy?

And quality, equity-based mutual funds have a superior track record that will doubtlessly continue after the gyrations of the late 1990s are long gone and forgotten. I have already spelled out here why the millennial years will be great for the financial markets.

But should you worry about a major stock market correction? After all, you cannot claim drops in the value of stocks inside your RRSP as capital losses against other capital gains.

Absolutely not. If you are 50 years of age or younger today, you can stuff your RRSP with quality stocks and funds and sleep at night like a baby. You will not be cashing out for 15 years, so any crashes, corrections, disasters and apocalypses between now and then are little more than intellectual curiosities. It is only the short-term thinkers who do the wrong thing and sell during periods of panic. Long-term geniuses view the panics as great buying opportunities. Go for growth.

(2) Make up missed contributions. Borrow if you have to.

The best tax shelter in North America is the RRSP and only half of Canadians have one. The average amount saved is small, and the numbers are not getting any more encouraging. Why?

Too many middle-class people are slaves to their mortgages, believing the old rules still work, and paying off home debt is the first, best action. Wrong. Forget the mortgage. Just renegotiate it to take advantage of cheap current rates and then pay it every month. Take your extra income and invest it in your RRSP. In fact, go way beyond that and be downright aggressive.

The rules allow you to go back to 1991 and make up every dollar you ever missed in RRSP contributions. Collectively, we have failed to put in well over $200 billion, which is called "contribution room." If we all did the sane and reasonable thing, the federal deficit would explode again because of all the money we'd be paid in tax refunds. For this reason, I fear that Ottawa may eventually disallow your ability to go back and do now what you should have done then. Don't take that chance. Catch up immediately.

How much are you behind?

Ask your financial adviser to find out, or do it yourself. Call Revenue Canada (the number is in the government pages of your phone book, under "Revenue Canada," then "Tax Services," then "TIPS Automated"). Have your social insurance number and last year's tax return handy. Talk to the friendly computer and it will tell you what your current RRSP contribution limit is, along with missed contributions.

Now go and put all that money in, adding on the $2,000 in overcontribution that you are allowed. If you do not have the money, then borrow it. Any financial institution will give you an RRSP loan at prime. Use your tax refund to pay down the loan—which can take care of up to half the indebtedness. Pay the rest off over a couple of years, and put all the money into quality growth assets, like mutual funds, inside your RRSP.

Money is cheap these days. Financial markets have a great future. You can borrow and get half the money back. Your investments will grow free of tax. Can you afford not to do this?

(3) Break from the crowd—contribute at the right time

Every year people line up in the snow to make an RRSP contribution for the year that just ended. No, no, no. This is exactly a year later than you should have done this. Contribute at the beginning of the taxation year, not the end of it.

The rules give you a period of grace—60 days—to get your RRSP money in and still be able to deduct it from the taxes on income you earned in that past year. Over time this grace period has morphed into the only time that people think about RRSPs. In fact, bombarded with zillions of radio, TV and print ads and seminars given by people like me, this has become "RRSP season."

You should use all this hype to remind you to contribute for the current year, because you'll be miles ahead getting that extra year's compounding under your belt. Putting in $3,500 at the beginning of the year instead of at the end, in a mutual fund earning 10%, will give you $60,000 more after 30 years.

Yes, that's sixty grand more just for changing the day on which you make your contribution. You did not take on any more risk or invest any more money. You just did the right thing. Also the right thing: contributing monthly. Just set up an automatic withdrawal plan from your bank account and get the money in there on a regular basis. Just like a car loan payment, you won't even notice it after a few months—not until you retire with lots of money.

And there's another reason this makes perfect sense ...

(4) Minimize those payroll taxes

Do you work for a paycheque? Is the thing absolutely decimated by tax by the time you get your hands on it? This strategy can change that.

Federal and provincial income taxes are, by law, deducted from paycheques by employers who have to send in the money (plus their own substantial contributions) every month. You can reduce the tax nicked from you by making monthly RRSP contributions. Here's how:

• Set up monthly contributions to your plan, using pre-authorized withdrawals from your bank account.

• Call the local Revenue Canada office. Ask for Source Deductions. Tell the nice people you want your withholding tax reduced because you're making monthly RRSP contributions. Ask for a Tax Deduction Waiver. In turn they'll ask for your estimated annual income and expected deductions and proof of your RRSP payments.

• RevCan will consider this and, when approved, send the waiver to your employer who will reduce the tax on your cheque. The process takes about a month.

Now you are going to have an increase in cash flow, with a larger cheque every pay period. Take that extra money and do something worthwhile with it—use dollar-cost averaging to buy units in quality mutual funds every month through pre-authorized debits of your bank account, that you will never miss.

Amateurs line up in the snow on the last day of February to get a break on taxes they have already shelled out.

Those serious about success don't. They contribute earlier, get more compounding on their assets, enjoy more after-tax income and end up with a lot more wealth.

(5) Take shameless advantage of your spouse

Yes, income-splitting. It's essential now and will get even more important in the years to come as seniors are sitting ducks for zealous tax collectors. A spousal RRSP is the best and easiest way of making sure that too much retirement income does not end up in the hands of one taxpayer.

Contribute as much as you want, up to your own limit, claim the tax break and the assets go into your spouse's name. After three years, the money can be taken out at his or her lower rate. The object, however, is to even out the assets held in both your names, so that in retirement your overall tax load is reduced.

Today, unfortunately, most seniors pay a lot more in tax than they need to, because they did not actively income-split in past decades. If you want a better quality of life, do it. Now.

(6) Make that overcontribution

The rules allow you to shovel $2,000 more into your RRSP than you'd think. Do this, too, before Ottawa changes its mind and disallows the action.

You will not get a tax deduction for making this move, so most people don't. But it makes sense because the extra $2,000 will grow tax-free and become much more over the years to come. Also, these are the days of no employer loyalty. You could get canned at any time, so carrying around an extra couple of thousand in your RRSP is a good idea because should you be laid off and don't have enough earned income next year to make an RRSP contribution, this will come in handy. You can make a claim against your taxable income at that time.

Or, if you have a dependent child aged 19 or older, the overcontribution can be made in his or her name if the child does not have earned income. By age 59 the $2,000 could have grown by 40 times.

(7) Load up on foreign content

Most people think only 20% of your RRSP can be foreign content. Wrong. You can vastly exceed that and, for reasons spelled out in the last chapter, you should.

Invest in mutual funds that hold other funds with foreign content and bump the content level of your plan up to 36%. Invest in units of labour-sponsored venture capital funds and receive not only generous tax credits but also the ability to put three dollars into foreign content for every buck into the labour fund, to a 40% maximum. Or, invest in foreign index funds, which are based on derivatives (that sounds scarier than it really is), and achieve 100% foreign content.

As I write this, there is still a separatist government in power in the province of Quebec. That should worry everybody.

(8) Invest without cash

Not having any money to make your RRSP contribution is not a valid excuse. You have two powerful options.

First, as mentioned, you can borrow to contribute, and you should. RRSP loans are plentiful and come at the prime rate. Many lenders will even suspend payments until you get your tax refund, which can be applied directly against the loan principal.

Absolutely ignore frequent media advice to avoid borrowing.

Another great way to load up your RRSP without cash is to make what's known as a "contribution in kind." This wonderful rule allows you to take assets you currently own (could be a GIC, mutual fund, bond, etc.) and to use them, instead of cash, to make contributions to your retirement plan. These are assets that are currently subject to tax, but the moment you move them into your RRSP, they start growing tax-free. (Be aware, however, that some assets, like mutual funds, which have grown in value, may trigger tax on that capital gain when moved into your plan).

This is a great strategy to use to catch up on missed contributions, and it should be a standard operating procedure for people who want to reduce the tax exposure on existing assets. Just open a self-directed plan and then move things in every year. The kicker: Ottawa considers a contribution in kind to be just like a cash contribution, which means you can deduct the value of the asset from your taxable income—getting a tax refund for selling yourself assets you already owned!

(9) Be your own bank

Yes, you can act like a banker, and have the mortgage on your house held by your own RRSP. That way you are actually making regular payments into your retirement plan instead of into your banker's pocket. This is neat idea because you will be steadily diverting a hunk of your income stream into your RRSP, and you can actually exceed the annual RRSP contribution limits with an RRSP mortgage.

Now, be warned—it is complicated and costs about a thousand dollars to arrange and then a few hundred each year to administer. You'll likely need a financial adviser to help you set it up properly. You will also need to have a lot of cash, or liquid assets, inside your RRSP—enough, that is, to replace the existing mortgage on your home. (Remember that unless your mortgage term is about to end, you might face discharge penalties from your existing lender.)

You also need a self-directed RRSP. Your plan then forwards enough money to pay off your existing mortgage and replaces it with a new one, taking title to your home. Now you will be making your mortgage payments into your RRSP. Is this a way to get a really cheap mortgage rate?

Nope, because Revenue Canada says the rate needs to be similar to current commercial rates. Besides, you don't want a cheap mortgage! If possible, you want an expensive one. Why? Because your RRSP is acting like your bank used to—it wants to get as much of your money as possible in mortgage interest. Only this time, you are paying all that interest to yourself, so a high mortgage rate is to your own advantage. You'll find a lot more detail on this in my real estate book, *The Strategy*.

You have to insure your RRSP mortgage, which costs a few bucks, and also you have to qualify for it financially, based on your income, just the way you do at the bank. Additionally, the whole thing has to be administered by an unrelated lender, like a trust company. Miss any of these rules, and your RRSP mortgage will be disqualified by Revenue Canada. Or, if you can't make the payments to your own mortgage, ownership of your home will go to your retirement plan. But since RRSPs can't own real estate, it will have to be sold.

There is an obvious hassle factor here, but for aggressive RRSP investors, holding a mortgage on your own home is one of the coolest experiences you can have.

(10) Making the most of a layoff

One theme of this book is that working for large companies in an era of zero employer loyalty is truly dangerous. Another theme is that you are almost always better off on your own, being an entrepreneur, carving your own way through the jungle.

Your RRSP can help you a lot when corporate troubles strike. If you are laid off, the tax bite on your precious severance package can be minimized by using your plan. You are allowed to roll over quite a bit of money into your RRSP without paying any tax. Here's the formula: $2,000 for each year you worked prior to 1996 (partial years count as full ones), plus another $1,500 for each year you worked prior to 1989 that you were not part of the company's pension plan.

Then, you can add in all the unused contribution room you have had from past years, and use that to shelter more of your package. Always remember, it is too late to do any of this after you have taken a cheque. Make sure all the arrangements are done ahead of time. So, let's say you get a package worth $40,000, and you have worked for your employer for the past 11 years. Since 1991, you have missed making $27,000 in RRSP contributions. Here's what you can shelter:

Severance package	$40,000
	————
Roll-over (six years, 1996-2000 times $2,000 each)	$12,000
Add unused room	$27,000
	————
Total	$37,000
Taxable portion of package	$ 3,000

Of course, with the 1996 cut-off date, you are not building up any new roll-over room now. And people just entering the workforce will have no ability to do this, other than using their unused contribution room. But for longer-term workers, it's a big help.

If you need money after doing the roll-over to live on, take it from your RRSP in small amounts. The tax on withdrawals of $5,000 or less is just 10% (21% in Quebec), and 20% for amounts up to $15,000 (30% in Quebec).

Some good news: a recent federal budget gives taxpayers a chance to recover lost RRSP contribution room if you were in a company pension plan and subject to the pension adjustment calculation. That means you can roll over your lump-sum pension payments into your RRSP and the lost RRSP room will be restored, minus the amount of the lump sum.

Commuted lump-sum value

Finally, if you are taking early retirement, and are offered the choice of having a locked-in plan with a defined pension in the future, or of taking your own accumulated pension contributions (called the commuted lump-sum value), take the money! You and your adviser will almost always be able to make it grow a lot faster.

For example, your package may offer you a $20,000 annual pension at age 65, or a commuted lump sum of $70,000. Which should you take? Well, if you invest that money in a locked-in retirement account (LIRA) for 20 years and get a 10% return, it will grow into enough ($470,000) to give you an annual pension of $37,600, an improvement of almost 100%.

Better yet, when you leave this vale of tears, you estate inherits the LIRA, which keeps chugging on, whereas the pension, if you'd taken it, would have expired along with you. Your spouse will certainly appreciate that.

Tax strategies: In conclusion

This small chapter gives nothing but a sampling of the ways in which you can lessen your punishing tax load, shift income to others, improve your retirement situation and have more cash to spend and invest. If you want to know more, get your hands on one of the excellent and inexpensive tax guides published by the major accounting firms, like Grant Thornton's *Smart Tax Tips* (published by Turnerbooks).

Also, and better yet, deal with a financial adviser. Tax planning only really works best when it goes hand in hand with investment and estate planning. In the future, things are going to get more complicated, not less. And each year shortens the time you have remaining to prepare for what is coming.

Investment Strategies

THE ARGUMENT

There are seven steps to successful investing. Do not delay in taking them, to find financial peace.

Like most people in his generation, unfortunately like too many people today, my father never invested in anything, except his house. Stocks are a gamble, he'd say. He scorned people who bought lottery tickets, too. Instead, he saved. It was a winning strategy.

Today, that's a formula for personal financial disaster. If you have the bulk of your net worth in residential real estate; if you have tried to protect and safeguard your money by putting it in guaranteed investments; if you are a cautious and prudent person who shuns risk, you are likely in serious trouble. And if you are the typical Canadian, you don't even realize it.

Archie was smart, or lucky, to invest in his house, because it was a rising commodity in inflationary times. It was enough to save his money because interest rates were reasonably high, and besides, he had the big, indexed pension coming. As long as he stuck with his career and stayed out of debt, how could he lose?

And he didn't. He scored.

Today, all the rules have changed. Deflation and demographics are the enemies of real estate. There is no guarantee of keeping any job long enough to build up pension assets. Interest rates have collapsed, so savers are losers. Life expectancy is marching cruelly higher, vastly increasing the amount of money that people need to sustain decent lives. Today you have absolutely no option but to invest. None.

Meanwhile, the financial tensions that Canadians feel are clearly close to a breaking point. A survey released as the old millennium ended, by the Canadian Council on Social Development, had some shocking findings on how insecure people feel.

- 30% of Canadians believe they will lose their jobs in the next few years.

- In the case of job loss, 40% believe they could not find equivalent work within six months.

- The average household balance sheet is a mess. Negligible savings. Big debt.

- A third of people could only last one month on their savings in the event of job loss.

I cannot imagine Archie, in 1962, feeling the same tensions nor the same lack of confidence in either the economy or the future. But today, because so many people, boomers and GenXers alike, have done the wrong things with their personal and financial lives—playing by the old rules that no longer work—this fear and insecurity is all around us. You can see it in road rage. It's there in random violence and home invasions. It's the mom in the minivan giving you the finger. The man yelling at the bank machine. There is palpable anger, frustration and disbelief at what is happening around us by those who have yet to learn, and live by, the new rules.

How to Find Financial Peace

But investing does not mean gambling. Done the right way, it can be a rewarding, relaxing, comforting experience. It can lead you to financial peace, just at a time in a decade or two when few around you will have any peace at all. It is not difficult. It does not need to be risky. It is not mysterious nor complicated. All you have to do, as an investor, is understand the basics, determine your goals, and then work with professionals to see they are accomplished.

Indeed, the very first step in this process of finding peace is deciding what it is you want. It might be wealth and a lavish lifestyle. A trophy home or a Boxster. It could be financial independence, and the freedom to travel or paint and not worry about cash flow. It might be gaining the financial muscle to let you be creative and start a business, give people jobs and do interesting things with your days. It might be, as it was with me, an overwhelming desire to simply have the necessary money to control your own life.

I have been there.

In 1988, I quit my job as a newspaper editor and columnist, sold my business interests and my commercial real estate and ran for Parliament. My media colleagues were shocked. Unexpectedly, I won and spent the next five and a half years as an MP, and subsidizing my salary with my savings (as most MPs find they have to do). In 1993, I rolled the dice and became one of five candidates in a federal leadership race. Of course, I lost, and that took more money. A lot of it. By the end of that year, after an election that all but wiped out the federal PC party, I found myself without a seat in Ottawa, without a job, without a pension, without prospects, without much money and with two houses, both in the wrong cities.

I determined several things at that point:

• Nobody would ever again have the ability to throw me out of work.

• From then on, forever, I would create my own opportunities.

• My goal would shift from public service to personal financial independence.

• I would never apologize for wanting wealth, or pursuing it.

Over the last few years, I have stuck to those determinations. Early on in the process, Dorothy and I met for the first time with a financial adviser, after always handling our own affairs. We have not looked back since. We learned how to harness investment bonds, stocks and mutual funds. We learned about diversification and foreign markets; about sheltering income and deferring taxes. We have made the right decisions about real estate, and resisted the faddish investments that so many people have come to regret. Not everything has worked, but enough has.

The difference between the years when I was preoccupied in Ottawa, and the years since, has been dramatic. Maybe you are like the old Garth in those few years. It used to be that I just collected my paycheque, tried to meet household expenses, missed making RRSP contributions, put my money to sleep in the bank and thought nobody could take care of my affairs better than me. I treated financial institutions with suspicion, had deep reservations about mutual funds, kept the bulk of my net worth in bricks and mortar and hoped I'd be able to hang on to my job long enough to get a pension. After all, at age 45, I knew I was becoming unemployable. I was going nowhere. Trapped. A victim of my own bad judgment and my busy life.

Then, in the space of a few hours, what I had was suddenly gone. At six o'clock on election day I was a federal Cabinet minister with a staff, responsibilities and a sense of worth. At nine o'clock I was nobody. The next morning Dorothy and I got in the car and drove as far away as possible. We sat in a coffee shop a few cities away. "Now what?" she asked. I was overwhelmed with the thought that she had just spent years following me around the country, putting up with endless political criticism, seeing our reserves depleted and suffering the sting of defeat at my side, smiling on the outside for the photographers who really wanted to see a few tears.

I had no answer for her.

As it turned out, that defeat was a mid-life wakeup call. Thank goodness I listened to it, and learned, and took action. I sincerely hope your call to action comes with less trauma than mine did, but I know for increasing numbers of people in this rapidly evolving economy it will be just the same. Everyone so impacted must heed the new rules and employ them with passion.

The two reasons why most people are failing:

(1) Apathy and neglect

Golfers spend time practising. Doctors and mechanics are constantly learning the latest technology. Business owners plan months in advance so they can meet payroll and tax obligations. But when these same people come face to face with their own financial futures, they fail. Most of us are failing. The numbers could not spell it out any more clearly: No savings. Debt equal to income. No adequate retirement funds. Eighty per cent, no financial plan. Almost 90% do not know that bonds go up when interest rates go down. Two-thirds believe mutual funds are covered by federal deposit insurance. God knows how many people think the "guarantee" on their segregated funds is effective from the day they buy one.

MONEY IS LIKE WATER

How could we know so little about something so essential? Money is like water. Life does not go on without it. Millions of lives are going to turn sour and sad unless habits change, investors learn what it is they are investing in and Canadians, in general, start paying attention. In the future, remember, you are on your own. Only the destitute will find government support after 2020.

According to a 1999 survey done for Deloitte & Touche by Marketing Solutions, Canadians spend an average of just five hours a year on their personal finances. Five hours a year—equal to a night of watching television, or sitting through a Blue Jays game. It is a sad indictment of society, and a portent of disasters to come. I strongly suggest that you take actions now to shelter yourself, by acquiring knowledge and enough wealth to ensure financial independence.

That was precisely my game plan in the spring of 1994. I devoured the Income Tax Act and every financial planning book I could get my hands on. I pored over the research documents published by the brokerage firms. I sought out and interviewed successful investors, wise advisers and seasoned entrepreneurs. I took all the money I had, in all the wrong places, and established a portfolio, started buying bonds, stocks and investment funds in an account watched over by an industry professional.

Today I have my freedom. I intend on keeping it.

(2) Bad information

The second reason people are failing financially is the quality of information they are exposed to. In the mass media it is a consistent regurgitation of the old rules that my father lived and profited by. As I have tried to show in this book, those rules no longer apply. They are, in fact, dangerous.

Let me give you an example. Here are the top tips to order your financial life, published by one of the country's largest and most respected daily newspapers:

• Develop a comprehensive financial plan. Review your will, RRSPs and other savings.

• Pay off high-interest consumer debt.

• Maximize your RRSP contribution.

• Set aside funds for children's education.

• Accelerate mortgage repayment.

• Start a savings plan such as payroll deduction plan for Canada Savings Bonds.

• Estimate your taxes and start tax planning.

• Develop or review investment strategies.

Clearly, some of those tips are common sense. High-interest debt should be repaid and RRSP contributions maxed out, and obviously a good investment strategy is essential. But in the above list are the seeds of failure. There is no advantage to devoting your cash flow to accelerating the repayment of your mortgage. There is no reason anyone wishing financial freedom would want to save money, especially in the form of a savings bond. Setting aside educational money is a poor alternative to aggressive long-term investing, and as for setting a comprehensive financial plan, that's a job for a professional, not an amateur who spends five hours a year thinking about money.

ARE YOU REALLY SERIOUS ABOUT SUCCEEDING?

Then you must break out of the information rut that most people are in. Take those all-important steps to educate yourself. Use the Internet as a profound research tool. Buy and read at least one of the major accounting firm's annual tax guides. Attend financial seminars whenever they're held in your area. Read more books like this one. Subscribe to a newsletter or two. Read the advice of columnists in the business press, like the *Financial Post* section of the *National Post* or the *Globe and Mail's Report on Business*, but never follow it without getting professional advice. Some of it is just wrong. Some is brilliant. Study the research turned out by the big brokerage companies like:

* RBC Dominion Securities
(http://www.rbcds.com/english/online/corporate/index)

* ScotiaMcleod
(http://www.scotiacapital.com/English/Research/Economics)

* Merrill Lynch
(http://www.canada.ml.com/research/index.html)

* Green Line Investor Services
http://www.tdbank.ca/tdbank/Greenline/english/rs.html

In short, devote some time to your own future. Do what most people are not doing: learn what the big economic and financial trends are, and then make sure you are positioned to take advantage of them. Now, take these steps:

The seven steps to successful investing

(1) Cash in your savings

Saving money is a dangerous and unproductive thing to do. It gives false security. This means you should not have *any* money in any of these "investments":

* Bank savings accounts

* Term deposits

- Guaranteed Investment Certificates (GICs)

- Canada Savings Bonds

- Government treasury bills (T-bills).

The reason is clear: interest rates have collapsed and will stay at historic low levels for years to come. That means even with modest inflation near the 1% mark that, after taxes, these vehicles give you essentially no return whatsoever. Inside a tax shelter, such as an RRSP, you will escape the debilitating effect of taxes, but at the same time largely squander the opportunity of rapidly growing your asset.

Remember: the greatest threat that most Canadians face is simply not having enough wealth. So, putting what you do have in assets that yield virtually nothing—as a tradeoff for being "safe"—is a losing strategy. Unfortunately, millions of Canadians have hundreds of billions of dollars in near-cash investments such as these. The greatest amount of money has in fact been deposited by those the most at risk—people over the age of 50.

Some people worry about not having a cash reserve to draw upon in times of adversity. Older people are the most prone to this, and often keep tens of thousands of dollars in daily interest savings accounts earning them less than 1% a year. What a waste that is. This money could be building them a security blanket of more wealth if they did the right thing— invest the cash and get a line of credit instead, to access when something goes wrong.

Don't let this fuzzy thinking infect you. Cash in your non-performing savings assets. Open a personal line of credit. If you never draw upon it, there's nothing to repay and usually no standby fees. Then turn your savings into investments.

And make sure those are true investments, not just savings vehicles in disguise, such as GICs that are linked to stock market performance. These can be very deceptive, but that has not prevented billions from finding its way there.

Linked GICs began to appear as interest rates plunged and depositors, worried about low returns, started cashing in their investment certificates.

This phenomenon hit hard in 1994-95, and many Canadians—completely ignorant of what they were doing—plunked large amounts of money into mortgage and bond funds, thinking they would act like mortgages and bonds, giving a steady yield with no downside. But when interest rates shot higher again (temporarily, as it turned out), those bond and mortgage funds dropped sharply in value (they move in the opposite direction to interest rates). The "GIC refugees" were horrified. Many of them immediately cashed in their funds, which locked in their losses, and went back into cash. Losers, twice over.

Enter linked GICs. These new bank products promised no downside (like mutual funds) and yet an upside (because the yield was linked to stock market performance). That attracted a lot of interest, and a lot of money. Sadly, I have heard 30-year-olds praise linked GICs because, "How can you go wrong?"

Well, you can. Anything that comes with a guarantee of no risk also comes with a price, and linked GICs are no exception. Here's how: Buy a $1,000 GIC with a three-year term. The return is based on a stock market index, like the TSE 100, using a market participation rate that will give you a slice of market gains. That may sound appealing, but beware of the hidden problems:

• The market participation rate could be quite misleading. For example, if the stock index rose by 50% over three years, don't expect the return on your GIC to soar. Many banks take an average of closing levels for the market over a long period of time, rather than the actual market level on the day your GIC matures. This can quickly drag the performance level, and your rate of return, lower.

• If markets do not rise over the period you own the GIC, your return could be zero. Most linked GICs do not have a base rate of interest.

• The index chosen to base the return on could be an underachiever. Check its history.

• There could be caps placed on the maximum returns that the GIC can give you.

> ## Rule: Guarantees are very expensive
>
> Are there places to keep wealth liquid that offer a better rate of return and more flexibility? Certainly, there are, including money market strips, provincial savings bonds, money market funds and government commercial paper. For complete details, see my 1998 book, *The Defence*. But for long-term investors who are serious about preparing for life 15 or 20 years from now, these are not viable options. You do not want to save your money. You must invest it.

(2) Invest now

Once you accept the premise that saving is wrong and investing is right, you might be tempted to hedge your bets by investing in a way that will help mitigate market volatility. This is especially the case in years of incredible swings. On the day I am writing this, the Dow Jones Industrials leapt to a 100-point gain before noon, and were down 260 points by mid-afternoon. Expect more of this. In fact, the days are ahead when markets could swing by 1,000 points in a single trading session. The media will watch in fascination. CNBC will cover it with a special icon at the bottom of the TV screen, something like, "Death battle" with a bull and bear locked in mortal combat. Ignore it all.

But short-term thinkers worry about this, and they are surrounded by a sea of bad advice on how to deal with volatile times.

• A GIC is still a GIC, which means in almost all cases your money is locked up and uncashable over a fixed period of time.

• The return you get is considered by Revenue Canada to be interest, not a capital gain, so it is taxed more heavily. This means the after-tax return on a linked GIC can be terrible compared with a similar performance delivered by a mutual fund.

• You will also be taxed every year on the return the GIC has recorded, even though you did not receive any of the money during that taxation year. This is the curse of many fixed-income investments. In contrast, you would pay no tax on the capital gain earned by a stock that went up in value until you sold it, and crystallized that gain.

I use linked GICs as an example of a sheep investment in wolf's clothing. It looks powerful and aggressive on the outside, and inside it's mush. The price people pay for the perceived benefit of safety is large indeed, including a poor rate of return and a daunting tax bill. Cash and near-cash investments (commonly know as savings) are no place to keep any significant amount of wealth—certainly not in the long term.

TIMING THE MARKET

The most common and popular advice is that your actions should be guided by what the market is doing now, or what it's likely to do in the next few days, weeks, or months. This is called timing the market, and it is almost always a losing strategy. But pick up any business magazine or business section of a daily newspaper, and the cult of market timing is in your face.

Commentators go on forever about the market being overvalued or undervalued, and ready for a correction. Acres of trees are sacrificed so worried investors can read meaningless short-term forecasts based on monetary and fiscal policy, profit projections and tea leaves. I have read columns warning of "panic selling" and "panic buying" in the same newspaper within days of each other.

Ignore it all. Invest now. Invest whatever you have in quality stocks, mutual funds and bonds, regardless of what interest rates might do or the perceived market momentum. The only way to succeed is to be into these financial assets over the long term—decades, not months. If you try to time the market you will probably fail, not recognizing where the peaks and valleys were until long after they have passed.

I cannot recount the number of times people who have attended financial seminars I have given across Canada have asked me if they should wait until the market crashes, to put in money. They asked me that question when the Dow hit 4,000 in 1995. I said, don't wait. It was asked again when the market hit 7,000, then 9,000, and I said, don't wait. When the Dow hit 10,000 in the spring of 1999, there was something akin to an investing crisis in Canada. Mutual fund sales took a 40% dive and the flow of money into guaranteed investments, like segregated funds, exploded. Millions of investors had turned into short-term thinkers, and were trying to time the market. I said, don't wait.

In fact, it is something I will keep on saying for years, until sometime between 2010 and 2015, when negative demographics in North America could seriously imperil the markets. Naturally, I expect corrections between now and then, with a rapid decline erasing a third of the market's value at any time. But those will be temporary events. That loss will be regained in months, perhaps weeks, because the economic fundamentals of North America are solid and will stay so. The only losers then will be the sellers —the ones who fall for the media's myopic interpretation of events. The ones who hang on will lose nothing. The market timers will not know what happened until it the train has left the station.

DOLLAR-COST AVERAGING

Another device the timid investor may be tempted to use is dollar-cost averaging. This was made popular by bestselling author David Chilton, whose landmark book, *The Wealthy Barber*, championed this strategy. That was one of the books I gobbled in the weeks following my own election defeat. Chilton, I should take some care to spell out, considers me to be aggressive when it comes to investment strategies, and has told me so in no uncertain terms. He was alarmed by certain aspects of my book on the wisdom of borrowing against residential real estate, *The Strategy*—a work I stand by today without reservation.

Chilton's unbridled success in Canada is well earned, and is also a reflection of the national psyche—risk-averse, cautiously positive and pedantic. Unfortunately, with most people's finances in a ruinous state, and with the entire Canadian society headed for a nasty retirement show-down, this is not the time for caution. Nor for dollar-cost averaging.

It works like this: commit a certain amount of money every month to the purchase of mutual fund units. In those months when the unit value fluctuates higher, your money buys fewer of them. Conversely, when values fall, you are able to afford more. Over the course of years you average the cost of those units, and avoid the potential of having bought in at too high a price.

It sounds incredibly reasonable. So why would I recommend against it? Simply because most people who are like me—in their late forties or early fifties—cannot afford the luxury of time. We need to be fully invested now in a hard-working diversified portfolio, not dripping a little cash into financial assets each month. In fact, given what lies ahead over the next 10 or 12 years, it's hard to think who would benefit from dollar-cost averaging. Young investors today, in their twenties and thirties, also have a limited time to bulk up their assets before the harsh times set in. They cannot afford to be deer in the headlights, either. Only investors a few years from retirement might be wise to follow Chilton's advice.

Finally, think about the wisdom of dollar-cost averaging over the years since *The Wealthy Barber* was first published. The Dow advanced by 600% between 1985 and 1999. So, $50,000 invested fully in 1984 and just ignored would have turned into $300,000. The same $50,000 invested at $300 a month during that 15-year period would be worth less than half at the end.

Rule: Being cautious carries a huge cost

TRACKING YOUR INVESTMENTS

Do you worry day-to-day about the value of your house? After all, its worth is constantly affected by the movement of mortgage rates, by shifting traffic patterns, construction, zoning bylaw changes and who your neighbours are. Despite that, most people only really think hard about what their home is worth when they contemplate selling it.

The same logic should apply to financial assets, like stocks, bonds and investment funds. They are long-term buys, just like your house. Ignore what their current value is.

I know this is hard. It runs against human nature. And in the short-term world around us, where the newspapers publish listings every single day of mutual fund values, it's tough to maintain your long-term focus. But you must. Don't look up your fund holdings every day. Don't even read the monthly or quarterly lists of the best-performing funds. You might be tempted to switch back and forth, incurring penalties while you chased last month's performance.

If you are compulsive about your portfolio, however, then check it in a more consistent and disciplined manner. I'd suggest using the excellent (and free) portfolio tracking service offered by The Fund Library (www.fundlibrary.com). But even if you sign on for that, resist the urge to log on and count your wealth every few hours. You'll go nuts, and make mistakes.

(3) Don't chase guarantees

Over the last few years, with the population aging and becoming more risk-sensitive, as stock markets flirt with new highs and in the wake of some violent market corrections that traumatized novice investors, funds that offer guarantees have become all the rage. Currently, of the over 2,000 investment funds Canadians can choose from, for example, almost half are segregated funds.

Seg funds are mutual funds with a guarantee that you will get most, or all, of your money back in the future, no matter what stock markets do. They are one of a number of fund categories growing in popularity. Here are the differences between them.

PROTECTED FUNDS

These funds offer you 100% capital guarantees but do not have other features of segregated funds, like protection from creditors. They are considered to be investment funds, rather than insurance products so they can be purchased from institutions and advisers that do not hold insurance licences.

The first major institution out with protected funds was the Bank of Commerce. Its protected index funds proved to be big winners during the first RRSP season they were available, offering a relatively short five-year guarantee. That means investors can count on getting all their money back, regardless of market performance, five years after making the investment.

Other companies, such as Dynamic Mutual Funds and the National Bank, offer protected funds with a 10-year guarantee, but with the feature of returning the capital to your beneficiary if you die before the 10 years are up.

GUARANTEED INVESTMENT FUNDS

This is a variation on segregated funds, guaranteeing you either 75% or 100% of your capital back after a decade. GIFs were pioneered by Manulife Financial in 1997, and have been quickly adopted by many other major players, including BPI, C.I., Templeton, Trimark and the Toronto Dominion Bank.

With GIFs you get a traditional mutual fund wrapped in the cloak of an insurance product. So, besides the 10-year guarantee, the investor also gets a professional fund manager, creditor protection and the ability to pass the money along to a beneficiary in the event of death.

SEG-FUND WRAPS

These are hybrids that combine segregated funds with mutual fund wrap portfolios—in which your money is allocated to various kinds of assets according to your risk profile and financial goals. An example is the Synchrony portfolios launched in 1998 by Talvest Fund Management and Maritime Life. These appeal to investors who want all their eggs in one basket, but yet to have diversification and come with a no-loss guarantee over 10 years.

SEGREGATED FUNDS

At first blush, they sound too good to be true. Mutual funds that will pace the growth of the markets, and yet never lose you money. That feature has resulted in explosive growth in seg funds, and predictions are that Canadians will place about $100 billion here within a few dozen months.

However, many people have no clear reason to be investing in segregated funds other than this: fear. And while seg funds are ideal for some investors, for the majority of people now buying them, they are not.

First, let me explain what is making these funds so hot: they are pools of money invested by professional managers in the same kinds of assets as mutuals—Canadian, American and global equities, bonds, REITs, royalty trusts, and so on. BPI, for example, offers 11 funds, including Canadian

Equity, Global Balanced, Income and Growth, Dividend Income, T-Bill, Canadian Bond and Canadian Mid-Cap funds. Trimark and Investors Group, among others, adhere to a "fund-on-fund" concept by investing the seg fund net assets directly in the units of corresponding family mutual funds—international equity, Canadian equity, balanced or fixed-income, for example. This means many investors in those mutual funds will be tempted to switch to the seg fund holding the same assets, but now giving a guarantee of no losses. The cost of switching will be slightly higher management fees, to pay for that guarantee. But for some investors, it's a reasonable insurance cost.

A segregated fund is an insurance product, originally designed for pension plans, which is why the mutual fund companies offering these have teamed with insurance companies. Seg funds have been available for about 30 years from companies like Great-West Life, Manulife and Canada Life, and they actually operate like insurance policies.

So if you invest in a segregated fund (which is like a 10-year life insurance policy) you are assured of getting your principal back at the end of the term, even if the value of the assets your seg fund has invested in have declined. (And your beneficiaries get it back a lot sooner when you die.)

Conversely, if the value of the assets the fund holds have risen over the 10 years, you get the gain. Segregated funds are known by that name because legislation requires that the money in these funds be held separately (or "segregated") from other assets of the insurer.

The appealing things about segregated funds:

• Your original deposit is guaranteed. After 10 years, you will get back at least the amount you put in.

• If the value of your fund rises, you can lock in that gain. For example, some funds offer a "reset option" letting investors reset the 10-year guarantee to market value at any time, up to four times a year. That secures investment gains without having to redeem the investment (like a mutual fund requires). And the increase is not subject to capital gains tax (remember, this is an insurance policy).

• If you die at any time, the original deposit is also guaranteed. This is regardless of when it happens. For example, if you invest $100,000 in a seg fund and depart three years later, your beneficiary gets $100,000, despite the fact that seven years remain in the term of the investment. It's paid in the form of a death benefit, immediately, without having to wait for the estate to be settled. Of course, your beneficiary will get more than the guaranteed amount if the fund has risen in value by the time of your death. The benefit is paid regardless of the maturity date, but age is a factor. With some funds, for example, the year after the investor turns 75, the death benefit guarantee is reduced to 80%.

• So, they are great for estate planning purposes, because that payment goes directly to the named beneficiaries without probate fees going to the government or executors taking a cut.

• Your estate is assured privacy. Seg fund contracts are not public documents, like mutual fund assets that must go through probate and the courts.

• Segregated funds are largely creditor-proof, which makes them appealing to small-business operators, farmers and other entrepreneurs who could suffer a business reversal. You need to name a parent, child or spouse (or also a grandparent in Quebec) as beneficiary to effect this.

• They can count as foreign content inside your RRSP or RRIF.

• They offer the convenience of mutual funds for making deposits or withdrawals. You can contribute monthly, quarterly or annually through a pre-authorized chequing plan and also arrange to take money out through automatic withdrawals for income.

You can take money out of a seg fund at any time, but withdrawals do serious damage to your guarantee. For example, if you invested $100,000, then took out $25,000 a few years later when the fund had grown to $125,000, you'd be tempted to think the original $100,000 was still guaranteed. But this is not so.

As the original guarantee was for $100,000, the new guaranteed amount would be 20% less, or just $80,000. Of course, you can avoid having the dollar amount of the guarantee reduced this much when making a withdrawal by resetting your guarantee to the higher market value before taking the money out. In this example, resetting the guarantee to $125,000 would restore your original amount at maturity to $100,000 (or 80% of $125,000).

WHY SEG FUNDS ARE NOT FOR EVERYONE

Remember that first rule outlined a few pages ago: Guarantees are very expensive.

• With seg funds, you pay for the guarantee. With GICs, your cost is a very low rate of return. With segregated funds, it's a higher MER (management expense ratio)—and that eats into performance. MERs typically run between about a half and a full point higher than mutual fund fees. Expect to pay the greatest additional management fees on funds with higher risk (global equities, for example), which reflects the increased cost of the guarantee you're getting. This might not sound like much of a premium, but over 10 years it can seriously reduce the growth of your wealth. And remember, the next 10 years are the ones in which you want the maximum rate of return.

• Also, not everyone can buy these funds. Because segregated funds pay out the full amount invested upon death, you may find some companies reluctant to sell units to aged investors who have a higher statistical chance of dying within 10 years.

• Most importantly seg funds offer a guarantee most investors will never need. Over the course of 10 years it is, in my view, about impossible that stock markets will be lower, for all the reasons already spelled out in this book. For that reason, I think investors younger than 65 or 70 years of age should not buy them.

On the other hand, seg funds allow older investors to still get growth and sleep at night. Life expectancy is exploding higher, and we all need that growth to finance 20 to 40 years in retirement. So, segregated funds provide a real exposure to the equity market without the risk of losing capital.

The bottom line: Segregated funds are ideal for older or conservative investors who are afraid of risking their money but still want growth and who are concerned about preserving their estate. They could also be a perfect fit for the self-employed. For 40- or 50-year-old investors, though, with more than 10 years to retirement, seg funds are unnecessarily costly. Go for stocks and mutual funds instead.

Finally, there are concerns that, if stock markets were to take a huge dive, and retain their losses, many segregated funds would not be able to come up with the necessary money to pay back investors—or that such an event would cause a huge increase in the management fees investors pay. Remember that, as with mutual funds, seg funds are not covered by the Canada Deposit Insurance Corporation. The Canadian Institute of Actuaries has shown a leadership role in this field.

(4) Buy stocks and mutual funds

Most Canadians are seriously underweighted when it comes to owning mutual funds, and especially stocks, fearing their volatility and the potential for market declines. If you are between the ages of 25 and 65, this is where most of your net worth should be, at least until the year 2010, with a gradual shift thereafter into investment-grade bonds. How much exposure should you have? As I have written before, why not deduct your age from 120 to get a percentage degree of exposure to these financial assets? It's a rough rule of thumb, but one with some merit.

Are the markets, and mutual funds based upon them, risky?

Actually, no. Not if you approach investing in the right way.

• Buy now, invest for at least five years, better ten years, and shelter as much of your gains as possible from tax.

- Buy quality. Funds and stocks with a track record. Companies with good technology, or good cash flow. Funds with great managers.

- Buy stocks and funds in sectors that have a future, based on what we know about demographics and the shifting nature of the North American population.

- Diversify, so that you do not have too much of your net worth tied up in one stock, one fund or one sector. I'd suggest that for most people with a reasonable portfolio ($200,000 to $1 million), that you put the bulk in mutual funds and the rest in blue-chip stocks.

- Research your buys carefully or, better yet, have an expert do it for you. Stay away from hot tips. Be very careful about putting money into flyers, such as unproven Internet stocks. Some will make you rich, most will make you cry. Don't become a day trader—don't even think about it. Trading on the Internet is fine, and you will save a lot of money doing so with companies like TD Waterhouse, E*Trade, Charles Schwab Canada, Action Direct and others—but make sure you know what you're doing before you start clicking.

- Don't pay too much. Have a look at the kind of earnings-per-share a company has. These multiples (the stock price as a multiple of those earnings per share) will tell you if the company is overvalued or undervalued.

- Always remember that investors can get carried away and turn investing into gambling. Look what happened to Bre-X. Ponder some of the Internet stocks that have soared and then crashed. If you want predictable returns, buy stocks and funds that have a history and are based on solid corporate performance.

- Buy when others are bailing out. History has proven to us, with market declines such as those of 1987, 1997 and 1998, that reversals are temporary and the general direction of the market is higher. With the kind of economic fundamentals that are in place today, and will be with us for the first decade of the new millennium, there is little doubt of what is to come.

Corrections are not times of panic for long-term thinkers. They are times to buy.

• Buy index funds. These are mutual funds that are not actively managed, like equity funds, but which instead simply pace the market by mimicking what the market index does. The management fees on index funds are far less than those of actively managed ones, and most index funds have enjoyed a better performance over the last few years. If what I am predicting over the next 10 years comes to pass, index funds will be a great way to participate in the advance. Index funds, however, typically hold less cash in them than actively managed funds, so they can decline more precipitously when markets take a tumble. Of course, long-term thinkers don't care.

A caution with index funds, however, is this: In rising markets they usually outperform actively managed funds, but in periods of decline, they can fall precipitously. That's because they do not have managers hedging against volatile times with cash reserves or moves into other assets. Index fund investors must have strong stomachs, and a long-term view.

• Maximize your foreign content with derivatives-based investment funds. Most of the opportunity in the world lies outside Canada's borders, and with these funds you can tap into that easily. They are RRSP-eligible, and a great place to put money. Recent winners have been Fidelity International Portfolio, AGF International Group American Growth Class, C.I. International Balanced and Global Boomernomics RSP. No-load fund stars include CIBC U.S. Index RRSP and Green Line US RSP Index.

Of course, whole books on stock and mutual fund investing are on the same shelf this one came from, and you can certainly read them. I have also detailed various stock and fund options in my book, *The Defence*. But the older I get, and the more I learn, the more I realize that any investor with a good basket of blue-chip stocks and a whack of funds with a proven 10-year record, who does aggressive tax planning and is not afraid of leverage, has a huge opportunity to become financially independent. So, do it.

(5) Buy bonds

Not savings bonds, but government and corporate bonds. Investment-grade bonds. A diversified portfolio should include these, and as you age and build up more wealth, bonds provide a steady cornerstone for your holdings. You should buy bonds to lock in a fixed rate of return; to get regular income; and to have the potential of a capital gain, in the (likely) event that interest rates decline.

In the future, beyond 2010 or 2015, bonds could be exactly what the doctor ordered. The economy could face serious problems that the equities market will reflect. The central bankers could have no option but to drop the cost of money a lot more to counter the deflationary effect of an aging population and sliding consumer demand. In that kind of environment, I definitely would want to own a mess of bonds.

You can invest in bonds in several ways.

• A bond mutual fund will give you a professionally managed portfolio of bonds, and there are scores of different funds to consider.

• You can buy a corporate or government bond itself through a broker or full-service financial adviser.

• Or you can buy a strip bond. That's a bond from which the interest portion has been stripped, so it does not pay you income but you buy it at a discount from the value it will have on the day it matures. In the meantime, it is very liquid, and its value will rise if interest rates decline.

A strip bond is a far superior investment to a GIC for a number of reasons. It's cashable anytime, whereas a GIC is locked in. It sells at that discount to face value, so you don't need to tie up as much money to get an identical return. It is risk-free. Government strip bonds are backed by the government's ability to tax—considered to be the greatest guarantee. And, as mentioned, if rates fall, the bond can be sold for a capital gain, which is impossible with a GIC.

With investment bonds that are not stripped, remember that in times of rising interest rates, they will lose value and become less expensive to purchase. Long bonds (maturities can be as long as 30 years) are more volatile than short ones, just as bonds with low yields are more volatile than those with high yields. As the new millennium begins, interest rates are low and in this environment bonds in general are choppy and somewhat unpredictable. That will change in a decade. Keep it in mind.

(6) Diversify, diversify, diversify

Always be diversified. Not too much money in one stock, one fund or one sector of the economy. Most people know that. It's common sense. But those same people routinely keep the bulk of their net worth in one illiquid asset whose value can fluctuate wildly and which can take months to sell—the family home.

This book makes the clear argument that, as I have been saying in other books and on the road for the past few years, this is a bad idea. The long-term future of residential real estate is as dark as the future of financial assets is bright. There will be hot markets and hot cities from time to time, but the general direction of housing values is down. Certain kinds of housing have no future at all.

But real estate is an aphrodisiac asset. When mortgage rates are low and the spring sunshine comes, buyers can emerge by the carload, boosting prices in demand areas. We still take a lot of our identity from our nest, and so people tend to lavish far too much time, attention and money on their houses. We also make the mistake of confusing getting shelter with investing. In the years ahead, with no inflation and an aging population that will rapidly downsize, that confusion will be ended. Many houses will become encumbrances, not money-generators. There are millions of people who do not want to hear that, but it has to be said. Be very careful about how much house you buy, and where it is located.

Meanwhile, I think it is only prudent that you diversity by removing some equity from your real estate and using it to buy the kinds of financial assets I have been mentioning here—good quality stocks and mutual funds. By doing this, you will:

- Be hedging against the future reduced value of your home.

- Build a more diversified and well-balanced asset portfolio.

- Grow your wealth more quickly.

- Earn investment income rather than just sitting on dead equity.

- Get a significant break on your taxes by deducting the interest on the home equity loan.

A great way of making all this work is to set up a systematic withdrawal plan (SWP). You can remove equity from your home, use it to buy financial assets and then remove income from those assets on a regular basis, so the interest on your home equity loan becomes tax-deductible. It's also possible to remove enough money from a SWP to make the interest-only payments on your home loan, so the whole scheme is self-financing.

Meanwhile, your wealth grows as the mutual funds earn capital gains in a rising market.

Investors who have done this over the past five years have gained extraordinarily. But along the way the critics who believe SWPs can be dangerous and inappropriate for a lot of people have been leather-lunged. My enthusiastic support for borrowing against real estate to diversify into financial assets has appalled those who think that risk is all around us.

Here's a typical media comment on this strategy, from *The National Post*: "The real danger is if you've financed a SWP by tapping into the equity in your home. Vancouver-based investment adviser Hans Merkelbach says a 30% or 40% drop in the markets would 'wipe out retirees' home equity and leave them with a staggering loan obligation at the friendly bank.'"

Statements like that can terrify people and keep them clinging to their front porches and their GICs. Unfortunately, it is a lot more scaremongering than fact. In reality, a home equity loan is secured by the home, not the assets purchased with the proceeds of the loan. So, a 30% or 40% drop in the markets would only affect those people who panicked, sold their financial assets at a 30% or 40% loss and could not repay all of the home equity loan with the proceeds. In that case, they would be left with a home equity loan equal to the market loss. If the loan had been for $50,000, on the typical Canadian home worth $150,000, and the market dropped 40% (and the SWP was liquidated), the homeowner could be left with a home equity loan of $20,000 to repay. That may be a lot of money, but it's not "staggering" and the homeowner is left with $130,000 in equity—hardly "wiped out."

The investor would also have a capital loss that could be used to offset capital gains, equal to the size of the outstanding loan balance.

More typically, however, is that nobody in their right mind would sell assets in a SWP during a 40% market decline. The market would eventually recover (as it has every time since the Great Depression), and in the meantime the homeowner has continued to enjoy the tax-deductibility of the home equity loan interest.

So, be very wary of this kind of overstatement found so often in the Canadian media. It may appeal to our cautious and risk-averse nature, but it will invariably lead you down the wrong path—the one that most of your friends and neighbours are on.

MOST PEOPLE CANNOT ACCEPT THIS

The notion of tapping into home equity and using a systematic withdrawal plan for either income in retirement or to make interest payments on the borrowing will, I assure you, continue to be controversial. This is because most people cannot accept that the old rules are so clearly dead. They do not want to believe all that money they have put into real estate is at risk. They may not realize they are decades behind in building liquid wealth because they devoted years and years to simply paying down the mortgage.

They are not confident about the economy or the future. They warn in one breath of a return to 1970s-style debilitating inflation, and in the next breath whisper that a rerun of the 1929 crash and the deflationary 1930s is at hand. They fear what is to come—whatever it is.

The new rules have no place for fear, certainly not for the next decade and more. Given where most people are today, without aggressive investment and tax strategies, they will fail.

Can the real risk be any more obvious?

(7) Don't do it alone. Educate yourself.

If you are willing to quit your job and study financial planning for a year or so, then go ahead and map out your own financial future and make your own investment and tax decisions. If not, hire an adviser.

Today it is hard enough just finding and keeping a job, keeping your relationship alive and your kids in skates and computer games. How can you make rational decisions about 2,000 investment funds, hundreds of stocks and bonds, royalty trusts and all the other investment choices that exist? It's impossible. You can't. Just like you can't fix your car anymore. And you shouldn't even try.

Sure, read books like this, and you will know more about what to ask, what to request and what to demand. Get a master game plan. Decide how much wealth you will need, and how aggressive you're going to be in getting it. But then, to implement that plan and advise you on the best way of achieving your goals, you need a financial mechanic.

In my own life, I would not dream of making my own stock and mutual fund decisions. I do not do my own tax planning. I do not trade securities on the Internet. Why? Because as much as I know about the subject of money, I know people who know more. And when it comes to my own wealth, I want the best.

The most important financial decision you can make is the one to get help. I have some suggestions in the final pages to come.

Generational Strategies

**Sample courses of action to help you prosper,
and protect what you have, from age 20 to 70**

In the future, expect intergenerational warfare. An army of aging and largely unprepared baby boomers will have expectations that neither government nor the taxpayers of the day will be able to satisfy. That army will find little, if any, sympathy from their children and grandchildren.

Already the lines between generations are thickening. In a rapidly changing world, when it comes to financial survival and success, one size does not fit all.

Financial plans are like snowflakes and fingerprints—no two are, or should be, alike. There can be many similarities between plans—sometimes the only difference is something quite subtle—but every person and/or family unit has highly specific, and quite individual, requirements and goals.

Nowhere is this difference more noticeable than between these generations. Every age group has its own demands particular to that stage of life. And yet, for all the generational differences, there are many common strategies and outlooks no matter what age group you belong to.

Advice from a national panel

To get a grasp of what you should be doing at a particular phase of your life when it comes to essential financial planning, I created several scenarios representing the various generations, from those in their twenties to those in their sixties. Then I sought the input of financial advisers from across Canada.

I had them assess the various financial situations that these people—individuals and couples—found themselves in, and then tell me what they thought. Were these people on the right path? What were they doing right or wrong? What should they be doing and what should they definitely not be doing? And I asked for suggestions on what these people could do to ensure that they do not squander the opportunities for financial security.

As mentioned, no one financial plan fits all. But, from the information assembled, you may be able to relate to, and act upon, certain situations that are relevant to your current circumstances. As well, you should find it helpful to incorporate some of the suggestions on what you should be focusing on during this particular time of your life.

A competent financial adviser is a must

As I have said many times before, don't try to put any financial strategies into play without consulting a reputable, qualified, independent financial planner. He or she will have the skills and expertise to ensure you get your financial life on track. It is a vital step in your life.

If you would like some suggestions of financial advisers to speak with in your area, contact me at www.garth.ca

The transient twenties

I usually recommend that you only buy (a house) if the cost is going to be the same as your rental cost, and you have the cash.

SUSAN NIELSEN

INVESTORS GROUP

The number one problem that people under 30 face is having too much non-tax-deductible debt.

DAVID MORSE

MIDLAND WALWYN

Andrea

There was a time when young people just couldn't wait to leave home. That may still be the case for many, but fewer of them are doing so these days. Though some will leave, they often return after a short stint experiencing the inherent rigours of the real world. The convenience and economics of this re-nester syndrome began with the recession in the early 1990s and despite the subsequent economic turnaround for business and more job opportunities, many young adults have elected to board with mom and dad. Especially if they have other financial goals such as saving enough cash for long-term travel plans, or perhaps one day owning their own home or starting up a business.

Statistics show that more young adults, between the ages of 20 and 34, are living with their parents now than at any other time in the past decade and a half. As of the last census in 1996, 56% of unmarried men and 47% of unmarried women were living with a parent or parents. Just like Andrea.

A stable job that she hates

She is single, just turned 25, and earns $26,000 a year in a relatively secure secretarial job that she hates. Like many other young single people in Ottawa, she is living with her parents, and pays them about $75 weekly board money. What Andrea would like to be is an entrepreneur, but she has no capital. And she is hoping that by living at home she may be able to amass enough to become her own boss.

Although she has reduced her monthly living expenses by living with her folks, she still has some other costs to take care of. There is some student debt to pay, about $150 a month for the next 20 months, and she needs a reliable car to get to work. As such, she owns a 1991 sub-compact, which is paid for, but does run up the odd serious repair bill. She also has to spend some money on clothing throughout the year.

Even though she's just a few years out of school, she has started thinking about RRSPs and financial security—she has some unused RRSP contribution room—and is toying with the idea of generating extra income with a home-based Internet business.

Although Andrea has a boyfriend, and would like to settle down one day, there are no serious marriage prospects in the near future. Other expenses she tends to incur are spending some money going out with friends three or four evenings a month, and some skiing expenses during the winter. But she does not budget to take an annual vacation trip. However, if she finds she has some extra cash, she may take a week somewhere hot through a last-minute travel company.

Lots of future, but no plan

Andrea has a lot going for her at the moment, despite living at home, hating her job, student debt and a car that will probably have to be replaced in the next couple of years. What she doesn't have is a plan of attack for her future—just vague ideas of what she'd like to do. She really has to pinpoint exactly a goal, set some deadlines and get going towards completion.

Based on her annual income, she is probably earning close to $1,700 a month after taxes. Her monthly costs include about $300 for room and board, a clothing allowance of about $100, the same amount for car expenses, plus $150 for her loan repayment—about $650 in total. That leaves more than $1,000 not accounted for but spent on a variety of activities and purchases. That's a lot of cash she's allowing to slip through her fingers.

Andrea's financial snapshot

Monthly income	Monthly costs	Missing in action
$1,700	$650	$1,050

Prognosis: Her future is slipping through her fingers
Remedy: Time to budget, and to invest

This is an especially relevant circumstance if she wants to set up her own business—she must get serious about her financial future and acquire some basic money management skills. Before committing to a plan, she first has to see where her money is going. She doesn't need a budget yet, but she does need a cash-flow analysis.

And the only way to do that is to keep track of her spending. This is the onerous task of recording where every dollar is spent after it is spent, and she should be prepared to undertake this for three to four months to get a real grasp on where the money goes. Only then can she attempt to prepare a realistic budget that will propel her goals.

Then she must develop a long-term perspective on what her objectives are and make some hard-and-fast lifestyle decisions. By staying at home and saving money on living expenses, the opportunity to start an Internet-based business is certainly more feasible. Even with equipment and software costs, these types of businesses require more brain power and talent than a huge amount of capital.

There are two questions that Andrea will have to deal with in this area. First, is she willing to stay in her boring job and earn some income while she develops her business? And second, how long is she willing to stay with her folks in order to realize her ambitions? Only she can answer these questions, but if she wants to get ahead, she may have to live with both situations in the interim.

One of the things she should do now is start contributing to an RRSP, even if it's only $100 a month. She might be better off paying as she goes at this point—as opposed to taking out a loan—at least until her student debt is retired. Andrea may even take steps to aggressively pay down her student loan and get it out of the way, especially before starting up a home-based business. If she leaves her job shortly, it's best not to have any outstanding debt, as the potential for unpredictable income is quite concrete. As an entrepreneur, she must remember there is no pension plan— she has to create her own. Getting money into her own plan now would form a habit that will serve her well in the long run.

If she decides that putting up with her nine-to-five job is the price she'll have to pay for future business success and financial security, then she has already put herself in a better position to get ahead. Even though she is only 25, she has to realize that most financial advisers will view her as being late in starting a plan and that to catch up she will have to become more disciplined.

By staying at her job, or even moving to one she likes a little better, she can have the resources to put her business aspirations into play as well as establish a path to financial security. With a steady income she should borrow—whatever amount she can afford to service—to contribute to her RRSP room, and then in turn reinvest her refund back into it.

Andrea's action plan

1. Track spending
2. Establish long-term objectives
3. Make monthly RRSP contributions
4. Aggressively pay down debt

From there, she can set up automatic monthly RRSP contributions that can provide her with two advantages. First, it can reduce her monthly tax outlay to Revenue Canada, thereby giving her a little more disposable income. Second, by having the money deducted monthly, she won't be as tempted to spend that amount if it was just left in her bank account— usually a common pitfall for people in this age group.

With her current income, Andrea has a commitment ratio, or debt service ratio as the banks call it, of about $750 a month. Basically it's calculated by dividing her income by 12 and multiplying it by 35%. With $300 room and board, increasing her student loan payments to $200, making a $100 RRSP contribution and putting $100 into short-term non-RRSP savings, for a total of $700, Andrea can come in under that ratio.

That way she is retiring her debt sooner, establishing a long-term savings program and setting up a short-term emergency fund for unexpected expenses such as a larger car repair bill. That still leaves her with about $1,000 a month for clothing expenses, regular car maintenance, entertainment and also money to invest in her business. Her monthly RRSP contribution should reduce her taxes by $336 a year, and she should get used to reinvesting it back into her RRSP so that she is actually investing more than $1,500 a year for now.

Now that she has a foundation established, Andrea is ready to put a plan to work. If she is really committed to being successful, and feels that the short-term pain is worth the long-term gain, then part of her monthly income could be invested into non-registered investments for, say, five years. This money could be designated for a purchase of a home and/or to expand her home-based business, or take advantage of other opportunities that may come her way.

Further to that, she could consider taking a 20-year investor loan to get a jump start. This would enable her to save taxes via the home-based business as well as the interest cost on the investment loan over the long term. How much she borrows will, of course, depend on how much of a commitment she is able to make to servicing the loan payments.

Where to invest is probably the easiest part of Andrea's circumstances. At 25, while she is still a little late in getting her retirement plans started, she still has the huge advantage of time on her side. Depending on when she sees herself retiring, she could have 30, 35 or more years to allow compound interest, capital gains and dividends to turn modest savings into substantial returns.

Equity funds the best bet

At this stage of her life, she should consider equity funds for her RRSP, and purchase these with either a small front-end load or no load basis. That will allow her some flexibility to withdraw the money free if she wishes to take advantage of the RRSP new home buyers plan. One approach for maximum future gains is to complement Canadian equity funds with international RSP index funds, which basically mirror the returns of various international indexes such as the S&P in the United States and the FTSE in the U.K. Although these are foreign funds, they are still 100% RRSP-eligible. In addition, she should also load up on pure international funds to the 20% foreign content limit. One fund that deserves some attention is the Atlas American Index RSP fund, which uses 70% of the S&P 500 (large-cap stocks), 20% of the S&P 400 (mid-cap stocks), and 10% of NASDAQ, which has a heavy weighting in high-tech stocks.

Another option for her RRSP that she should consider is the Investors Retirement High Growth Portfolio, which focuses on long-term growth, and also contains 20% free foreign content—10% Investors European Growth Fund and 10% Investors U.S. Growth Fund. She could complement this selection with the appropriate 20% of pure foreign content. It's an aggressive approach but, given the number of years she has for it to work for her, it's quite a suitable choice and the results should be quite rewarding.

For any money that she has in open investments (i.e., those not incorporated into an RRSP), something less volatile and more balanced should be employed. If she thinks she might have to access some money within five years from now, she should consider a dividend fund, which can offer some of the best after-tax returns in that particular fund group. Funds that generate interest are definitely not recommended as they are not tax advantaged. Dividends and capital gains are the only way to go.

Like Andrea, many young people are prone to thinking that they have a lot of time to think and prepare for retirement. And they are right. They do have a lot of time. But, and this is the big but, they have to get

Wealth-building rules for Twenty-somethings

1. Start saving now, even if it's a small amount to begin with. Time is on your side. A little money invested now in an RRSP can grow to a significant asset thirty or forty years into the future. Harness the magic of tax-deferred compounding.

2. Set a financial plan in motion—even if you are not earning a generous salary yet. Decide what you'd like to do and when you'd like to do it, and then take steps to accomplish your goal. Having a course outlined for you will make it a lot easier to achieve your ends.

3. Work with an adviser to ensure you are on the right path and invested appropriately—at this stage of life good quality equity mutual funds have virtually no risk over the long term.

4. Have the sum you can afford to contribute to your RRSP deducted monthly. That way you pay less tax every month and you won't be tempted to use the cash you normally accumulate to make a one-time RRSP contribution each February. After a while, you won't miss the deduction.

5. Try to retire any debts (student or car loans) quickly. And above all, don't get into a credit card debt hole, it can slow down any financial progress you hope to achieve into your thirties—the time when you may well have to take on more financial responsibilities and obligations.

6. Treat this process seriously. Given what the future holds, you could experience an economic depression right in the middle of your working life. You need to build a wealth base now.

cracking now, not 10, 15 or 20 years from today. Although at that stage of the game they can still catch up, it will be a lot harder to accomplish at that time, and certainly more stressful to do when they may have many other obligations.

The other problem that people under age 30 have today, although Andrea is not in the firing line here, is too much non-tax-deductible debt. This trend began in the mid-seventies when the baby boomers started borrowing willy-nilly and, as a result, a whole host of debt products flooded the market.

Rarely a week will go by without some offer from a credit card company decorating the inside of your mailbox. And, with interest rates expected to remain low for some years to come, this situation can only get worse. The ready availability of so much credit, and the aggressive campaign of lenders to extend it, especially to young consumers, could put a lot of them into a hole that will be exceedingly difficult to climb out of.

The bottom line for those born in the 1970s? Hate debt, and invest with passion.

The nesting thirties

History shows common stock outperforms all types of investments.
PHILIP RINI
PROFESSIONAL INVESTMENTS

What needs to be put in place now is a comprehensive financial plan that deals with not only budgeting to save 10% of your income for retirement, but also other important areas such as tax, estate and investment planning.
MIKE HAYHOE
INVESTMENT PLANNING COUNSEL OF CANADA

Bill and Joanne

It should come as no surprise to a lot of middle-class Canadians that their earning power over the last few years has been stagnant. In today's dollars, according to recently released statistics, the average wage earner is no further ahead than 20 years ago. There may even be slightly less to go around.

Over the past 20 years Canadians have endured two major recessions, a period of high inflation and high interest rates, wage concessions, layoffs and several levels of government consistently digging deeper into taxpayers' pockets. Finally, and fortunately, the tide of tax change has turned towards relief.

Perhaps the corner has been turned though, as we are now enjoying the lowest interest rates in decades, a rejuvenated economy, near zero inflation and a decline in joblessness.

Nevertheless, many are still feeling the effects of the past two decades and wondering if they will ever get ahead, and what, if anything, they can do to make it happen. Bill and Joanne are one such married couple.

He's 34 and she's 32, they've been married six years, and they have a four-month-old baby girl. Joanne is currently on maternity leave, and she and Bill are weighing their options about her returning to work in a few months.

Their annual combined family income is $65,000—Bill makes $40,000 as a CBC cameraman, and Joanne earns $25,000 working three days a week as a computer technical support consultant. They live in Toronto so $65,000 a year doesn't go as far as it does in most other parts of Canada. Both are university educated and have been working since their early twenties.

Unlike many individuals and couples in their late twenties/early thirties, Bill and Joanne were concerned about their financial security and kept an eye on the future after getting married—in part because they would like to have a couple of children. With that in mind, they started putting money into RRSPs several years back and now have $37,000. This year they plan on adding another $4,200 to their investments. About half of their investments are in equity funds, the remainder in various bonds and a couple of stocks.

Bill & Joanne's financial snapshot

Income	Assets	Debts	Net worth
$65,000	$37,000 RRSPs	$155,000 mortgage	$97,000
	$215,000 house		

Prognosis: *Doing okay, but need to build more net worth*
Remedy: *Cut mortgage burden, raise cash flow, be more aggressive*

They are carrying a $155,000 mortgage at the current five-year rate on their house, which is worth about $215,000. Both Bill and Joanne subscribe to fiscal prudence and they have not incurred any major debt obligations since purchasing their home. There are costs associated with the occasional house improvement project for which they do a lot of the work themselves.

Their only other major costs are their two leased vehicles—a two-door sub-compact and a small station wagon.

Children can be very expensive

Bill and Joanne are probably in much better financial shape than a lot of couples in their particular age group—25 to 35. They are to be commended for staying free of major debt obligations—mortgage aside—and ensuring that they did not let student loan obligations drag on too long after graduation.

Even thought they appear to be ahead of many of their contemporaries, they are concerned that they may not be doing enough to ensure a financially secure family lifestyle and a leisurely retirement. And their concerns are not unfounded. Typically, couples in this particular age group can incur considerable costs associated with maintaining and furnishing a home and the accompanying costs of raising a child or children.

Studies have shown that it can cost about $100,000 to raise and launch a child into self-sufficient adulthood. And if Bill and Joanne follow through on their plan to have two children, that will account for $200,000 worth of their earnings over the next 20 or so years.

Their situation might be manageable at this point, but how do they get ahead—and stay ahead? The simple answer is to increase their net worth, and that is usually accomplished by paying down debt and investing.

In terms of paying off debt, they really only have to consider their mortgage. One option is to convert the payment schedule to biweekly from monthly. This could well save them more than $30,000 in interest over the term of the mortgage, assuming that it is now amortized over 25 years at 6.75%.

And what about investing? Just by contributing $4,200 this year to their RRSPs, and ensuring that it is wisely invested in a fund capable of delivering 10% over a 25-year period, that money could grow to $45,000 during that time—all for a one-time investment.

Another approach they could consider is to do both—reduce their debt and invest. If Bill contributes the $4,200 to a spousal RRSP (he being in the higher tax bracket), this strategy could save them about $1,600 in tax. That way they could have the $4,200 working for their retirement, and at the same time the $1,600 could be used to make a principal payment on their mortgage. That could save them about $6,000 in interest over the life of the mortgage. This way they can enjoy the benefits of long-term compounding as well as paying down non-deductible debt.

Whatever they do, there is no way they should forgo their RRSP contributions and use that money instead to pay off the mortgage. That's an absolute no-no. If mortgage rates soared back to the 10% range—which by most financial experts' musings is highly unlikely—then it might be wiser to find some ways to pay the mortgage down. Until such inflationary times come our way again it would be far more prudent, with Bill in the 42% marginal tax bracket, to keep contributing to their RRSP.

If Bill and Joanne were feeling a little more adventurous, they could also consider extending their mortgage at these low interest rates for as long as possible, and take the extra cash and get it invested now at the early stage of their investment lives. They could be so much further ahead because of long-term compounding. If interest rates spike 10, 15 or 20 years from now, they can deal with it at that time. In the meantime, their investments will have been going great guns.

The other major consideration they must address at this point is whether Joanne should return to work or become a stay-at-home-mom. While there are emotional and social issues to deal with, there are also economic considerations to assess. How much will child care cost? Will Joanne have to devote unpaid time to retain and upgrade up-to-date technical skills? Will medical, dental and other benefits have to be relinquished?

Bill & Joanne's action plan

1. Explore ways of lessening mortgage interest
2. Maximize RRSP contributions
3. Have Joanne return to work
4. Take more investment risk

What do the numbers say? Well, based on their current lifestyle, it may not be as financially wise to try to live on one income. A quick estimate of their monthly expenses—$1,000 for the mortgage, $800 for the car leases, $300 for property tax and $350 for their RRSP contribution—totals up to $2,450. Bill's after-tax income would be approximately $2,500 a month, which doesn't leave an awful lot left over for food, diapers, heat, phone, hydro, clothing and any entertainment. Even if they gave up one of the vehicles, it would still not be enough to pay the bills.

So fiscally, it appears that for now Joanne should return to work. However, because she is required to only put in three days a week, it might not be too much of a burden balancing her work demands and parenting at this point. Childcare costs are tax-deductible up to $5,000 per child annually, and by working, Joanne will also be able to keep her name on the books for RRSP contribution room. It will also allow her to maintain her skills in the ever-evolving information technology arena.

As far as their investments go, they could afford to take a little more risk. For individuals in their early thirties who are saving for a retirement that is more than 20 or 25 years away, a diversified portfolio of good-quality equity mutual funds would not be out of line. Again, this depends on Bill and Joanne's risk tolerance level, but with such a long time horizon, history has demonstrated that equities always produce the best rate of return. At the very least, their portfolio at this stage should include an 80% equities/20% balanced asset mix.

Portfolio of global equity funds

Their portfolio should include two Canadian equity funds, one managed by a growth manager such as Dynamic Canadian Growth or Clean Environmental Equity, and the other managed by a value manager such as AIC Diversified Canada or Trimark Canadian. They should ensure they have their full 20% foreign-content factor using a broad-based international fund such as Templeton Growth or AGF International Value.

Another thought would be to consider buying a labour-sponsored venture capital fund, such as Working Ventures, VenGrowth or C.I. Covington, with their RRSP contribution. That way they can generate an additional 30% in tax credits, which should translate into $1,260 in tax savings. They could then pump that back into more investments, or if they are intent on reducing their debt, they could apply it to their mortgage and save themselves about $5,000 in interest over the life of their mortgage. Additionally, their retirement horizon of more than 20 years is more than adequate to offset the holding period of eight years, as well as the increased risk of a venture capital investment.

Are they saving enough? Based on their combined $65,000 income, they should be saving $4,200 as the bare minimum. If they can keep putting in this amount yearly, alongside their $37,000, and manage to earn about 10% annually—not an outrageous expectation—then they should have sufficient funds for a comfortable retirement by age 60.

Of course, they could be much better off if they were able to put closer to 10% of their income ($6,500) away each year, but at this stage of the game, with the addition of the baby, this might not be feasible. The same goes for RESP investing for their child or children's education. Since the government introduced the Canadian Education Savings Grant whereby it contributes up to 20% of the first $2,000 annually to a maximum of $400, Canadian parents can get a bit of a bigger jump on the rapidly escalating costs of post-secondary education.

But again, it all boils down to cash flow, and for Bill and Joanne they might be better off putting all their extra cash into their RRSPs since their tax refunds are of more value to them at this point. What they could do to prepare for the education cost crunch is to set aside as little as $25 a month and, together with the 20% CESG, this amount can grow into a substantial sum by the time the child reaches age 18.

One thing they might want to consider if they want to increase their disposable income is that leasing two cars might not be their best option. If they can get by with one car they could be so much further ahead, at least $300 to $400 a month—which could be applied to the mortgage, RRSPs or RESP, or all three. However, if two cars are necessary, then they should turn in one of the leased cars and purchase an inexpensive second vehicle, as it makes more sense than paying depreciation on two cars on a monthly basis.

Overall, Bill and Joanne appear to be headed in the right direction. They have $60,000 in home equity, $37,000 in RRSPs, and the commitment to make that portfolio grow. Their cash flow could be tight from time to time, but if they continue their financially prudent ways, stick to

Base-building rules for your thirties

1. Time is still on your side so make sure you have a financial plan in place, RRSP contribution room all used up and regularly (monthly contributions) scheduled for the future. If you have unused RRSP room, borrow to fill it.

2. Don't procrastinate. If you don't have an RRSP, get one going and cut down on your taxes. If you have an RRSP with a few dollars in it, don't put off adding more now—rather than in your forties—since 5 or 10 years of extra compounding can make a big difference to your portfolio. You may have more money in your forties, but you can also have more financial obligations at that time. Be aggressive with stock and mutual fund purchases. Don't factor future CPP income into the equation.

3. If you own a house and have equity built up, use some of it to get a jump on the future. Even $10,000 or $20,000 invested now will grow more as a financial asset than as bricks and mortar.

4. This is no time for financially conservative investments. Over a 30-year period your stocks and equity mutual funds can deliver a substantial amount of growth. Why not harness demographics with investments in such sectors as financial services and health care?

5. You need a good plan and a budget you can stick to, especially if you have children. Find ways to reduce taxes (income splitting), invest in a Registered Education Savings Plan (the government will chip in 20% annually up to $400), and make sure you have adequate insurance, up-to-date wills and powers of attorney.

6. Find ways to reduce expenses. If you are running two cars, see if you can get away with just one for a couple of years. Use that money to invest. On average it costs Canadians over $5,000 a year to operate a car—more than $1,000 more than that if you live in the Toronto area. Over two or three years you could have a nice chunk of change growing every year instead of a rusting, depreciating mechanical (and eventually economic) liability.

their budget and have an independent financial adviser assess their progress regularly, they shouldn't have to worry.

There is one caution that Bill and Joanne should pay attention to, as should most couples in this age group. Sufficient life and disability insurance must be put into place. For Bill and Joanne they should have life insurance that is equal to 10 times their salaries—Bill should be insured $400,000 while Joanne should have at least $250,000 worth. In terms of disability, the income replacement formula suggest about two-thirds of their current income. They should see if they have any of these types of benefits at work through group plans, and how much they need to purchase handle any unforeseen and untoward circumstances.

For individuals and couples in their early or even late thirties, the most important factor they have in their favour is time. Even at this stage of their lives, if they start saving and contributing to an RRSP on a regular basis, long-term compounding can deliver a substantial return.

Probably the most common mistake made at this age is believing that you have all the time in the world and figuring you should wait until you are earning a larger income before starting to save for retirement. As many financial advisers can tell you, as soon as that income starts to grow, so do your expenses. So, it never really gets any easier to start putting money away.

At this age it is not too early to factor in tax and estate planning concerns alongside budgeting and investment strategies. Although people in their thirties may not think it's really appropriate, having a comprehensive financial plan laid out at this phase in their lives can mean the difference between a comfortable retirement and a struggle to make ends meet.

The expansive forties

Taking into consideration that they are self-proclaimed conservative people, they need to be educated to the fact that being too cautious carries a high amount of risk.

TONY POZDIN

REGAL CAPITAL PLANNERS LTD.

Everyone is risk averse. No one has ever come into my office to seek help in finding greater risk. What people fail to understand are the different kinds of risk out there.

ALAN CAMERON

INVESTMENT PLANNING COUNSEL OF CANADA

People who are in their forties need to seriously look at their retirement plans and their ability to make it happen.

DONNA OGSTON

REGAL CAPITAL PLANNERS LTD.

They need to bear down for the next five to ten good years and sock a lot of money into investments.

PATRICK BAINES

PARTNERS IN PLANNING

Jim and Drew

Turning 40, for most people, has that uh-oh kind of significance to it. You're not a kid anymore, but neither is this the beginning of senility. However, it's a milestone that seems to get a lot of people thinking a little more solemnly about the future—especially when retirement and senior citizenship are just two decades away. At this age, you begin to realize that 20 years or so can fly by before you know it.

It's a time when there's usually a lot going on in people's lives—things like paying down the mortgage, sending the kids off to college, buying a cottage, and helping and caring for elderly parents. The forties is a very demanding time for most people, and trying to cope with the day-to-day concerns can push preparations for future financial security into the future.

Again, this is the paradox of time for this particular age group. There's lots of time to build up a good-sized portfolio of retirement funds, but only if you start right away, not a decade and a half from now. It's a good thing that, with all the current and future financial demands of this age demographic, from age 45 to 55 is the time of life when most people earn the most income.

For Jim and Drew, a couple in their early forties, this is where they find themselves. But unlike most couples in this age group, there are two differences. They are earning a very good income and have acquired substantial assets.

Both are professionals. Drew, 44, is an architect in downtown Vancouver, and Jim, 42, is a musician with a successful Canadian country and western star. They live in a paid-up $480,000 condo on Burrard Street, and together bring home about $250,000 a year, but often feel they are taxed to death.

Drew & Jim's financial snapshot

Income	Assets	Debt	Net Worth
$250,000	$480,000 condo	None	$710,000
	$170,000 RRSPs		
	$ 60,000 shares, funds		

Prognosis: By all standards, doing well, but need more security
Remedy: Reduce tax, diversify assets and plan ahead

They have individual RRSPs of about $85,000 each, plus non-registered investments of about $30,000 each. About half of that is in balanced mutual funds, $8,000 in T-D Bank shares and $7,000 in segregated funds. Both men consider themselves to be very conservative in terms of investments.

This approach also spills over into their spending habits. While they don't spend lavishly, they do enjoy an above-average lifestyle. When schedules permit, they like to get away a couple of times a year to destinations in the U.S. or the Caribbean. Perhaps every couple of years they have enough time to take an extended vacation overseas.

Both belong to a racquet sports club, where they work out at least twice a week, and play the occasional tennis match. During the winter they get away skiing to Whistler about one weekend per month, depending on Jim's work schedule. Their only other major expenses are their vehicle leases—Drew drives a new BMW 3-Series and Jim drives a Jeep Cherokee.

They have it made. Or do they?

A half-a-million-dollar paid-up condo, a quarter-million-dollar-a-year income and more than a quarter million dollars' worth of investments. Not a bad situation to be in. Most 40-year-old Canadians, and most of those older than that, would be envious. Drew and Jim have it made. Or so it seems. In the next dozen or so years, both, according to statistical data, should be earning the most money in their entire working lives.

That should nail down a pretty tidy retirement lifestyle. But there are no guarantees—especially for Drew. The bloom is off the real estate boom in B.C. and if there is a slowdown in new construction and renovations, his earning potential could be in jeopardy. The same goes for Jim. He will always be able to support himself as a musician, but will he be able to maintain the same earning power as he ages? Showbiz can be a mercurial domain. The other what-if to consider is if disability strikes one or the other before they've accumulated sufficient assets.

Without considering the, "What's the worst thing that can happen?" worry, they both realize that they are in relatively good shape. The question that's foremost on their minds now is, "Can we do more, can we do better, and how should we approach it?" So while the going is good right now, there's no time like the present to strike while the iron is hot.

Between travel, vehicles, condo fees and an active lifestyle, Drew and Jim will likely require a more-than-ample retirement income if they want to maintain the type of life they currently enjoy. To do that it is estimated that they will probably require at least $90,000 (in 1999 dollars) in after-tax income. Which means they should aim to have close to $3 million amassed in the next 13 years, by which time Drew will be 57 and Jim 55.

First off, they feel that their tax situation needs to be addressed. They may not really be taxed to death, but if they are grossing $250,000 a year, you can bet that their tax bill will hover between the $80,000 to $100,000 mark. And that is no small potatoes. It's a significant amount of money siphoned out every year. The first step to minimizing their taxes is to ensure that they max out their RRSP contribution every year up to the $13,500 limit.

To reduce their tax bill now and in the future, they need to focus exclusively on equity investments outside of their RRSPs. It is probably wiser to select mutual funds that subscribe to the "buy-and-hold" approach, like AIC and Infinity, where there is limited trading and tax will be deferred until the units are redeemed.

They could also consider having about 10% of their portfolio in Oil & Gas, which will give them a 100% tax deduction. Another technique they should use to get their money working harder and at the same time put a dent in their taxes is to leverage their condo. Too much of their new worth is tied up in non-performing real estate during their peak earning years.

Jim & Drew's action plan

1. Reduce tax through RRSP contributions
2. Use real estate equity to invest
3. Build diversified portfolio
4. Address insurance needs
5. Devise comprehensive estate plan

For example, if they took a home equity loan out of at least $250,000 (about half of their home equity), they would probably pay about $16,250 in interest annually, and half of that would come back to them in the form of tax savings. And, they would have another quarter million dollars invested for the future, earning 8, 9, 10, maybe even 12% a year—appreciation that you can be assured will not be the case if that equity just sits in the condo.

They may even consider borrowing—rather than putting cash every month in financial assets—to invest, again because the interest payments are tax-deductible. This could be done in addition to any action they take on investing with a home equity loan.

What they have to do first is to establish what they are spending and what they may be able to add to their portfolios over and above what they have done to date.

As of now, they are probably bringing home about $150,000 to $170,000 after taxes. It's a fair amount of money, even if you take away $60,000 for living expenses (about $5,000 per month). That should leave them with about $90,000 to $110,000. This hasn't always been the case until recently, when they started to earn bigger money, and spend a fair amount paying off the condo as well as paying off some other debts.

With access to this kind of money right now, both should be getting into the savings mode in a big way. To meet a goal of retiring by their mid- to late fifties, and having approximately $90,000 in after-tax income, they need to be putting away at least $60,000 a year in the most tax-efficient manner possible.

How should they invest? First, they should make sure that they are well diversified, and given that they have a dozen or more years to retirement, they can afford to ride the roller coaster of a global portfolio for a while.

They should also look at continuous investing as they could comfort- ably put away at least $7,500 a month into registered and non-registered portfolios—$2,250 into maxing their RRSPs and at least $5,000 into their non-registered assets.

A suitable portfolio for them at this point should include about 30% in bond funds. A good corporate issue would work as part of the 30%, and they should also use some international bonds to take advantage of currency plays. The purchase of some of the indexes would be a good idea to anchor the portfolio.

Five to 10% in resource investments is not an outrageous amount. And the remaining 60% to 65% should be designated for dollar-averaging equities that can provide solid returns while minimizing market swings. Also, the monthly purchase of good-sector blue chips is advised. Inside their RRSP they should also ensure that they maximize their foreign content to the 20% limit, as should every Canadian investor.

For outside of their RRSPs, there is no question that international equity funds with a bottom-up management style are their best bet. Products like Templeton Growth, AGF International Value, and Fidelity International Portfolio would be well suited to their goals and conservative investing nature.

Part of their monthly investment amount should also be targeted to a Universal Life policy on each of them—this will help with tax-free com- pounding. Also, if they do not have critical-illness insurance plans for both of them, they should put that strategy on the top of their "to do next" list.

With all things being equal, and the income keeps coming through, then within a decade they should have a good $2 million in financial assets, well on their goal to amassing close to $3 million by the time they hit their retirement threshold four years later.

Without fail, their general financial planning strategy should include a comprehensive estate plan, probably more so than for traditional couples, as family law in Canada may not deal with their property at death or disability in a way that Jim and Drew would prefer. So it is paramount that they invest some time with their financial planner and a lawyer to ensure that they have up-to-date and financially astute wills and enduring powers of attorney in place.

For the most part, Drew and Jim are on the right track by starting to invest and attempting to use asset allocation. Again, they have to ensure the issue of home equity is put into perspective. And if they can bear down for the next 5 to 10 years and sock away more than the suggested $7,500 a month, they should be in line to have a retirement fund that will go a long way in providing the lifestyle they now enjoy—well into their seventies, eighties and nineties.

While most 40-plus Canadians do not have the income or have amassed the assets that Drew and Jim enjoy, many of the same strategies that will work for them should work for those with more modest means. Many couples in their forties are still carrying mortgages on their homes; however, they have managed to build up some equity in their houses.

•   Getting real estate equity out now could mean the difference between making do with your retirement funds or living the lifestyle you want. And don't forget the tax reduction possible when borrowing to invest.

•   One of the most common mistakes people of this age group tend to make is believing that they can do it all themselves and not seeking out the advice of a financial adviser. Consequently, they usually make bad choices.

•   Also, in an effort to diversify, many of these people put too many funds in their portfolio, as they try to cover all the angles. That only serves to dilute the returns, which can be so much better if, working with an

Take-charge rules for the forties

1. If you don't have an RRSP at this stage of the game, where have you been? It's still not too late to get started on your retirement savings, but you and your money will have to work harder to get there—you have let things slide, and are in danger. Take charge now.

2. Make sure your financial plan is up to date and that you have the appropriate investments for this 20-year drive to retirement—GICs, bonds and other "guaranteed investments" won't cut it. A substantial growth component is essential if you don't have a good number of financial assets built up yet. Do not invest in segregated funds. You do not need to pay a premium at this stage for a guarantee of future performance.

3. Get good advice. Too many in the boomer generation are doing it themselves, investing and putting their money away, and not getting any input on whether the investments are suitable for their circumstances. What's right for your neighbour might not be right for you. In fact, your neighbour is probably in trouble.

4. Many of the forty-plus boomers are probably living in the biggest house that they will ever own, and many have substantially paid down the mortgage. Don't sit on that equity, especially if you have a meagre portfolio. Get a home equity loan bolstering your investments and use the interest costs to reduce your taxes. Get invested internationally, especially if you can afford to carry some investments outside of a registered plan.

5. You're entering the years when you will statistically earn the most money ever in your working life—don't squander the opportunity. Make sure you stick to the plan developed by your adviser and get as much cash into growth-oriented investments as possible.

adviser, you choose eight or nine good funds that consistently will bring you the numbers you need.

•　Many people in this age group still do not invest to acquire the most international market exposure as possible. Foreign content has been shown to bring up those annual returns by a good measure.

•　Not understanding risk is another common faux pas of the forties set. With 20 or 25 years to go before retirement, many of these boomers feel they still have lots of time to amass a good sum by age 60 or 65. What they don't figure on is that they may have to fund 20 or 30 or even 40 years of retirement (and the last few years probably being the most expensive). And they won't be able to do it by taking the safe route with savings bonds, GICs and other guaranteed investments.

The risk is not in the performance of the ups and downs of the market, but in the fact that supposedly low-risk investments cannot deliver the goods.

And lastly, like most of the adult age groups, one of the nastiest mistakes to make is to procrastinate. Time is on your side if you are in your forties, but you've got to make it happen today. Playing catch-up is not in the foundation of a good financial plan or wealth-building strategy.

The critical fifties

I feel superior returns in the coming decade will come from picking better performing sectors and top mutual funds that have a good track record in those sectors.

JAMES DOUVILLE

BERKSHIRE INVESTMENT GROUP

Canadian women outlive men by six years on average, so they (women) should learn the hows and whys of money management, and the details of their financial plan, in preparation for the statistical likelihood they will end up being the final stewards of the family fortune.

DON GORDON

GORDON FINANCIAL GROUP

Craig and Ginny

Fifty-three-year-old Craig represents the epitome of success for many Canadians. He's the president of his own company, currently a fairly prosperous concern that manufactures growth hormones for the Canadian beef industry.

He and his wife, Ginny, 51, are happily married, and she keeps extremely active working in the home, performing volunteer and charity work, as well as serving on the board of her husband's company. Their sons Peter and Warren have finished their post-secondary schooling, left home and embarked on promising careers.

The couple has no mortgage on a $600,000 monster house in southern Calgary, although it seems a bit empty now that the kids have gone. Their annual income, taken in the form of a dividend from the company, is $180,000. Craig has no RRSP, and considers his corporate equity as his retirement fund. They have less than $100,000 in investible assets, mostly in Alberta government long bonds.

They live well, but not extravagantly, remembering how much hard work and sacrifice was necessary getting to where they are today. There is not a lot of time for hobbies, but both try to work out three times a week at the fitness club where they are members—not a high-end exclusive club, but not a discount gym either.

When she does snag some spare time, Ginny likes to pursue oil painting, while Craig's biggest indulgence is two or three golf resort weekends with his buddies during the summer. Usually they take a couple of holidays a year: a one-week sun vacation down south in the winter, and a couple of weeks during the summer, either in the States or Canada.

Craig & Ginny's financial snapshot

Income	Assets	Debt	Net Worth
$180,000	$600,000 Home	None	$700,000 + Equity
	$100,000 Invested		
	Corporate Equity		

Prognosis: Heading into retirement in fine shape, maybe
Remedy: Lighten up on real estate, heavy up on growth assets

Apart from day-to-day expenses, property taxes and related household bills, their only other expense currently is their transportation—Craig drives a leased sports utility vehicle and also leases a mid-size sedan, which his wife drives.

On the surface it appears that Craig and Ginny have it all. Compared to the average citizen in Canada, this is living exceedingly well. But even individuals and couples who appear to be relatively wealthy may still have a lot of work to do to ensure that they can maintain the lifestyle that people like Craig and Ginny have worked diligently to attain. Have they made the right choices and do they have enough resources to reap the fruits of their endeavours when retirement comes a-calling?

There's no doubt that Craig and Ginny have had a good run, they are financially independent and earn sufficient income from their business to support an above-average lifestyle. With the big-ticket debt items—mortgage, kids' education, business startup costs—behind them, their financial focus should be redirected to accumulating adequate retirement funds, conserving the value of their asset base and ensuring that they minimize Revenue Canada's bite. At this time too, they should review their estate plan strategies to ensure an orderly transfer of their wealth upon one or both spouses' death to the intended beneficiaries.

Craig & Ginny's priorities
- Build retirement assets
- Conserve what they have
- Lessen the tax load

Currently, the annual family income is $180,000 in the form of dividend income from the company. As Ginny is an officer of the company, the income can be split with each spouse receiving $90,000, which in Alberta would make it about $71,500 after tax, for a total income of $143,000— the benefits of dividend income over straight salary.

How much are they going to need in retirement if they would like to have about 70% (about $100,000 annually) of after-tax pre-retirement income? To provide that amount from age 65 to 90, factoring in various taxes, a 5% inflation rate until age 90 and no CPP credits, they will need around $2 million in capital to finance that amount. Can they do it, and if so, will they be able to retire before age 65?

Their financial security basically boils down to one major issue here and that is, how much is his company worth, and will he be able to get the price he hopes to when it comes time to sell? The $180,000 annual dividend suggests there is substantial equity in the company. It could range from $4 to $6 million, which would make quite a tidy sum on retirement.

Expecting the business to continue to grow over the next dozen or so years and then cashing out sounds like a fair plan. However, putting all your eggs into one basket has been shown time and again to be not the most prudent financial strategy. So Craig will need to take a good look at identifying potential risks to his business, acknowledge them and perhaps enact some mitigating strategies.

There are five elements that could affect the long-term viability of his business. The first is competition. The industry is facing lots of competitive pressures from non-Canadian suppliers these days, especially from south of the border. Can Craig compete in export markets if his Canadian customers decline? He's got to look at this very carefully.

Another threat is market pressures. More people turning to healthier lifestyles and looking for more natural food with less intervention from the additive market—mad-cow disease did a number on that—can his business continue to thrive as it has over the past decade?

Have Craig and Ginny really assessed the taxation issue? They could be overlooking potential erosion of their expected retirement funds from capital gains tax and recaptured depreciation at the time of sale. They have to address this potential threat now, not later.

Another big issue could be if Craig dies prematurely or is disabled. If someone, perhaps Ginny, has not been groomed to take over in case of an unfortunate event, there could be a severe financial impact on the company, its resale value, and in effect, expectations of a secure retirement. The company should be insured against such losses.

The last big maybe that could affect the value of the company is litigation, and whether it could be named in a class action suit taken against one of its customers. This is a very real possibility in today's more litigious climate. Strategies must be in place to protect the company and its directors and their personal assets from this very real risk.

There are a lot of "ifs and buts" to deal with regarding relying on the company to drive their retirement portfolio. Are there other things that they could do perhaps to lessen this reliance and provide for them if the bottom drops out of the business? In a word, yes.

Aside from their business interests, Craig and Ginny have about $700,000 in assets, although most of that, just like with the majority of Canadians, is tied up in non-liquid, and usually non-appreciating, real estate. That has to change.

The Calgary real estate market has been one of the few well-performing ones across the country in the past couple of years. How long that will last is anyone's guess. However, most experts don't expect it to appreciate significantly in the next dozen years to where it would make sense to keep all that equity growing slowing, or even stagnating.

The writing, it seems, is on the wall, or at least walls. They have to get this huge chunk of brick and lumber working for them. The first option is to sell the home outright—and do it soon as this is probably a good time to dump the property before all the aging boomers decide that their monster homes are keeping them from building their financial assets.

They might well consider renting a nice condo—they do have a good income at this point—and investing the proceeds of the sale. For example, if they took the $600,000, at an 8% (capital gains) compounded annual pre-tax rate of return and you factored in their current 31% marginal tax rate, their portfolio could well grow to more than $1.23 million in the next dozen years. Modest for their lifestyle, but still quite a nice lump sum.

If they don't like the idea of renting, they could just downsize and buy a smaller home at half the value, and invest the remaining $300,000. Then, they should leverage the equity in their new home. They could borrow up to 75% of its value—$225,000—and invest that too. At today's borrowing rate of about 6.5%, a $225,000 interest-only loan would cost about $14,625 per year. But the interest payments would be tax-deductible. And at their 31% marginal tax rate the after-tax cost of the loan would be just over $10,000 or 4.5%.

They could also leverage their existing home and invest $450,000. But after about 12 years (they could probably gain close to half a million in the portfolio during that time) they will still be left with a home that might be worth less than it is today, and if so, certainly much harder to dispose of at that time.

Craig & Ginny's action plan
1. Resolve the real estate situation
2. Restructure portfolio for more growth
3. Review spending habits, increase investment stream

Getting more mileage out of the bond component of their portfolio is also something they should remedy promptly. As income instruments, long bonds can be valuable components in a portfolio. But when it comes to growth and liquid reserve requirements, especially in today's climate, they are not appropriate. Craig and Ginny should restructure these assets to produce a more growth-oriented, tax-efficient portfolio. It should be well diversified in asset classes, securities and geographical areas to reduce the risk inherent with their current Alberta-based assets.

While they still have a substantial cash flow from their business, Craig and Ginny should take a good look at what they are spending currently and whether some of that cash could be channelled into more investments. Because they have received their income in the form of dividends, they have enjoyed the benefits of minimizing their personal income tax. However, it has not allowed them to build up tax-deductible RRSP room and CPP retirement credits. And at this stage of their life it might be more advantageous for them to forgo RRSP and CPP benefits and opt for less conventional means to build up reserves for retirement.

If they mobilize their home equity and convert their Alberta bonds, they can have substantial portfolio developing before retirement. This non-registered portfolio would not be tax sheltered, but without the foreign-content restrictions they could expect a much higher pre-tax return than they could from an RRSP, which would be based mostly on Canadian investments.

A portfolio suggestion for them at this stage would be to put 30% into a well-managed balanced fund such as Ivy Growth & Income, 10% into an international fund such as AIC value, another 10% into an international growth fund such as AIM GT Global Theme, 20% into a domestic value fund such as AIC Diversified Canada, 15% into a domestic growth/momentum fund like Synergy Style management and 15% into a foreign equity fund such as Global Strategy World Diversified Equity.

Any funds that tap into the financial services, health care, software and large-cap technology sectors are definite areas to explore for investment for the coming decade, particularly for individuals like Craig and Ginny whose time horizon for building up a sizeable nest egg is starting to close in a little.

They have the means—$700,000 in assets, an above-average income for the time being, and no big debts—plus just enough time, maybe another 8, 10 or 12 years to allow their investments to grow. But they have to get their assets working now, perhaps topping them up with additional contributions from their income. That could get them to a point where they should have enough money to enjoy a comfortable lifestyle when they hit their sixties.

This, of course, is not counting any assets that may come from the sale of the business. If the business declines in the coming decade, then they've at least made some substantial strides to their financial security with their other investments. If the company continues to thrive and can attract a buyer when Craig has had his fill, then that would just be the icing on the cake.

Craig and Ginny are probably guilty of making the mistake many people in their fifties are prone to, and that is putting too much confidence in the wrong assets. For some, it might be assuming that the Canada Pension Plan will take care of them—they just have to survive till they're 65. For others, it's assuming that their paid-up, or nearly paid-up, real estate will make the difference 10 or 15 years down the line.

And for a smaller group, like Craig and Ginny, it's hoping that all their hard work behind their business will pay off with the big score just in time for the retirement cruise. In many cases it probably will deliver a good package, but when it comes to financial security, sometimes you have to hedge your bets, maybe not move all your eggs into different baskets,

Cautionary rules for the fifties years

1. Don't put too much confidence in assets that just might not appear. In 15 years the CPP you were counting on to supplement your other income might be not much more than a token payment, if anything at all if you already earn a set income level. If you own a business you hope to sell, a large home you hope to get rid of, or are expecting an inheritance, the same applies. Don't count on it too much. Get a diversified portfolio going, and if anything else comes your way take it as icing on the cake.

2. Put your home equity to work now through downsizing, before the real estate market takes a demographically induced dive, or by leveraging via a home equity loan.

3. Remember: you still have some time to go until retirement, and then maybe 20 or 30 years of retirement to finance. That means your portfolio has to have a good-sized growth component including some quality equity mutual funds. Even at this age GICs are too risky—little growth potential and you pay the maximum in tax on the interest.

4. Have a well-defined financial plan in place, including sound estate strategies; the older you are, the more you have, and the more there is to lose. Ensure your spouse is the beneficiary of your RRSPs.

5. If you still have unused RRSP room, borrow the money and fill it up, using the tax savings to help repay the loan.

but just add a couple of other baskets to the mix. The proverbial back-up plan.

The other major mistake is that people in this age group tend to become more conservative in the types of investments they pursue. People in their early fifties, even their late fifties, still have a window of opportunity to grow their assets, particularly in the economic climate we are currently enjoying. They need growth in their portfolios. People in their sixties, and even in their seventies, need a growth component in their portfolios. We may not all live to be 90 or more, but it's not a bad idea to prepare for it in case it happens. And you cannot prepare for it with savings bonds, GICs and other supposedly safe investments.

By age 50, you should have a well-defined financial plan in place, including estate strategies, and making sure the balance of your assets is shifting their bulk from real estate into financial products.

The skittish sixties

This woman's financial net worth is better than most Canadians. However, she needs professional help.

MURRAY REIMER

REIMER FINANCIAL SERVICE INC.

They are afraid to diversify into the market for fear of losing their principal. They do not understand that the greater danger lies within the low-interest GIC market which will not keep pace with their needs in retirement.

CHERYL HARRIS

MONEY CONCEPTS

With Canadian life expectancy on the rise, they will live longer and need more money. They will face a challenge of shrinking pensions, and low growth on traditional assets such as GICs will lead to an income shortfall.

DIXIE ALLEN

EQUION FINANCIAL

Vicky

Just like many women in their sixties, Vicky was looking forward to her golden years—spending more time with her husband, enjoying her role as a grandmother, and joining with a small group of other retired couples in various activities.

Suddenly, weeks before her 68th birthday seven months ago, she was widowed. At that point, her husband's modest pension ended upon his death, and their wasn't much in the bank account. Also, her husband did not have a huge amount of insurance—just enough to cover funeral costs, some other bills and a few small outstanding debts. There was a little left for her to take a month-long trip to visit her sister in England a few months later.

Now half a year later, she still grieves. But Vicky is still trying to get her life back on track. Her financial situation is quite worrisome even though she does have some resources. She just is not sure about what she should do.

Her liquid assets total $100,000, in strip bonds ($60,000) and GICs ($40,000), plus she owns outright a nice four-bedroom house (in good repair for now) in the Armdale Rotary area of Halifax. In today's market it's worth $300,000. She has no RRSP, but gets a small pension of $500 a month, plus CPP benefits.

Vicky's financial snapshot

Assets		Debts	Monthly Income	
Bonds	$ 60,000	None	Pension	$500
GICs	$ 40,000		CPP	$420
Home	$300,000		Interest	$500
Total	$400,000		Total	$1,420

Prognosis: Worried, but in better shape than she thinks
Remedy: She has far too little growth for her age

Despite these assets, she is very concerned about the future and her financial security. And despite the efforts of her small circle of friends, she is feeling quite alone. Both her children and their families live outside of the province. Her son Brian lives and works in Toronto. He and his wife have two young boys both under age five. Vicky's daughter Elizabeth is a stay-at-home mom, and lives in Bathurst, N.B., where her husband works. They have a six-year-old son and three-year-old daughter, and are expecting their third child five months from now.

With growing families and the economic responsibilities that they entail, neither of her children is in a position to contribute significantly to Vicky's financial well-being. And that's the way she wants it. She's happy that her offspring are establishing themselves. Throughout her bereavement, the fact that her children are making strides in their lives has brought her some comfort. However, she would like to be able to afford to travel more often to visit them, and now fears that her small monthly income will preclude that.

How risky is playing it safe?

For many women of Vicky's generation, owning a home and conservative, guaranteed investments were the ticket to a financially secure retirement. And clinging to that belief can often lead to a spartan existence. According to Moshe Melevsky, a professor of finance at York University, Toronto, playing it safe may be riskier than taking a chance, given the lengthening life expectancies of Canadian women. A woman in her late sixties today is facing a 71% probability of outliving her nest egg.

This could mean disaster for a woman like Vicky, especially if she fails to address her financial situation and needs before long. Is she really destined for dire straits and declining security? Or is her situation a lot more promising than she thinks?

Given that she has about $400,000 in assets, and no debts outstanding from her husband's estate, she is in much better shape than she believes. That's not to dismiss her concerns of having sufficient income to fund her lifestyle. At least $2,000 per month after tax is what's needed to finance an average retirement lifestyle, although this might be somewhat more than what is needed to live comfortably in Halifax, as opposed to Calgary, Toronto or Vancouver.

Nevertheless, with her annual pension of $6,000, about $5,000 in CPP and approximately $6,000 in interest income, she is looking at approximately $17,000 a year before Revenue Canada takes its bite. So she is heading for a significant shortfall if she maintains the status quo.

Her biggest problem is that her modest assets are not that liquid and really can't provide her with a significant amount to supplement her pension and CPP.

The first matter she should deal with—since it represents the bulk of her assets—is her home. Sentimental reasons aside, this property will eventually become a burden. She may not realize it, but this house can facilitate much improved circumstances for her.

If the thought of selling the house does not appeal to her at this point, and because it is a large home in a good neighbourhood, taking in a lodger might be the way to alleviate some of the costs associated with owning the property. Even though there is no mortgage, taxes and maintenance costs can put a severe dent in Vicky's annual income. Having someone else live in the home might also work to her advantage when she is away visiting her children.

However, income from a lodger will still not come anywhere near bringing up her disposable income to a comfortable level. So if staying in her home is her choice, then accessing the equity she has built up in it can give her some breathing room. By using the equity in her home—via a home equity loan—she should be able to invest for growth and income. Many Canadians have improved their lot by cashing in slow-growing assets and channelling them into mutual funds that are set up to provide a systematic withdrawal plan—usually on a monthly basis—and this allows a fixed income and with a more tax-efficient treatment.

But in light of her age and the size of her home, probably the most sensible option would be to sell. Certainly, there is no time like the present as her house is a state of good repair and she will be able to get the maximum price for it. By freeing up the $300,000 worth of equity, Vicky should be able to increase her independence, and have more money to travel and visit with her family. She will also have more to invest for her more senior years as she could well survive another 20 or more years (at least 50% of the $300,000 should be earmarked for her future income needs), and even assist with her grandchildren's education.

Still, she has to live somewhere. By renting a condo or an apartment in a seniors complex, she should be able to maximize the most of the $300,000—making it work for her. If owning a property is still important to her, a small townhouse or condo purchase should allow her to invest a sizeable chunk of money for growth and income. She can even take out a home equity loan on the paid-up smaller home to facilitate more investment income.

So she does have several options. However, she must act quickly, because on the current track she could be out of money within nine years.

The other issue she must address is her current choice of investments. As it stands, the strip bonds and GICs will not cut it. She should cash in the GICs when they come due and move that money into more strip bonds (they have a higher rate of interest and more liquidity), to complement the portfolio driven by the proceeds from the house sale.

If this is the approach she is comfortable with, what type of products would best suit her? Because her portfolio is governed by RRSP restrictions, and Canada makes up only 3% of the world market capitalization, investments in international equity funds would be in order—AGF International Value Fund, Fidelity International Portfolio or Mackenzie Universal Select Managers Fund are prime examples. Also suitable for her would be a balanced fund and a dividend fund, such as Global Strategy Income Plus and the AGF Dividend Fund. The main objective here is growth and tax-preferred income.

If she's willing to take a more aggressive approach, here's another option. She should not only ditch the GICs but also cash in the strip bonds, and place the entire $100,000 into three diversified mutual funds such as AGF American Tactical Asset Allocation Fund, Mackenzie Ivy Foreign Equity Fund, or Trimark Select Growth Fund. If she can derive an 8% monthly income of the market value of these funds (adjusted every year-end), this will help her cash flow immediately and also allow her portfolio to grow if she sticks with it for the long term. Certainly this would be a good income-booster strategy while she considers her options on what to do with her home and where she will reside when and if she sells the house.

If she follows through on some of these options, what can she expect? For example, if she takes her current $100,000 portfolio plus half the proceeds from the house sale, she should do quite well. Very well indeed. She can create an additional income of $1,500 monthly for the next 20 years (including cost of living increases), and after that still have more than $260,000 left in her portfolio. All this is accomplished by using a systematic withdrawal plan using $250,000 in capital, $18,000 deducted for income each year, a 3% cost of living and 9% annual growth—quite achievable.

Putting her assets to work

Invested in Funds:	$250,000	Assumptions	
Income from SWP:	$ 18,000	Inflation:	3%
		Funds growth:	9%
Left after 20 years:	$260,000		

Of course, where the $250,000 is invested will have a lot to do with a successful outcome—a financial asset mix of blue-chip stocks and high-quality bonds. This can best be accomplished through balanced mutual funds, asset-allocation mutual funds or via a private money management program of stocks and bonds.

What she shouldn't be investing in are things like limited partnerships, individual stocks, more GICs or the Canada Savings Bond offerings. Other products not conducive to a well-performing portfolio include bank five-year guaranteed mutual funds or segregated funds—the higher management expenses are not really necessary for the guarantees involved.

The bottom line though is that Vicky has to take control of her financial well-being by meeting with a reputable financial planner to assess her situation in more detail, and present her with a plan that will meet her needs and goals. Not only will she enjoy a better lifestyle and additional portfolio growth for later years, but she should also be able to readily set aside money for her grandchildren, via RESP contributions, as well as have a significant amount of capital left over in her estate.

Vicky is not alone. Hundreds of thousands of Canadians are in the same boat—most of their financial assets are tied up in real estate, and the rest of their money is locked into low-growth GICs. Many individuals in their sixties (some even younger) believe that investing in mutual funds is for the young set—too much market volatility.

Because these people are just retired or approaching retirement, they believe that their objectives should be short-term, and consequently choose investments with short-term objectives as well. Because they fear losing their principal, they fail to take notice that a greater peril is found in low-interest products that will not keep pace with their needs. After all, the evidence points to most of us living longer lives than the generations that went before.

Probably the biggest mistake along these lines is to under-plan. Too many people think investing stops at age 65 or at the age they retire. Investments have to be planned right up to one's demise, or at least to when one expects to expire.

Complementing this mistake is keeping a higher percentage of their money in real estate rather than in financial assets. This means their wealth grows at a slower rate and they can easily lose ground. And when opting to rebalance their portfolio, too much emphasis is put into guaranteed investments—GICs and bonds. Perhaps these are appropriate for short-term strategies, but there has never been a time in the history of investing where over any extended period GICs provided a greater after-tax return than equities.

Other mistakes that individuals in their sixties are prone to make include ineffective tax planning with their investments, little consideration of estate planning issues with investment choices, and little or no thought of addressing the tax liability of their future estate.

So what should individuals in their sixties be considering?

First should be an evaluation of their short-, medium- and long-range goals, and diversifying accordingly. This, in many cases, will have to include a shift of real estate equity in financial assets. And if those assets are for long-term planning—remember, you may have another 20 or 30 years to go—they should be converted into equities. Also vital at this stage is planning the disposition of your estate, especially after both spouses have passed on.

Sixties rules—consolidate, trim taxes

1. Downsize your real estate, or better yet, sell and rent. Get all of your equity working for you through something like a systematic withdrawal plan—it can provide a comfortable income (usually at a lower tax rate) and also grow your assets so that by the time you're 90 or 100, you'll still have plenty of money on hand to buy candles for the cake.

2. Stay away from GICs and savings bonds—you'll probably outlive the highly taxed interest they provide. You still need a portfolio that has some kick to it—a growth element is vital. If you cannot sleep at night, or are worried about your estate, then segregated funds might be ideal.

3. Have a qualified financial adviser go over your circumstances at least twice a year to make sure you are not living below the means that you have on hand. And ensure your estate planning, wills, powers of attorney are all in place.

4. Work with your financial planner to minimize your tax profile. You're at an age where CPP and OAS are still being paid out—various strategies can work to your advantage with the income you receive from these programs.

5. Reverse mortgages are a last resort. Your house might not be worth as much 15 or 20 years from now and your estate could be saddled with a huge debt. Much better to sell, or leverage the equity (always with caution, and depending on your ability to service debt), get a tax break on the interest and enjoy the benefits of a SWP.

Personal Strategies

THE ARGUMENT
One of the greatest periods in your life to build wealth and secure financial independence is at hand. It's now. Do not squander it by heeding bad advice or being fearful of the future. You must be bold, and take action.

Most people never will, instead choosing to relive their parents' lives, making the same decisions because they are familiar and easy. But if I had made the choices that Archie did, I would be neither a happy man nor a successful investor today. His choices were right for his times; mine are right for my times. Our children will face radically different ones in the middle of their working lives, by 2020.

It troubles me greatly that so many people are sleepwalking into the future, but it's a reality that we have to deal with. The retirement crisis is now a dozen or more years away, and nothing can push it into the future. The best possible defence you can have against the future is wealth—and this is the time to get it. I strongly suggest you take some of the following actions.

Actions to Take:

Attend a Financial Seminar

They are normally free, there is no obligation to sign up for anything, and you will be exposed to a huge amount of financial information. I know, because I spend a substantial amount of time preparing to give a seminar. It's worth it though, because I feel this form of public education is truly worthwhile. Here is an opportunity to hear about a lot of investment and tax strategies, to ask all the questions you want, pick the brains of the financial adviser hosting the event, and probably be offered a free consultation to see if you are, in fact, on the right path or the wrong one.

Of course, not all seminars are what they appear to be. Some are sales events put on by the no-money-down real estate gurus or multi-level marketers. Protect yourself by always leaving your chequebook at home.

If you would like to know my seminar schedule, check my web site (www.garth.ca). If you would like more information, call 1-877-489-2188, toll-free.

Get a Financial Adviser

One of the biggest financial mistakes you can make is thinking you do not need help. Of course you need help. We all do. And while I hope this book has given you some insights and rules for success in the decades to come, it is no substitute for a trusted adviser who knows you and your goals.

This has never been more important than in these turbulent times, when a problem on one side of the world can turn into a personal crisis for you on the other. We all face the same dilemma: interest rates are too low to allow for conservative investing. You know your life will be very long and expensive, yet investing for growth means facing up to risk—today, considerable risk.

Are you comfortable making these decisions alone? Have you learned enough about all the possible options and dangers? Can you find the time necessary to research everything?

Well, I can't. So I rely heavily on my adviser. This is a person I trust to make the right decisions at the right time, so when I'm on the road or focusing on making some money (rather than managing it), I know the job is being done right.

We all know that over the last few years the Canadian economy has boomed in an environment of low interest rates, negligible inflation and roaring financial markets. So how can it be that so many people are doing so poorly in the personal financial affairs?

The answer is clear: most Canadians are gambling horribly with their financial futures and they don't even know it. Why? Because they entrust their money entirely to amateurs with no formal training who devote, on average, about five hours a year to the job and refuse to consider any research or investment information that isn't free. That's right—they try to do their own financial planning. Big, big mistake.

Need evidence?

• Six in ten Canadians believe they will not have $250,000 in net worth on the day they retire. That's according to a Gallup poll, and it is shocking evidence of the unpreparedness of Canadians for what lies ahead.

• Record numbers of people have been going bankrupt, even as interest rates and unemployment have been declining.

• Too many Canadians have too much of their net worth locked up in one type of asset that has been declining in value for most of the decade: residential real estate. That makes us some of the least diversified investors on the planet.

• Half of Canadians have never made an RRSP contribution, despite the fact that this is the continent's best tax shelter. And most taxpayers have no idea that with one phone call they can open an RRSP with no cash and transfer into it things they already own, earning a rebate cheque from the government.

• Collectively, we are about $200 billion behind in our RRSP contributions. Most experts agree that we will never make it up.

• Most people think Canada Savings Bonds provide an excellent long-term return, when they actually wither as an investment. Only a quarter of people with bond or mortgage mutual funds know those funds will fall when interest rates rise. Worse still, only 14% of people can identify the best-performing investment class since the Second World War. Of course: stocks.

• People clamour to buy investments when they are at their highest value and then dump them when they fall. Remember the folks lined up on Yonge Street in Toronto to buy gold at $1,000 an ounce? Today the metal is worth a quarter of that, and there are no lineups. How about the people who bought houses at $1 million each on a nice street north of Toronto in 1989? Years later, half that street was for sale at $500,000 a house. And recall how many investors bailed out of their stocks after Black Monday in 1987 or Grey Monday in 1997 or the Asian crisis of

1998? They missed three of the greatest run-ups in stock market history. You can rest assured that in the next major market correction, history will repeat itself.

• Millions of Canadians keep billions in low-yield guaranteed investment certificates when they could be earning more of a return with less risk in other securities. Why? Because they've never even heard of segregated funds, strip bonds or mortgage-backed securities.

I could go on for pages, but I hope this is enough for you to get my point: the average Canadian is the last person he or she should trust with something so important as personal financial planning, tax and investment strategies. And yet most do. It's sad. That's one reason a giant retirement crisis will descend on this country. It's why millions of Canadians must shed the rules of the previous generations and welcome the new rules of opportunity.

Be Wary of the Bad Apples

A lot of people have been ripped off by unscrupulous financial advisers. Some advisers turn out to be nothing but churners—excessively buying and selling investments just to maximize commissions, at the expense of the client's portfolio. Others are simply cheats, and over the past few months some spectacular cases have made the front pages.

Some of the "top producers" at rapidly growing financial services companies get to be top producers not by making wise investments but by racing through legions of clients.

Others are more motivated by the goodies flowing from mutual fund companies than by the best interests of investors. Ontario and British Columbia are two jurisdictions that have taken some action to curb such practices, backed by the Investment Funds Institute of Canada and the national regulators.

While you are right to approach this exercise with caution and care, you need not be a cynic or skeptic. The simple truth is that almost everyone would be better off with a second opinion. The key is to find someone with both knowledge and integrity. The good news is that there are many of them to choose from, and the vast majority of individuals I have worked with over the years at seminars across the country are simply outstanding.

Here are my answers to the questions I'm most often asked about finding an adviser you can trust:

How do I know if a planner is qualified? Are there regulations?

People who sell you financial securities have to be licensed. The industry as a whole, however, is unregulated, which means finding a good adviser is going to take some work on your part. The Canadian Association of Financial Planners has about 1,600 members, but that accounts for only about 20% of all those people who call themselves planners. There are currently no national standards, so interviewing a potential adviser is critical, as is getting references and referrals.

What does good advice cost?

Most people think a financial planner will charge them a huge amount of money. Usually, that's not the case. In fact, most planners work for you for free.

The right way to think about most planners is the same way you think about travel agents: you can get your ticket to Montreal and pay Air Canada $500, or your travel agent can arrange it for you and it still costs the $500. That's because Air Canada will do a lot more business each year with your agent than with you, and so the airline is happy to pay the agent a commission—in effect, lowering the cost of the ticket.

So, your financial planner is paid a commission by the mutual fund company or the bond issuer or insurance company when you add that investment to your portfolio. Of course, you can hire an adviser who is fee-only and does not actually arrange for any investments to be made. That will cost you up to $2,000 for a complete financial plan and an hourly consultation fee ranging from $50 to $250, with most in the $100 area. In that case you will still need someone to implement the plan, and purchase the securities.

You will often see "expert" opinion in the media warning you away from commission-paid advisers and into the arms of fee-paid ones. Ignore it. For the vast majority of people—those with under $1 million in liquid assets—an adviser who is renumerated through commissions is just fine.

What can you expect from a person like that? For starters, a free first consultation will last 60 to 90 minutes. That will be followed by an analysis of your existing assets and a draft financial plan, with recommendations. All of that typically costs you nothing—so what possible excuse could you have for not getting such a valuable second opinion on how you're doing?

Common Investor Mistakes an Adviser Can Help You Avoid

- Waiting for the "best" time to invest, or never investing

- Buying at a high price: selling at a low one

- Buying yesterday's hot investment

- Choosing investments not suited to individual goals or time horizons

- Failing to diversify: "putting all your eggs in one basket"

- Reacting to short-term events rather than long-term trends

- Basing investment decisions on fees and sales charges

Where do I start?

You can ask others—family members, co-workers or the boss—who they use as advisers. Word-of-mouth references are good because you can get a feel for an adviser's track record from somebody you know.

Naturally, you can respond to ads published in the financial section of your local newspaper, or in the *Financial Post*—especially during RRSP season, when there are lots of them offering particular investments.

As I've already suggested, attend a few financial seminars. During RRSP season and tax time there is a flurry to choose from. A great deal of information can be had in a short period of time, and the financial planner hosting the seminar will invariably offer you a free consultation in his or her office or your home. This gives you an opportunity to meet, and assess, that person.

What questions should I ask?

When you have that first meeting, the adviser will ask for a lot of information on your income, assets, taxes, family situation and goals. In return, you should ask about how that person expects to be paid; what are his or her areas of personal expertise; and for his or her track record and credentials. Be tough. Be frank. Be candid. Ask where the adviser puts his or her own money, why, and what the results have been.

Ask what his or her investment philosophy is. Does it match yours? Are you being offered more than just a family of mutual funds? Are you getting advice tailored specifically to you and your situation?

Here's a list of questions American investors are urged to ask of a potential planner, published in the *Wall Street Journal*. It's a good one to start with.

Things you should ask advisers during interviews

- What is your area of expertise?

- What is your approach to saving and investing?

- Will you provide an individualized financial plan?

- What kinds of communications can I expect from you on an ongoing basis (account statements, newsletters, etc.)?

- How often will you review my portfolio?

- How are you compensated for the service you provide?

- How are fees calculated?

- On average how much can I expect to pay for your service?

- What do I receive in return for that fee?

- What, if anything, do you expect of me during our relationship?

Should I ask for references?

Absolutely. In fact, this is the most important thing you should ask for. A good adviser has nothing to hide. In fact, a good adviser should have a lot to be proud of, and will want to share his or her clients' success with you.

Ask for a list of 10 or 12 people he or she has worked with. Then call and ask for a candid appraisal of the planner's effectiveness. Has the adviser reduced their tax bill? Increased their net worth? Diversified their investments? What overall rate of return are they getting on their portfolios? How often do they hear from the adviser? Are they kept fully informed? Are they concerned about excessive trading in their accounts? Are they related to the adviser? It does happen!

What level of service should I expect?

Several meetings at first, to approve an investment and tax strategy, then regular updates—perhaps quarterly. Your portfolio should be reviewed several times a year, or as changing conditions dictate.

You should get a regular account statement—monthly is best. It should break down all transactions, giving you rates of return and securities held, along with weightings by asset class (for example, 41% mutual funds, 32% fixed income, 27% equities).

Many good advisers provide clients with newsletters, access to investment research or client, appreciation nights where investment professionals come to speak. Advisers with some of the larger investment firms also are backed by substantial research departments, along with access to new stock and bond offerings.

The most important thing to expect is a comfortable working relationship with somebody you trust.

How can I tell if it's not working?

A telltale sign you're working with the wrong person is churning. That's when the adviser is buying and selling a lot of mutual fund units or stocks for no good reason other than to earn more in commission. Check your regular statement and look for any evidence of unnecessary trades.

How can I tell the difference between a planner, a broker and a counsellor?

As mentioned above, anybody can call himself or herself a financial planner, there are no national standards or regulations, That does not mean you should look elsewhere. Far from it—using a planner whom you get along with can be the most cost-effective way of building wealth.

Many planners work for companies that offer a full range of financial products, including strip bonds, stocks, mutual funds, GICs and more. The planners with these companies usually earn their living through commissions paid by the mutual fund and other companies. Ask, and most are happy to tell you exactly who pays them, and how much.

A broker is licensed to sell any financial product and must have completed the Canadian Securities Course. He or she will work for a brokerage company regulated by the Investment Dealers Association of Canada. A broker will also earn money through commissions on every transaction in your account.

An investment counsellor is paid through fees, which can take the form of an annual payment or a percentage of the total portfolio under management. Usually, counsellors are the preserve of the rich—those with more than $500,000 in investable assets. They, by the way, account for only 1.6% of the population. Pity.

How do I know if an adviser is full-service?

Ask. Some planners sell only mutual funds, so obviously they will not be able to give your portfolio the balance and diversity it should have. Everybody needs a little fixed income, for example, and you also want an adviser who will look at your total financial picture: real estate, insurance, estate, tax and investment plans.

What about the discount brokers?

These are no-frills operations that allow you to buy stocks, bonds or funds at a vastly cheaper commission cost than with a full-service broker or planner. Examples are T.D. Waterhouse and the Royal Bank's Action Direct. In recent months incredible Internet operators have been added, like E*Trade Canada and Charles Schwab Canada.

The discount brokers are innovative and cutting-edge in terms of the latest investor technology. Canada Trust, Action Direct, E*Trade, Schwab, T.D. Waterhouse and others all offer the option of real-time trading via personal computer and modem—an experience that can get any living person's adrenalin coursing.

The online brokerages now also offer extensive research, accessible in an instant and continuously updated. Investor education has never been this easy.

Should I go with a small company or a big one?

There is no right answer to this question because it is the individual adviser that really matters. The advantage of a small office or firm is that you stand a better chance of getting personal service from an experienced individual. The advantage of a large firm is access to research and, of course, a full range of investment options. I have dealt with scores of advisers and brokers, and their support staff across the country, and my personal recommendation would be to find a small office of a big company. That way, you can establish a close relationship with the people working there and still enjoy the benefits accorded the clients of the busiest downtown mega-operation.

And always remember this: a good financial adviser is more interested in a long-term relationship with you than in making quick commissions. As your wealth grows, so does the adviser's compensation; so over a 15- or 20-year time line, your financial well-being is your adviser's main concern. Put yourself in his or her chair and you will realize quickly that this is the prudent way to build a business.

So, if you're getting churned, you're getting burned. Move on.

Should I give over all my money?

Probably not—at least not at first. You need to build a relationship and also see the wisdom of your adviser at work. So don't write a cheque representing your life savings right off the bat. By the same token, don't hand over $5,000 and expect to see dramatic results in a few weeks.

Once you feel comfortable with the advice you are getting, it makes sense to consolidate your portfolio with one person. That way you can achieve diversity, organize the best tax planning strategies and ensure the right mix of mutual funds, bonds, real estate and equities for your stage of life and risk tolerance.

Seek out information and knowledge

For investors, knowledge is the ultimate power. In the critical decade to come, you must invest astutely and aggressively to prepare for what 2020 will bring.

There are many sources of credible information. Your financial adviser can steer you towards some. The Internet is a great tool; use it. Buy and read more books like this one. Read the daily press, especially the *Report on Business* section of the *Globe and Mail* and the *Financial Post* section of the *National Post*. Read both carefully, but do not believe it all. Many columnists have an agenda, and most are not wealthy. It makes a difference to those who are determined to be.

There are also many useful investment-oriented newsletters. One of them is *The Turner Report*. More information is available at www.garth.ca.

How to Reach Me

I'd be pleased to see you come out to one of my educational seminars where we can discuss the comments and strategies presented in this book. Or, if you'd like the names of some financial advisers that I might know in your area, send me a letter, fax or e-mail. You can access my current seminar schedule through my Internet Web site. Here's how to reach me; I will make every effort to give you a response.

Phone: (416) 489-2188
Fax: (416) 489-2189
e-mail: garth@garth.ca
Internet: www.garth.ca
Letter: Garth Turner
Suite 310, 1670 Bayview Avenue
Toronto, Ont. M4G 3C2

To book a personal appearance in Canada, contact
Speaker Solutions
www.speakersolutions.com
1-877-489-2188

Acknowledgements

The "Generational Strategies" section of the book would not have been possible without the kind assistance and knowledgeable input provided by the following individuals:

Dixie Allen
Equion Financial
Don Mills, Ontario
Tel.: (416) 442-4146
Fax: (416) 441-9885

Patrick Baines
Partners In Planning
Nanaimo, British Columbia
Tel.: (250) 390-3062
Fax: (250) 390-9095

Alan Cameron
Investment Planning Counsel of Canada
Newmarket, Ontario
Tel.: (905) 715-7103
Fax: (905) 715-7096
1-800-717-8117

James Douville
Berkshire Investment Group
Edmonton, Alberta
Tel.: (780) 496-7725
Fax: (780) 425-0530

Don Gordon
Gordon Financial Group
Victoria, British Columbia
Tel.: (250) 881-7600
Fax: (250) 881-7607

Cheryl Harris
Money Concepts
Miramichi, New Brunswick
Tel.: (506) 778-8446
Fax: (506) 778-8459

Mike Hayhoe
Investment Planning Counsel of Canada
Kitchener, Ontario
Tel.: (519) 578-2591
Fax: (519) 745-5009

David Morse
Midland Walwyn
Charlottetown,
Prince Edward Island
Tel.: (902) 628-8111
Fax: (902) 368-3964

Susan Nielsen
Investors Group
Victoria, British Columbia
Tel.: (250) 727-9191

Tony Pozdin & Donna Ogston
Regal Capital Planners Ltd.
Calgary, Alberta
Tel.: (403) 640-0928
Fax: (403) 640-9095

Murray Reimer
Reimer Financial Services
Abbotsford, British Columbia
Tel.: (604) 852-6494
Fax: (604) 852-3627
1-800-663-6641

Philip Rini
Professional Investments
Kingston, Ontario
Tel.: (613) 384-7511
Fax: (613) 384-8919
Alzheimer Disease

Alzheimer Disease

Alzheimer Disease is a degenerative brain disorder that destroys vital brain cells. There is no known cause or cure for the disease. Over 300,000 Canadians, or 1 in 13 over the age of 65, currently suffer from Alzheimer Disease and related dementias.

The Alzheimer Society is a nationwide, not-for-profit health organization dedicated to helping those affected by Alzheimer Disease. Over 140 local chapters across the country provide information and support to those in need. The Society is also the leading Canadian source of funds for research into caregiving.

For more information and to learn how to help, contact your local Alzheimer Society, or call **1-800-616-8816** or visit our web site at **www.alzheimer.ca.**

A portion of the proceeds of this book will be donated to the Alzheimer Society of Canada, in memory of Archie Turner and in hope for others with this disease.

The Alzheimer Society wishes to thank Garth Turner for helping to raise awareness of the disease and for the much-needed financial support.

The Alzheimer Society

Index